ISBN 978-0-483-99069-2
PIBN 10801422

FB &c Ltd, Dalton House, 60 Windsor Avenue, London, SW19 2RR.
Company number 08720141. Registered in England and Wales.

For support please visit www.forgottenbooks.com

HE PRAISE OF ZI

A COLLECTION OF MUSIC FOR

Singing Schools, Choirs, and Musical Conventions;

CONSISTING OF

SYSTEM OF MUSICAL NOTATION
II.—A VARIETY OF EXERCISES AND GLEES FOR SINGING SCHOOLS.
III.—AN EXTENSIVE COLLECTION OF HYMN TUNES.
IV.—A LARGE ASSORTMENT OF SENTENCES, ANTHEMS AND CHANTS.

BY

SOLON W. LORD AND FREDERIC S. DAVENPORT.

NEW YORK:
MASON BROTHERS,
J. B. LIPPINCOTT & CO. CINCINNATI: SARGENT, WILSON & HINKLE.
CHICAGO: ROOT & CADY.

THE PRAISE OF ZION:

A COLLECTION OF MUSIC FOR

Singing Schools, Choirs, and Musical Conventions;

CONSISTING OF

I.—A SYSTEM OF MUSICAL NOTATION.
II.—A VARIETY OF EXERCISES AND GLEES FOR SINGING SCHOOLS.
III.—AN EXTENSIVE COLLECTION OF HYMN TUNES.
IV.—A LARGE ASSORTMENT OF SENTENCES, ANTHEMS AND CHANTS.

BY

SOLON WILDER AND FREDERIC S. DAVENPORT.

NEW YORK:
PUBLISHED BY MASON BROTHERS,
BOSTON: MASON & HAMLIN. PHILADELPHIA: J. B. LIPPINCOTT & CO. CINCINNATI: SARGENT, WILSON & HINKLE.
CHICAGO: ROOT & CADY.

PREFACE.

Singing School Department.—The definitions in this department are designed to be clear and distinct, and sufficiently full for all the uses of Singing Schools. The practical exercises are easy, and we hope, adapted to the purpose for which they are intended. In these times, when peace again blesses our land, the choral, "Let all men praise the Lord," from the "Hymn of Praise," by Mendelssohn, must find a ready response in every heart.

Hymn-Tune Department.—Much time and labor has been spent in the preparation of this part of the work, with the hope of presenting choirs and singers generally with good, singable music, avoiding lightness and frivolity on the one hand, and harmonies too hard and intricate on the other. A careful selection of those old favorite tunes which are almost as indispensable for singing schools as for choirs, is included. The hymns have been chosen for their emotional nature, and the music has been written or selected with reference to giving expression to the same. Unusual opportunities have been afforded us for making selections from foreign as well as American sources, which we have largely availed ourselves of. The lovers of the music of Ch. Zeuner will find a number of compositions by him never before published.

Anthem Department.—The music here will be found to be almost entirely new. Attention is called to the large variety of pieces suitable for opening church worship, also to the closing choruses by Neukomm and Novello respectively, which are now for the first time published from the original MS., kindly furnished by Dr. L. Mason. To him and the many others who have assisted us by word and deed, we would here render our most grateful acknowledgments.

We hope the work will prove of interest to others, as it has to us.

SOLON WILDER,
FREDERIC S. DAVENPORT.

New York, *August*, 1865.

Electrotyped by Smith & McDougal, 82 & 84 Beekman Street, N. Y.

Printed by John F. Trow, 50 Greene Street, N. Y.

SINGING SCHOOL DEPARTMENT.

MUSICAL NOTATION.

CHAPTER I.

INTRODUCTION.

§ 1. All persons are capable of realizing certain distinctions of tones (musical sounds). The following are the first that present themselves; viz:

1st. Long or Short.
2d. High or Low.
3d. Loud or Soft.

§ 2. Hence every tone has three essential properties, or conditions of existence; viz:

1st. Length.
2d. Pitch.
3d. Force.

§ 3. As there are three distinctions, and three essential properties of tones, it seems proper to divide rudiments of music into three corresponding departments; viz:

1st. Rhythmics.
2d. Melodics
3d. Dynamics

CHAPTER II.

RHYTHMICS.

§ 4. The relative length of tones is represented by characters, called *Notes;* thus,

Whole Note. Half Note. Quarter Note. Eighth Note. Sixteenth Note.

THE RELATIVE VALUE OF NOTES ILLUSTRATED.

One whole note,

is equal to two halves,

or four quarters,

or eight eighths,

or sixteen sixteenths.

§ 5. Characters indicating corresponding length of silence are called *Rests;* thus,

Whole Rest. Half Rest. Quarter Rest. Eighth Rest. Sixteenth Rest.

N. B.—Notes or rests do not represent any absolute length.

§ 6. A *Dot* • adds one half to the length represented by a note or rest; thus, a 𝅝 • equals 𝅝𝅗𝅥, and a 𝅗𝅥 • equals 𝅗𝅥𝅘𝅥, and so on.

§ 7. The figure 3, placed over notes, reduces the length represented by three equal notes to that of two of the same kind. Groups of notes thus marked are called *Triplets*

CHAPTER III.

RHYTHMICS.

§ 8. The relative length of tones is estimated by a division of time into equal portions, called *Measures.*

§ 9. Measures are represented to the eye by spaces separated from each other by perpendicular lines, called *Bars;* thus,

Bar. | Measure. | Bar. | Measure. | Bar. | Measure. | Bar. | Measure. | Bar.

§ 10. There are four kinds of measures in common use.

§ 11. A measure having two parts, is called *Double Measure.*

EXAMPLE.

Double Measure, accented on the first part.

2/2   2/4

§ 12. A measure having three parts, is called *Triple Measure.*

EXAMPLE.

Triple Measure, accented on the first part.

3/2   3/4

§ 13. A measure having four parts, is called *Quadruple Measure.*

EXAMPLE.

Quadruple Measure, accented on the first and third parts.

4/2   4/4   4/8

§ 14. A measure having six parts, is called *Sextuple Measure.*

EXAMPLE.

Sextuple Measure, accented on the first and fourth parts.

6/4   6/8

§ 15. The kind of time is indicated at the beginning of a piece of music in the form of a fraction; thus $\frac{2}{2}$ signifies double time, and that two half notes or their equal fill a measure; and $\frac{3}{2}$ signifies that three half notes or their equal fill a measure.

§ 16. The practical way of keeping time is by beats of the hand, which is left for the teacher to explain.

§ 17. The practice of beating time and counting aloud is earnestly recommended. In classes the practice of beating and counting, omitting a part of the beats, is advised; thus, in double time, counting the first and remaining silent on the second part. In quadruple time, the ladies may beat and count the first and third, while the gentlemen beat and count the second and fourth parts, and *vice versa.*

§ **18.** The close of a piece of music, and in this work the end of a line in poetry, is indicated by a *Double Bar.* Thus,

---

CHAPTER IV.

MELODICS.

§ **19.** A SERIES of eight tones, ascending or descending in a particular order, is called the "*Scale.*" The names used to designate these tones are, *One, Two, Three, Four, Five, Six, Seven, Eight.* The syllables, *Do, Re, Mi, Fa, Sol, La, Si, Do,* are used to designate their *relative* pitch. The letters C, D, E, F, G, A, B, C, are used to indicate their *absolute* pitch.

§ **20.** The scale is indicated by a character called a *Staff,* consisting of five lines and four spaces, each line and space being called a *Degree.*

EXAMPLE.

Lines.
Spaces.
Degrees.

§ **21.** When more than nine degrees are required, added lines above or below are used. Thus,

EXAMPLE.

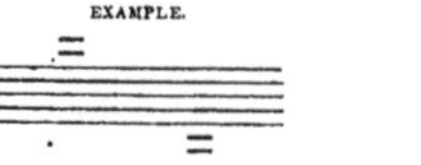

§ **22** Any degree of the staff may be taken to indicate the place of *One,* but the others must follow in regular order.

§ **23.** The position of the letters upon a staff is determined by a character called a *Clef,* of which two are in common use; viz.: The G clef, thus, ; and the F clef, thus, .

§ **24.** The G clef determines G to be upon the second line, and the F clef determines F to be upon the fourth line. For example:

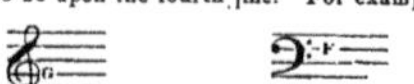

§ **25.** The arrangement of the letters upon the staff is as follows:

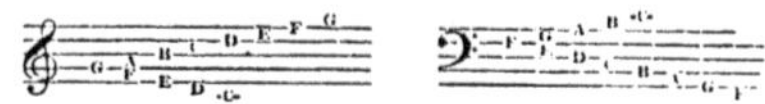

§ **26.** By common consent the scale is represented upon the staff as follows, beginning at C, and is called the *Model Scale.*

Names. 1 2 3 4 5 6 7 8 | 8 7 6 5 4 3 2 1
Pitch. C D E F G A B C | C B A G F E D C.
Syl. Do Re Mi Fa Sol La Si Do | Do Si La Sol Fa Mi Re Do.
Names. 1 2 3 4 5 6 7 8 | 8 7 6 5 4 3 2 1.
Pitch. C D E F G A B C | C B A G F E D C.
Syl. Do Re Mi Fa Sol La Si Do | Do Si La Sol Fa Mi Re Do.

§ **27.** The difference of pitch between any two tones is called an *Interval.* In the scale given above there are two kinds of intervals, greater and smaller, called *Steps* and *Half-steps;* thus, the intervals between three and four, and seven and eight, are *Half-steps*, all the others are *Steps*. The intervals between the letters occur as follows: between E and F, and B and C, are *Half-steps*, and all the others are *Steps*.

CHAPTER V

MELODICS.—CHROMATIC SCALE.

§ 28. BETWEEN those tones of the scale differing in pitch by the interval of a step, an intermediate tone may be produced; thus, intermediate tones may occur between one and two, two and three, four and five, five and six, and six and seven; but not between three and four, and seven and eight, because the intervals between these tones are half-steps.

§ 29. These intermediate tones are named from either of the tones between which they occur; as between one and two may be either *Sharp One* or *Flat Two*.

§ 30. The absolute pitch is called C Sharp (♯C), or D Flat (♭D).

§ 31. The influence of a flat or sharp extends through the measure in which it occurs; and also through succeeding measures, until a note occurs upon some other degree of the staff.

§ 32. The influence of a flat or sharp is terminated by a character called *Natural* or Restorer (♮).

§ 33. A scale composed of the eight scale-tones, and the five intermediate tones, given above, is called the *Chromatic Scale*.

THE CHROMATIC SCALE REPRESENTED.—*Ascending Scale.*

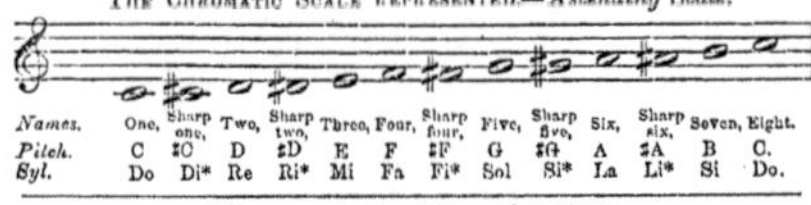
Names. One, Sharp one, Two, Sharp two, Three, Four, Sharp four, Five, Sharp five, Six, Sharp six, Seven, Eight.
Pitch. C ♯C D ♯D E F ♯F G ♯G A ♯A B C.
Syl. Do Di* Re Ri* Mi Fa Fi* Sol Si* La Li* Si Do.

* In pronouncing give i the sound of *e* in *me*

Descending Scale.

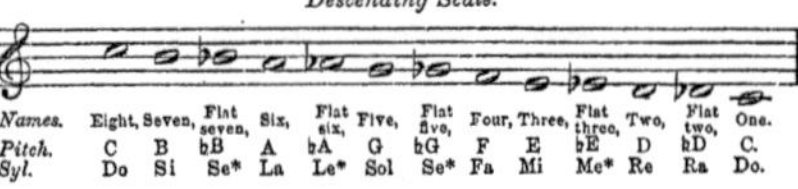
Names. Eight, Seven, Flat seven, Six, Flat six, Five, Flat five, Four, Three, Flat three, Two, Flat two, One.
Pitch. C B ♭B A ♭A G ♭G F E ♭E D ♭D C.
Syl. Do Si Se* La Le* Sol Se* Fa Mi Me* Re Ra Do.

CHAPTER VI.

MELODICS.—MINOR SCALE.

§ 34. THERE are two forms of the *Minor Scale* in common use, designated by the terms *First* and *Second Forms*.

§ 35. Either form commences upon the Sixth of the major scale; that is, Six of the major scale is taken as One of the minor.

§ 36. The major and minor scales are said to be related; thus, A minor is related to C major, and C major is relative to A minor, and the signature is the same.

The two forms of the minor scale are given, and the order of intervals in each is given directly under the form.

MINOR SCALE—FIRST FORM. (*Melodic Minor.*)

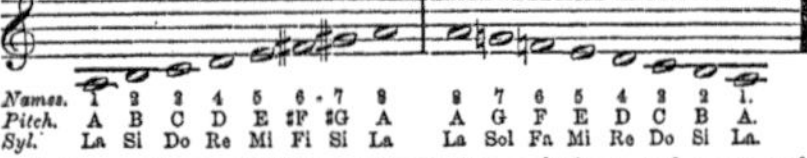
Names. 1 2 3 4 5 6 7 8 8 7 6 5 4 3 2 1.
Pitch. A B C D E ♯F ♯G A A G F E D C B A.
Syl. La Si Do Re Mi Fi Si La La Sol Fa Mi Re Do Si La.

Scale ascending: Half-steps between two and three, and seven and eight; the other intervals are steps.

Scale descending: Half-steps between two and three, and five and six; the other intervals are steps.

* Give *e* the sound of *a* in *may*.

Minor Scale—Second Form. (*Harmonic Minor.*)

Names.	1	2	3	4	5	6	7	8	8	7	6	5	4	3	2	1.
Pitch.	A	B	C	D	E	F	♯G	A	A	♯G	F	E	D	C	B	A.
Syl.	La	Si	Do	Re	Mi	Fa	Si	La	La	Si	Fa	Mi	Re	Do	Si	La.

In this scale, ascending and descending, the intervals are alike: Half-steps between two and three, five and six, and seven and eight. Steps between one and two, three and four, and four and five. The interval between six and seven is a step and a half-step.

CHAPTER VII.

MELODICS.—TRANSPOSITION OF THE SCALE.

§ **37.** The scale is said to be transposed when any other pitch than C is taken as *One*. But, in taking any other pitch than C, the order of intervals, given in Chapter IV., must be preserved.

ILLUSTRATION OF SCALE COMMENCING UPON G.

G A B C D E F G.
1 2 3 4 5 6 7 8.

As it now stands it is wrong, because the interval between six and seven is a half-step, and it should be a step. Made right by using the tone ♯F in the place of F.

So the scale of G is made up of the following tones:

G A B C D E ♯F G.

§ **38.** Instead of writing a sharp beside every F in a piece of music, it is put upon the letter F, immediately after the clef, and is used as a signature to indicate the key.

N. B.—By key is meant the relationship of tones when any letter is taken as One. Thus, by Key of C is meant the relationship of tones with C as a basis

§ **39.** In transposing the scale to any other letter the same principles must be observed as in the foregoing.

The authors do not deem it necessary to write out any more transpositions; for, if the principles already stated in Chapters IV. and VII. are understood, the pupil can do it with greater advantage to himself.

CHAPTER VIII

DYNAMICS.

Under this head comes *Force of Tones*, or Power. The following are the more common forms of expression:

§ **40.** A tone of medium force is called *Mezzo*, marked *mez.* or *m.*

§ **41.** A tone softer than *Mezzo*, is called *Piano*, marked *Pia* or *p.*

§ **42.** A tone louder than *Mezzo*, is called *Forte*, and is marked *for.* or *f.*

§ **43.** A tone softer than *Piano*, is called *Pianissimo*, and is marked *pp.*

§ **44.** A tone louder than *Forte*, is called *Fortissimo*, and is marked *ff.*

§ **45.** A tone began, continued, and ended with the same degree of force, is called an *Organ Tone.*

§ **46.** A tone beginning *Piano*, and increasing gradually to *Forte*, is called *Crescendo;* marked thus <

§ **47.** A tone beginning *Forte*, and diminishing gradually to *Piano*, is called *Diminuendo;* marked thus >

§ **48.** A union of the two last produces the *Swell;* marked thus <>

§ **49.** A very sudden *Crescendo* or *Swell* is called the *Pressure Form*, and is marked thus < or <>.

§ **50.** A tone produced very suddenly and forcibly, and instantly diminished, is called an *Explosive Tone* or *Sforzando;* marked thus >, or by *sf* or *fz.*

CHAPTER IX.

DYNAMICS.

§ **51.** When successive tones are sung in a connected and flowing style, they are said to be *Legato*. The legato is marked thus ⌒.

N. B.—The same character, called a *Tie*, is used to show how many tones are to be sung to one syllable.

§ **52.** When tones are produced in a short and detached manner, they they are said to be *Staccato*, marked thus ' ' ' '.

§ **53.** A medium between legato and staccato is called *Half-staccato*, and is marked thus, • • • •.

§ **54.** When a tone is prolonged beyond the time indicated by the note, such prolongation is called a *Pause*, and the character representing it is called a *Pause* or *Hold*, and is marked thus, 𝄐.

§ **55.** When a passage is intended to be sung twice, it is indicated by the following character, 𝄇 called a *Repeat*.

§ **56.** When a piece of music is to be closed by repeating the first part, it is indicated by *Da Capo* or *D. C.*, in which case the end is designated by the word *Fine*.

§ **57.** When a passage of music is designed to be performed at pleasure as regards time, it is marked *Ad lib.*

§ **58.** When a passage of music is to be hurried as regards time, it is marked *Accelerando*.

§ **59.** When a passage of music is to be performed gradually slower and slower as regards time, it is marked *Ritard* or *Rit.*

MAJOR AND MINOR SCALES.

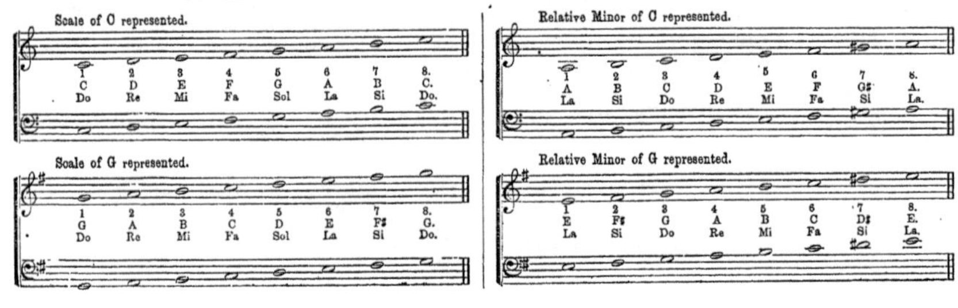
Scale of C represented.
1 2 3 4 5 6 7 8.
C D E F G A B C.
Do Re Mi Fa Sol La Si Do.
Relative Minor of C represented.
1 2 3 4 5 6 7 8.
A B C D E F G♯ A.
La Si Do Re Mi Fa Si La.
Scale of G represented.
1 2 3 4 5 6 7 8.
G A B C D E F♯ G.
Do Re Mi Fa Sol La Si Do.
Relative Minor of G represented.
1 2 3 4 5 6 7 8.
E F♯ G A B C D♯ E.
La Si Do Re Mi Fa Si La.

Scale of D represented.

1	2	3	4	5	6	7	8.
D	E	F♯	G	A	B	C♯	D.
Do	Re	Mi	Fa	Sol	La	Si	Do.

Scale of A represented.

1	2	3	4	5	6	7	8.
A	B	C♯	D	E	F♯	G♯	A.
Do	Re	Mi	Fa	Sol	La	Si	Do.

Scale of E represented.

1	2	3	4	5	6	7	8.
E	F♯	G♯	A	B	C♯	D♯	E.
Do	Re	Mi	Fa	Sol	La	Si	Do.

Scale of F represented.

1	2	3	4	5	6	7	8.
F	G	A	B♭	C	D	E	F.
Do	Re	Mi	Fa	Sol	La	Si	Do.

Relative Minor of D represented.

1	2	3	4	5	6	7	8.
B	C♯	D	E	F♯	G	A♯	B.
La	Si	Do	Re	Mi	Fa	Si	La.

Relative Minor of A represented.

1	2	3	4	5	6	7	8.
F♯	G♯	A	B	C♯	D	E♯	F♯.
La	Si	Do	Re	Mi	Fa	Si	La.

Relative Minor of E represented.

1	2	3	4	5	6	7	8.
C♯	D♯	E	F♯	G♯	A	B♯	C♯.
La	Si	Do	Re	Mi	Fa	Si	La.

Relative Minor of F represented.

1	2	3	4	5	6	7	8.
D	E	F	G	A	B♭	C♯	D.
La	Si	Do	Re	Mi	Fa	Si	La.

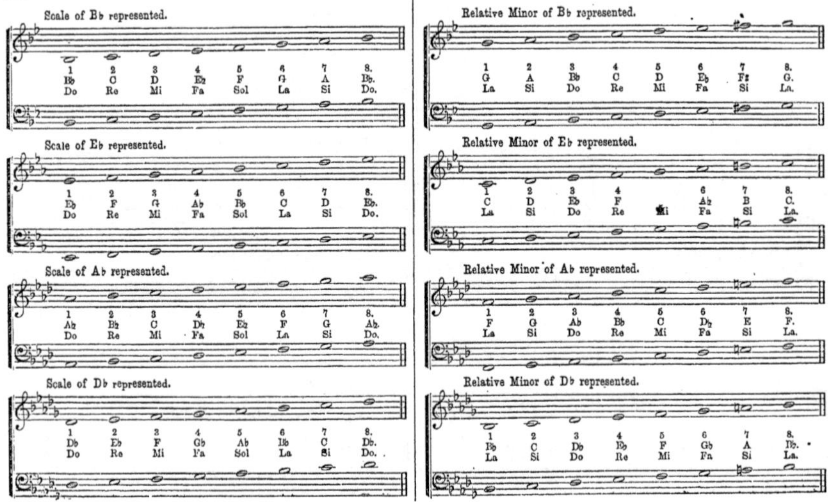
Scale of B♭ represented.
1 2 3 4 5 6 7 8.
B♭ C D E♭ F G A B♭.
Do Re Mi Fa Sol La Si Do.
Scale of E♭ represented.
1 2 3 4 5 6 7 8.
E♭ F G A♭ B♭ C D E♭.
Do Re Mi Fa Sol La Si Do.
Scale of A♭ represented.
1 2 3 4 5 6 7 8.
A♭ B♭ C D♭ E♭ F G A♭.
Do Re Mi Fa Sol La Si Do.
Scale of D♭ represented.
1 2 3 4 5 6 7 8.
D♭ E♭ F G♭ A♭ B♭ C D♭.
Do Re Mi Fa Sol La Si Do.
Relative Minor of B♭ represented.
1 2 3 4 5 6 7 8.
G A B♭ C D E♭ F♯ G.
La Si Do Re Mi Fa Si La.
Relative Minor of E♭ represented.
1 2 3 4 6 7 8.
C D E♭ F A♭ B C.
La Si Do Re Mi Fa Si La.
Relative Minor of A♭ represented.
1 2 3 4 5 6 7 8.
F G A♭ B♭ C D♭ E F.
La Si Do Re Mi Fa Si La.
Relative Minor of D♭ represented.
1 2 3 4 5 6 7 8.
B♭ C D♭ E♭ F G♭ A B♭.
La Si Do Re Mi Fa Si La.

PRACTICAL EXERCISES.

No. 1. The Scale in Whole and Half Notes—Double Time.
Do Do Re Re Mi Mi Fa Fa Sol Sol La La Si Si Do, Do Do Si Si La La Sol Fa Fa Mi Mi Re Re Do
No. 2. The Scale in Half and Quarter Notes—Double Time.
No. 3. The Scale in Quarter and Eighth Notes—Double Time.
If there is one who has not tried his voice, Let him now make the effort, and all will rejoice; For, if you wish to belong to this school, You must labor in earnest, for that is our rule.
No. 4. The Scale in Quarter Notes--Quadruple Time.
No. 5. The Scale in Half and Quarter Notes—Quadruple Time.
Float - ing so sweet - ly o'er hill and o'er vale, Come the soft gush - ing notes of the love l night - in - gale.
No. 6. The Scale in Quarter Notes—Triple Time.
Let us en - deav - or To sing Tri - ple Meas - ure; And beat our time well, If we wish to ex - cel.

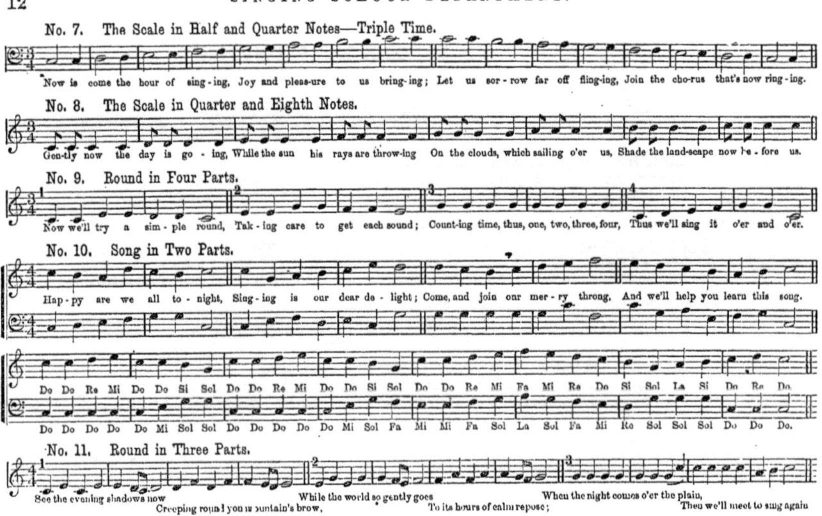
No. 7. The Scale in Half and Quarter Notes—Triple Time.
Now is come the hour of sing-ing, Joy and pleas-ure to us bring-ing; Let us sor-row far off fling-ing, Join the cho-rus that's now ring-ing.
No. 8. The Scale in Quarter and Eighth Notes.
Gen-tly now the day is go-ing, While the sun his rays are throw-ing On the clouds, which sailing o'er us, Shade the land-scape now be-fore us.
No. 9. Round in Four Parts.
Now we'll try a sim-ple round, Tak-ing care to get each sound; Count-ing time, thus, one, two, three, four, Thus we'll sing it o'er and o'er.
No. 10. Song in Two Parts.
Hap-py are we all to-night, Sing-ing is our dear de-light; Come, and join our mer-ry throng, And we'll help you learn this song.
Do Do Re Mi Do Do Si Sol Do Do Re Mi Do Do Si Sol Do Do Re Mi Fa Mi Re Do Si Sol La Si Do Re Do.
Do Do Do Do Do Mi Sol Sol Do Do Do Do Do Mi Sol Fa Mi Mi Fa Sol La Sol Fa Mi Re Sol Sol Sol Do Do Do.
No. 11. Round in Three Parts.
See the evening shadows now
Creeping round yon mountain's brow,
While the world so gently goes
To its hours of calm repose;
When the night comes o'er the plain,
Then we'll meet to sing again

No. 12. Exercise in Four Parts.

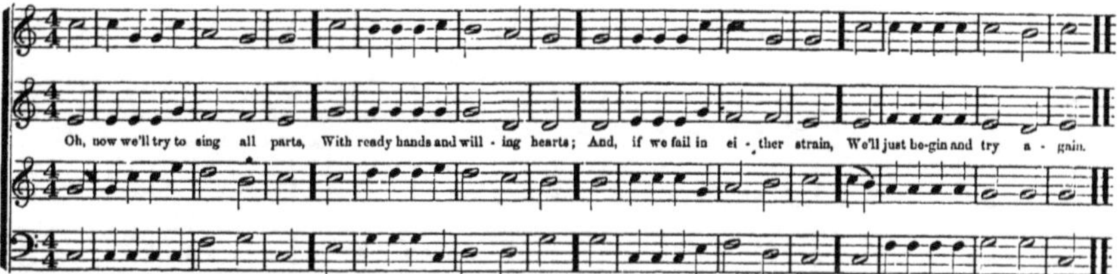
Oh, now we'll try to sing all parts, With ready hands and will - ing hearts; And, if we fail in ei - ther strain, We'll just be-gin and try a - gain.

No. 13. Tune in Quarter Notes.

The turf shall be my fragrant shrine, My temple, Lord! that arch of thine; My censer's breath, the mountain airs, And silent thoughts my constant prayers.

No. 14. Same Succession of Tones as in the preceding Exercise.

My choir shall be the moonlight waves, When murmuring homeward to their caves; Or, when the stillness of the sea, E'en more than music, breathes of thee.

No. 15. Same Succession of Tones as before.

Thy heaven, on which 'tis bliss to look, Shall be my pure and shin-ing book; Where I shall read, in words of flame, The glo-ries of thy wondrous name.

No. 16. Same Succession of Tones as before.

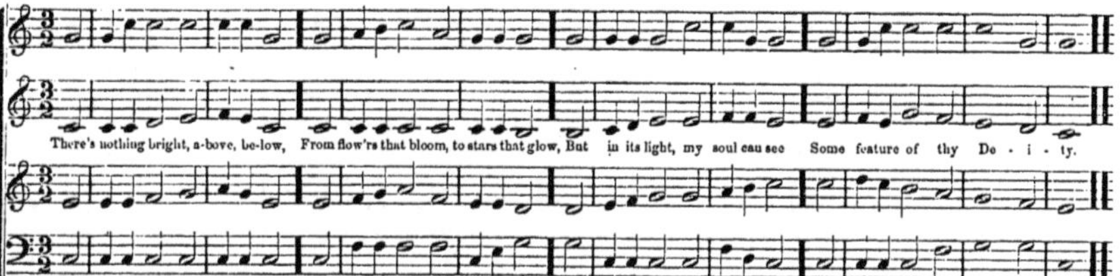
There's nothing bright, a-bove, be-low, From flow'rs that bloom, to stars that glow, But in its light, my soul can see Some feature of thy De - i - ty.

No. 17. Same Succession of Tones as before.

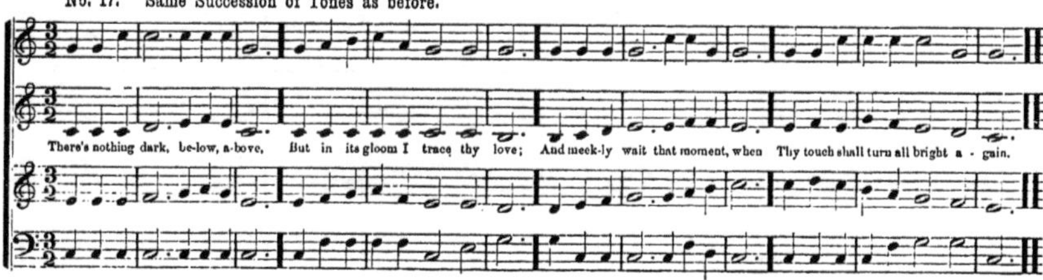
There's nothing dark, be-low, a-bove, But in its gloom I trace thy love; And meek-ly wait that moment, when Thy touch shall turn all bright a - gain.

No. 18. THIS WORLD.

1. This world is not so bad a world, As some would like to make it, And, whether good or whether bad, Depends on how we take it;
2. This world is quite a clev - er world, In rain or pleas- ant weath - er, If peo - ple would but learn to live In har - mo - ny to - geth - er;
3. Then were this world a pleas- ant world, And pleas- ant folks were in it; The day would pass most pleas- ant - ly To those who thus be - gin it:
For if we scold and fret all day, From dew - y morn till e - ven, This world will ne'er af - ford to man A fore - taste here of heav - en.
Nor seek to burst the kind- ly bond, By love and peace ce - ment - ed, And learn that best of les - sons yet, To al - ways be con - tent - ed.
And all the name-less griev-anc - es Brought on by bor-rowed trou - bles, Would prove, as cer - tain - ly they are, A mass of emp - ty bub - bles.

No. 19. THE MERRY HEART.

Words by CHAS. SWAIN.

1. 'Tis well to have a mer - ry heart, How- ev - er short we stay; There's wis - dom in a mer - ry heart, What-e'er the world may say.
2. There's beau-ty in the mer - ry heart, A mor - al beau - ty, too; It shows the heart's an hon - est heart, That 's paid each man his due:
3. The sun may shroud it - self in clouds, The tempest's wrath be - gin; It finds a spark to cheer the dark— Its sun - light is with - in.
Phil - os - o - phy may lift its head, And find out many a flaw, But give me the phil - os - o - pher That's hap - py with a straw.
And lent a share of what's to spare, De - spite of wisdom's fears, And makes the cheek less sor - row speak, The eye weep few - er tears.
Then laugh a - way, let oth - ers say What- e'er they will of mirth; Who laughs the most may tru - ly boast He 's got the wealth of earth.

No. 20. BOUNDING AWAY.

Bounding away with our friends to the mount - ain, Stop we a moment to drink at the fount - ain; Then with new vigor we'll hasten a - way.......
Sing-ing, and laughing, and mak-ing all gay: Mer - ri - ly, mer - ri - ly, mer - ri - ly, mer - ri - ly, mer - ri - ly bound-ing a - way, a - way....
ritard.
ritard.

No. 21. Sharp One and Sharp Four.

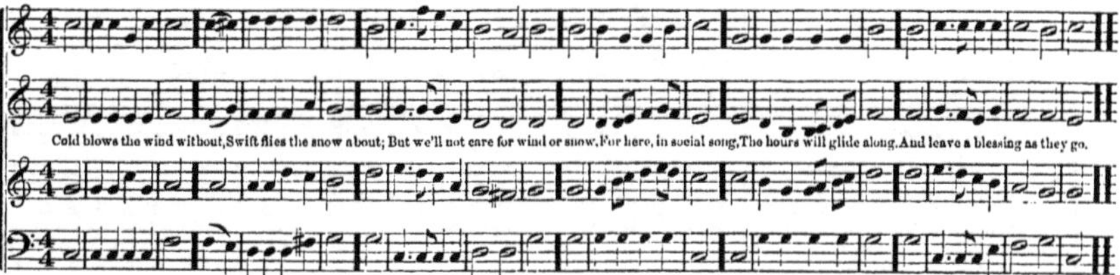
Cold blows the wind without, Swift flies the snow about; But we'll not care for wind or snow, For here, in social song, The hours will glide along, And leave a blessing as they go.

No. 22. Various Chromatic Intervals.

Sad and lone - ly all the day, Have we come our wea - ry way; But be - fore us lights ap - pear, Show-ing that our friends are near.

No. 23. SHEPHERDS IN THE VALE. Words by W. D. B.

SOLO—Soprano.
1. We're hap - py shep - herds in the vale, Our flocks are all our care; We gath - er flowers in ev - 'ry dale, With lov - ing friends to share.
2. At ear - ly dawn of each new day, We trip it o'er the green; While all a - round, in joy - ous play, The lit - tle lambs are seen.
3. Up - on the hill - side is our home, Where friends and pa - rents dwell, And nought would tempt us far to roam From friends we love so well.
4. And when our days on earth are o'er, When heart and flesh doth fail, We'll sleep, with loved ones gone be - fore, With - in this flow - 'ry vale.
We're hap - py, hap - py, hap - py, hap - py shepherds in the vale, We're hap - py, hap - py, hap - py all the day; We sing, and laugh, and lead our flocks in ev - 'ry flow - 'ry dale; And thus we pass the mer - ry hours a - way.
DUET—Soprano and Alto.
We ring our bells, Their mu - sic swells, Up -
La, la, la, la, La, la, la, la,

on the per - fumed gale;.... While e-choes sweet, The strains re-peat To the shepherds in the vale.
La la la la, La la la la, La la la la, La la la la, La la la la, La la la la.
No. 24. THE SILVER STREAM.—Song with Vocal Accompaniment.
SONG. Words by W. D. R.
W.
1. Flow
2. Sing
Tenor.
Soprano.
Alto.
Peaceful riv - er, wilt thou e - ver Be the same as here to - day? Swiftly go - ing, ev - er flow - ing, To the o - cean far a - way.
Base.

on, flow on, thou sil - ver stream, A - long thy winding way; Thy waters in the sun-light gleam, And sparkle, spar - kle all the day. Thy
on, sing on, thou hap - py stream, No sor - row canst thou know; Thus flowing on, thou e'er dost seem The type of- joy, of joy be - low. For
Accomp. pianissimo e stac.
Peaceful riv - er, peaceful riv - er, Wilt thou ev - er, wilt thou ev - er, Peaceful riv - er, Wilt thou ev - er Be the same as here to-day?
banks are covered o'er with flowers Of ev - ery kind and hue; And ma - ny are the hap - py hours I've passed with them and you.
mov - ing on, at ra - pid pace, Are all our pleasures here; But oth - ers come to take their place, And fill our hearts with cheer.
ritard.
Swiftly go - ing, Swiftly go - ing, Ev-er flow - ing, Ev-er flow - ing, Swiftly go - ing, Ev-er flow - ing To the o - cean, far a - way.

No. 25. EARLY FRIENDS.

Words by W. D. B.
CON MOTO. A Minor.
W.
1. Ye much-loved friends of ear - ly years, Oh, say! where are ye gone? I call your names a - mid my tears, But still I am a - lone.
2. How ma - ny friends have gone be-fore, To be for ev - er blest!.. And oth - ers lin - ger on the shore, And soon will be at rest;...
For ye are float - ing far and near Up - on life's troubled wave; And some, who were to me most dear, Are cold with - in their grave.
Though lost to earth, they now are known A - mong the hap - py choir Of "Shin-ing Ones" a-round God's throne—Oh, may I meet them there.

No. 26. THE CRICKET.

1. Lit - tle in - mate, full of mirth, Chirp-ing on the kitch-en hearth, Where-so - e'er be thine a - bode, Al - ways har - bin - ger of good.
2. Neither night nor dawn of day Puts a pe - riod to thy play; Sing, then, and ex - tend thy span Far be - yond the date of man.
Pay me for thy warm re - treat With a song more soft and sweet; In re - turn thou shalt re - ceive Such a song as I can give.
Wretched man, whose years are spent In re - pin - ing dis - con - tent, Lives not, ag - ed though he be, Half a span, compared with thee.

No. 27. I'VE BEEN ROAMING.*

WORDS BY E. JACKSON.

1. I've been roaming thro' the valley Where the rippling water plays; Thro' the meadow where the dew-drops Sparkle in the sun's bright rays; Where the rose and li - ly
2. Where the storm - king his court
3. There en - dur - ing pleas - ure
2. I've been roaming o'er the mountains Where the winds do fiercely blow, Where the earth, all robed in whiteness, Wears a coronal of snow; La, la, la, la, la, la, la, la, la, la, la, la,
3. In my roamings after pleasure Oft a voice would whisper low, Telling of a glorious region, Where true pleasures ev-er flow; La, la, la, la, la, la, la, la, la, la, la, la,
bloom - ing, Lend - eth fra - grance to the breeze, Which, at sum-mer's qui - et evening, Soft - ly mur-murs 'mid the trees.
hold - eth, Where his sub - jects hom - age pay
reign - eth, There do peace and joy a - bound;
la, la, la. La, la, la, la, la, la, la, la, la, la, la, la, la, la, la. To the king, who reign-eth o'er them Till cold win - ter flees a - way.
la, la, la. La, la, la, la, la, la, la, la, la, la, la, la, la, la, la. And, at length, when life is o - ver, There may you and I be found.

* The first part may be sung by Sopranos as a song, the other parts singing *La.*

No. 28. OVER THE SNOW.

No. 29. MAY MORNING.

Mer-ri - ly, mer-ri - ly, o-ver the snow, Careful - ly, careful-ly, onward we go, Cheer-i - ly, cheer-i-ly, raise we our song, Happi - ly, hap-pi-ly, glide we a - long.
Words by W. D. R.
1. Far a - way in the east is break-ing, The day we've been longing to see; So a - rise, and your sleep for - sak-ing, And join in our in - no-cent glee.
2. 'Tis a beau - ti - ful clear May morning, All na - ture is hap-py and gay; So we'll haste, and ourselves a - dorn-ing With flow'rs in the woods far a - way.
3. Then we'll sing and dance round the May-pole, A-way in the meadows so green, So hap - py of heart and so joy - ful, The hap - pi - est girls ev - er seen.

No. 30. MAY.
May in the fra - grant for - est sings, For win-ter's cold has passed a - way; And from the grass the field-lark springs, To greet the beams of opening day.
No. 31. THE RIVER.
1. River, that in silence wind - est Through the meadows bright and free, Till at length thy rest thou find - est In the bo - som of the sea.
2. Thou hast taught me, silent ri - ver, Many a lesson deep and long; Thou hast been a generous giv - er, I can give you but a song.

No. 32. HUNTING SONG.

From MENDELSSOHN.

CON SPIRITO.

A - way to the chase! A - way to the chase! A - way, a - way, a -
A - way to the chase! A - way to the chase! Our hearts with joy are bounding.
A - way to the chase! A - way to the chase! A - way, a - way, a -
- way. Tra la la, tra la la, tra la la, tra la la, tra la la, tra la la, tra la la.
A -
A - way, a - way to the chase! A - way, a - way to the chase, to the chase, to the chase! Tra la
- way. Tra la la, tra la la, tra la la, tra la la, tra la la, tra la la, tra la la.
A -

- way to the chase! A - way to the chase! Our hearts with joy are bound - - ing. Hil - li - o!........ Hil - li
la, tra la la, tra la la, tra la la, tra la la, tra la la, tra la la, tra la la. Hilli - o!............... Hilli - o!.............
- way to the chase! A - way to the chase! Our hearts with joy are bound - - ing. Hil - li - o!........ Hil - li -
f
p
- o! A - way, a - way, a - way, a - way, a - way, a - way, a - way, a - way, a - way, a - way, a - way, a - way, a - way.
f Dim - in - u - en - do po - co a po - co. pp
...... A - way, a - way, a - way, a - way, a - way, a - way, a - way, a - way, a - way, a - way, a - way, a - way, a - way.

No. 33. MUSICAL DIALOGUE.

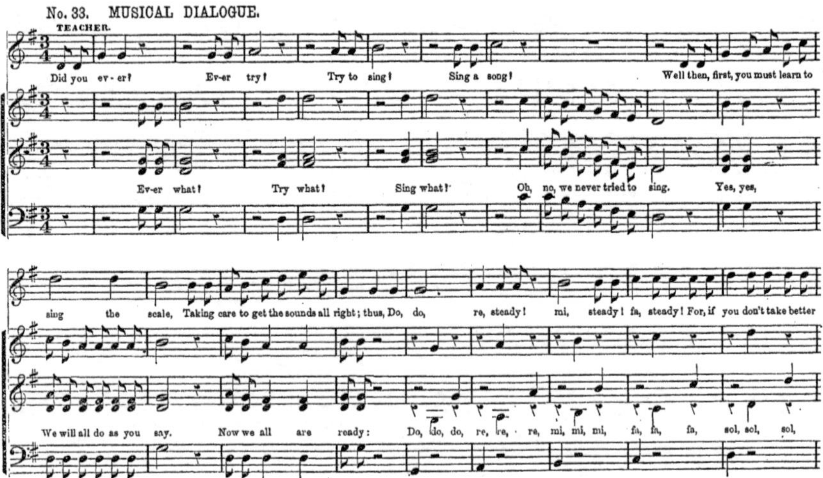
TEACHER.
Did you ev-er? Ev-er try? Try to sing? Sing a song? Well then, first, you must learn to
Ev-er what? Try what? Sing what? Oh, no, we never tried to sing. Yes, yes,
sing the scale, Taking care to get the sounds all right; thus, Do, do, re, steady! mi, steady! fa, steady! For, if you don't take better
We will all do as you say. Now we all are ready: Do, do, do, re, re, re, mi, mi, mi, fa, fa, fa, sol, sol, sol,

care, you will nev - er learn to sing; So, will you not all try once more To sing the scale you tried be-fore? And try it till you get it right, For
la, si, si, si, do.
la, la, si, do. So say we all of us, So say we all of us, So say we all,
you must know that in the scale The best of us are apt to fail. So cour-age now, and you pre-vail, And then in song you'll take de - light.
So say we all of us, So say we all of us, So say we all of us, So say we all.

No. 34. GONE.
Gone are our childhood days Down Time's long river; Gone are the friends we loved—Yes, gone for-ev-er! And will they e'er re-turn? Never! No! Never!
No. 35. DREAMS OF YOUTH.
JEREMIAH MERRILL.
1. Memories of those hap-py days, Come to me, I love you well: Come, and let us sing your praise; Would that ye could ev - er dwell.
2. Then, how free from care was I! Then, how in-no-cent the joy! Peace was ev - er hov-ering nigh, Care was but an i - dle toy.
3. Would that I had nev-er known, What life's stern-er les-sons tell; Dreams of youth for ev - er flown— Hap-py dreams of youth—Fare-well.

No. 36. TO THE HAY-FIELD.

WORDS BY W. D. B.

1. To the hay - field we are go - ing. Will you join us on the way ! . . Where the men and boys are mowing. There we'll have a mer-ry play. Oh, how
2. In the hay - field there are pleasures, Such as make us all feel gay ; . . Happy hearts, good health, the treasures That we find a-mong the hay. Come, then,
fresh- ly smells the clo - ver, Fragrant as the breath of May ; And just lis- ten to that plo - ver, Singing as she flies a - way, as she flies a - way, a- way.
rit. e dim.
friends, and 'mid the clo - ver Let us pass the mer - ry day ; And at night, when day is o - ver, Hasten to our homes a- way, to our homes a - way, a-way.

No. 37. SUNSHINE EVERYWHERE.

WORDS BY W. D. R.

There's sun-shine on the mountain, There's sun - shine on the hill, There's sun-shine in the fountain, And in the laughing rill;
There's sun-shine in the wild-wood, There's sun - shine in the grove, There's sun-shine in our childhood, And in the friends we love.

No. 38. A FAREWELL.

Words by TENNYSON.

1. Flow down, cold streamlet, to the sea, Thy tribute wave de - liv - er; No more by thee my steps shall be For ev - er and for ev - er.
2. But here will sigh thine al - der-tree, And here thine as - pen quiv - er, And here by thee will hum the bee For ev - er and for ev - er.
How soft - ly flows by lawn and lea A streamlet, then a ri - ver; No - where by thee my steps shall be For ev - er and for ev - er.
A thousand suns will stream on thee, A thousand moons will quiv - er, But not by thee my steps shall be For ev - er and for ev - er.

No. 39. OLD FRIENDS TOGETHER.

Words by CHAS. SWAIN. W. R.

1. Oh, time is sweet, when ro - ses meet With spring's sweet breath around them; And sweet the cost, when hearts are lost, If those we love have found them!
2. Those days of old, when youth was bold, And time stole wings to speed it; And youth ne'er knew how fast time flew— Or know-ing, did not heed it!
3. The few long known that years have shown, With hearts that friendship blesses: A hand to cheer—perchance a tear— To soothe a friend's dis - tress - es;
And sweet the mind that still can find A star in dark-est weath - er! But nought can be so sweet to see, As old friends met to - geth - er!
Though gray each brow that meets us now—For age brings wint'ry weath - er—Yet nought can be so sweet to see, As those old friends to - geth - er!
That helped and tried, still side by side— A friend to face hard weath-er; Oh, thus may we yet joy to see, And meet old friends to - geth - er!

No. 40. SERENADE.

1. Sleep on, dear - est, while a - round thee All is wrapt in si - lence deep, While the chains of sleep have bound thee, God doth
2. To the cham - ber of her dwell - ing, Where my love in slum - ber lies; Thro' the trees in love-tones tell - ing, As on
3. And the woo - ing night-wind bears them Far a - way o'er dis - tant plain, And the dream - ing fair one hears them, Hears and

con - - - - stant vi - gils keep, God doth con - stant vi - gils keep, God doth con - stant vi - gils keep.
gold - - - - en lad - ders rise, As on gold - en lad - ders rise, As on gold - en lad - ders rise.
3. Hears and sweet - ly dreams a - gain, Hears and sweet - ly dreams a - gain.
1. Con - stant vi - - - gils keep, Con - stant vi - - - gils keep.
2. As on lad - - - ders rise, As on lad - - - ders rise.
sweet - - ly dreams a - gain, Sweet - ly dreams a - - gain. Sweet - ly dreams a gain.
1. God doth, &c. God doth, &c.

No. 41. THE WAYSIDE WELL.

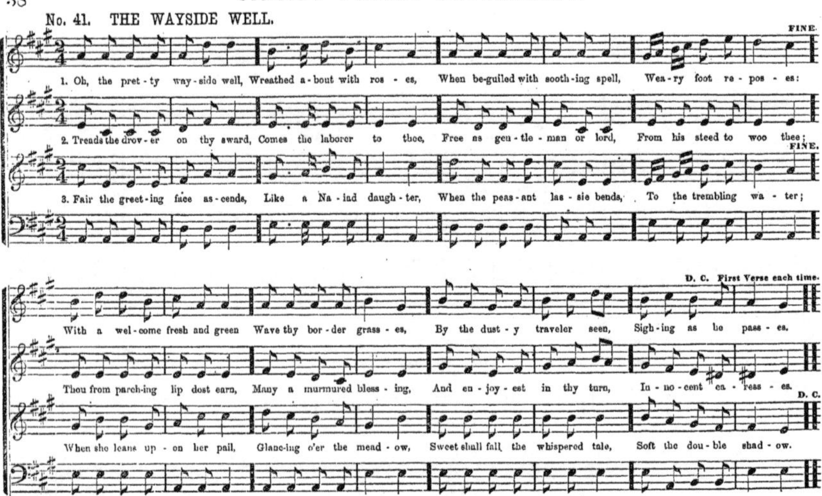
FINE.
1. Oh, the pret - ty way - side well, Wreathed a - bout with ros - es, When be-guiled with sooth-ing spell, Wea - ry foot re - pos - es:
2. Treads the drov - er on thy sward, Comes the laborer to thee, Free as gen - tle - man or lord, From his steed to woo thee;
FINE.
3. Fair the greet - ing face as - cends, Like a Na - iad daugh - ter, When the peas - ant las - sie bends, To the trembling wa - ter;
D. C. First Verse each time.
With a wel - come fresh and green Wave thy bor - der grass - es, By the dust - y traveler seen, Sigh - ing as he pass - es.
Thou from parch-ing lip dost earn, Many a murmured bless - ing, And en - joy - est in thy turn, In - no - cent ca - ress - es.
D. C.
When she leans up - on her pail, Glanc-ing o'er the mead - ow, Sweet shall fall the whispered tale, Soft the dou - ble shad - ow.

No. 42. THE FALLING SNOW.

1. Si - lent - ly down, grace-ful - ly down, O - ver the for - est, and o - ver the town, Rob - ing the earth in a pure white gown.
2. Gen - tly it falls, qui - et - ly falls, Cov - er - ing huts and cov - er - ing halls; Build - ing its mi - nia - ture cities and walls.
3. Cold and bleak, froz - en and bleak, Fly - ing a - bout in a mer - - ry freak, Twirling a - round the mountain's peak,
4. Sweeping a - way, melt - ing a - way, When the sun, with its gold - - en ray, In - to the ar - - bor creeps to play.
Waft - ing to and fro, to and fro, Cir - cling, drift - ing on the ground, Falls the feath - er - y snow.
Over the earth be - low, earth be - low, Spreading in sheets,.. rolling in balls, Danc - ing, frol - ick - ing snow!
Down to the valley be - - low,........ Losing it - self in the rip - pling creek.— Fickle and fleet - ing snow!
Where the vio - lets grow,........ Melt - ing, wast - ing, hiding a - way.— Frail and beau - ti - ful snow!

No. 43. THE LOOSING OF THE SILVER CHORD.

WORDS BY MISS H. F. GOULD.

W.

1. Weep not o'er my sink - ing clay, While the sil - ver chord gives way; Start not, when the fleet-ing breath Leaves it in the arms of death:
2. Pluck the last un - fold - ing rose On my fondling tree that grows; Lay it on this peace-ful breast, When ye bear my form to rest:
3. Swift the flight of time will be, Ere ye all may fol - low me, Where the pass to life is made Through the vale of chill and shade.
For the spir - it's sweet release Must this heart-pulse faint and cease; Soft-winged an - gels hov'ring nigh, Wait the loos-ing sil - ver tie.
Love - ly em - blem of the joy Earth may give, and death de - stroy; Fair - er flowers im-mor - tal bloom In the fields be-yond the tomb.
Pur - er, stronger, at the goal, Are the ties of soul to soul; Where the blissful opening skies Take me as the mor - tal dies.

No. 44. MUSIC.
Words by "MOORE."
D.
1. When thro' life un-blest we rove, Los-ing all that made life dear, Should some notes we used to love In days of boy - hood, meet our ear—
2. Like the gale that sighs a - long Beds of o - ri - ent - al flowers, Is the grateful breath of song That once was heard in hap-pier hours.
3. Mu - sic, oh, how faint, how weak, Language fades be - fore thy spell! Why should feeling ev - er speak When thou canst breathe her soul so well!
Oh, how welcome breathes the strain! Wakening tho'ts that long have slept; Kindling former smiles a - gain In fad - ed eyes that long have wept.
Filled with balm, the gale sighs on, Though the flowers have sunk in death; So, when pleasure's train is gone Its memory lives in Mu-sic's breath.
Friendship's balmy words may feign, Love's are ev'n more false than they; Oh! 'tis on - ly Mu-sic's strain Can sweetly soothe and not be - tray.

No. 45. THE SCHOOL-HOUSE BROOK.

WORDS BY MRS. W. W. — W.

1. Be - side the red school-house just o - ver the hill, A clear brook is flow - ing a bright, sil - ver rill, Fast the years have been passing since
2. A - lone now I wan - der its green banks a - long, And list for the voic - es once joined in my song; Some sing with the an - gels, some
3. Oh, stay thy loud murmurs, bright streamlet, a-while, And chant a low re-quiem, my heart to be-guile, O'er the friends of my child-hood that
hap - py and free, I played on its banks, full of child - ish glee.
still sing on earth; Our cir - cle is brok - en, and hushed is our mirth.
once hap- py throng; Stay, stay thee one mo-ment, then has - ten a - long.
CHORUS.
But the school-house brook flows its on - ward way, As it

did in the days of yore, Its mur - murs to me seem ev - er to say: The friends that I loved are no more.
did in the days of yore, Its mur - murs to me seem ev - er to say: The friends that I loved are no more.
did in the days of yore, Its mur - murs to me seem ev - er to say: The friends that I loved are no more.
No. 46. REMEMBRANCE.
Words from the "Bangor Whig and Courier."
1. There are tones that will haunt us for ever, Far away by the mountain and sea; There are looks which will live with us ever, Till memo-ry ceases to be.
2. There are hopes that our sorrows may lighten, While dreary and dark is the day; And dreams that like sunlight can brighten Our paths, though gloomy the way.
3. There are names that we cherish, though nameless, For aye on our lips they may be; There are hearts full of love, yet seem loveless, And thoughts unexpressed, but still free.

No. 47. ONE BY ONE.—(May be used as an 8s & 7s.)

WORDS BY W. D. R. W.

One by one our friends are landing On the bright and "shining shore;" On the brink we all are standing, Waiting to be carried o'er.
One by one we each shall meet them, When our Master bids us come; One by one we soon shall greet them In our own e - ter - nal home.

No. 48. ABSENT FRIENDS.

Words by LILLA L.
W.
1. Miss-ing some-thing from the day-life, Miss-ing with the eye and ear, Soft-ly creep we where the ling-'ring Look and word shall seem more near.
2. So the lit-tle clock is tick-ing, Count-ing in its form-al way, Like some faith-ful clerk still keep-ing At his post on ho-li-day.
3. So, the mir-ror-pol-ished cour-tier I-dly stands and blank and bland, Rea-dy with its strict at-ten-tion, Faith-ful to the first command.
Qui-et room, but not de-sert-ed, Al-most feel we presence there: "Wait-ing" is the watchword writ-ten On each ta-ble, book, and chair.
So the play-ful breeze co-quet-ing, With the mus-lins at the sash, So the sun-shine, call-ing, coax-ing, With its bright-est beam and flash,
Kneel we in the hap-py si-lence For a moment—then our smile Makes the wel-come warmer, rich-er, Ere we go to wait—the while.

No. 49. MUSIC OF NATURE.

1. There's mu - sic in the midnight breeze, There's mu - sic in the morn; The day-beam and the gen - tle eve, Sweet sounds have ev - er borne; The
2. The winds that sweep the moun - tain top, Their joy - ous ech - oes bear; Young zeph - yrs on the streamlet play, And make sweet mu - sic there; With
3. The heart, too, hath its thrill - ing chords, A con - se - crat - ed fount, From which in - spir - ing mel - o - dies To heaven in glad - ness mount; Why
val - ley hath its wel - come notes, The grove its tune - ful throng, And o - cean's might-y cav - erns teem With na - ture's end - less song.
rust - ling sound the for - est leaves Bend to the pass - ing breeze; And pleas - ant is the bu - sy hum Of flow - er - seek - ing bees.
na - ture's mu - sic— but that man May join the myr - iad throng Of all her glo - rious works in one Har - mo - nious burst of song.

No. 50. INVITATION TO FLORA.

W. Words by W. D. S.

SOLO.
1. The spring.... has come,.... but where.... the flowers.. With which.... to deck..... our May - - day bowers!..............
2. The vio - - lets, hid...... be - side...... the stream,.. Will drink..... with joy...... thy sun - - ny beam;................
3. The ros - - es, too,...... with art - - less grace,... Will turn..... t'wards thee. ... their smil - - ing face;................
4. Then, Flo - - ra, haste,.... and dress..... a - gain..... The mount - ain, val - - ley, and...... the plain;.................
TENOR.
1. The spring has come, but where the flowers, The spring has come, but where the flowers, With which to deck our May-day bowers, To deck our May-day bowers, May-day bowers!
2. The vio-lets hid be - side the stream, The vio-lets hid be - side the stream, Will drink with joy thy sun-ny beam, With joy thy sun - ny beam, sun-ny beam.
3. The ros - es, too, with art-less grace, The ros - es, too, with art-less grace, Will turn t'wards thee their smiling face, T'wards thee their smiling face, smil-ing face.
4. Then, Flo-ra, haste, to dress a-gain, Then, Flo - ra, haste, to dress a-gain The mountain, val - ley, and the plain, The val - ley and the plain, and the plain.
Come, flo - - - ral god - - - dess, come,...... and reign........ And hid - - - den flowers...... will bloom.... a - gain.
And li - - - lies fair......... with - in......... the dells,........ Will soft - - - ly, gen - - - tly ring...... their bells.
The flow - - - rets all,......... with hap - - - py mirth,........ Will leave........ their slum - - bers in...... the earth.
And on......... the mor - - - row, on........ the green,........ With flowers...... we'll crown....... our May - - - day queen.
Come, flo - ral god - dess, come, and reign. Come, flo - ral god - dess, come, and reign, And hid - den flowers will bloom again, The flowers will bloom a - gain.
And li - lies fair with-in the dells, And li - lies fair with-in the dells, Will soft - ly, gen - tly ring their bells, Will gen-tly ring their bells.
The flow - rets all, with hap - py mirth, The flow-rets all, with hap - py mirth, Will leave their slumbers in the earth, Their slumbers in the earth.
And on the mor-row, on the green, And on the mor - row, on the green, With flowers we'll crown our May-day queen, We'll crown our May-day queen.

No. 51. SOFTLY NOW THE LIGHT OF DAY.

Soft - ly now the light of day Fades up - on my sight a - way; Free from care, from la - bor free, Lord, I would commune with thee.
ritard. a tempo.
Soon for me the light of day Shall for ev - er pass a - way; Then, from sin and sor - row free, Take us, Lord, to dwell with thee.
ritard. a tempo.

No. 52. FAINTLY FLOW.

Words by J. G. Percival.

D.
1. Faint-ly flow, thou fall-ing riv - er, Like a dream that dies a - way; To the o-cean glid - ing ev - er, Keep thy calm, un - ruf-fled way:
2. Ros-es bloom, and then they with-er; Cheeks are bright, then fade and die; Shades of light are wafted hith - er, Then, like vis - ions, hur- ry by:
Time, with such a si - lent mo - tion, Fleets a - long, on wings of air, To e - ter - ni - ty's dark o - cean, Burying all its treasures there
Quick as clouds at evening driv - en O'er the ma - ny - colored west, Years are bearing us to heav - en, Home of hap - pi - ness and rest.

No. 53 "COME TO ME IN CHERRY-TIME."

Words by G. P. Morris.

1. Come to me in cher-ry-time, And, as twi-light clos-es, We will have a mer-ry time Here a-mong the ros-es.
2. When the stars with quiet ray.. All the hill-tops brighten, Cherry ripe we'll sing and play Where the cher-ries ri-pen.
When the breezes crisp the tide, And the lin-dens quiv-er, In our bark we'll safe-ly glide Down the rocky ri-ver.
Come to me in cher-ry-time, And, as twi-light clos-es, We will have a mer-ry time Here a-mong the ros-es.

No. 54. THE NEW-YEAR'S PASTORAL VISIT.

WORDS FROM THE "MAINE EVANGELIST."

1. We've gathered here in days gone by Our pas - tor's face to greet, Love in all hearts, joy in each eye, Kind words and friendship sweet.
2. Once more we seek our pas - tor's home To hail the new - born year, With grateful song and prayer we come, Full hands, and words of cheer.
3. If o'er the past some clouds are thrown, We hail these brighter skies; There gather round our pas - tor's home Glad, sun - ny me - mo - ries.
4. The mountains gird our val - ley round, The riv - er glides be - low: So may God's guardian care abound, So let his bounties flow.
Our pastor's home, our pastor's home, Our long-loved pastor's home; The cen - tre of the flock is here, Our long-loved pas - tor's home.
Our pastor's home, our pastor's home, Our long-loved pas - tor's home; With joy we greet the new-born year, Here at our pas-tor's home.
Our pastor's home, our pastor's home, Our long-loved pas - tor's home; There's many a thought of joy that clings A - round our pas-tor's home.
Our hap - py home, our hap - py home, Our childhood's hap - py home; The cen - tre of the world is here, God bless our hap - py home.

No. 55. CRADLE SONG.

Words from the German. D.

1. Evening is balm-y and cool in the west, Lull-ing the gold-en bright meadows to rest, Twinkle like sil - ver stars in the skies,
2. Now all the flow-ers are gone to re - pose, All the sweet incense cups peaceful - ly close, Blossoms rocked lightly on evening's mild breeze,
3. Sleep till the flow-ers are opening once more, Sleep till the lark in the morning shall soar, Sleep till the gold - en bells heavenly chime,
Greeting the two little slumber-ing eyes. Sweetly sleep, Sweetly sleep, Thy watch the good an - gels in par - a - dise keep.
Drowsi-ly, dreami-ly, swinging the trees. Sweet - ly.... sleep,.. Sweet - ly sleep, &c.
Festively welcome the morn-ing's prime, Sweet - ly.... sleep... Sweet - ly sleep,.. Thy watch the good an - gels in pa - ra - dise keep.

No. 56. MORNING.

WORDS BY CHAS. SWAIN.

1. O'er the bend - ing rush - es, O'er the wav - ing corn, Where the fount - ain gush - es Speed the wings of morn.
2. Flow - rets with - out num - ber, As thy foot - steps pass, Lift their heads from slum - ber Out the dew - y grass.
3. From the wild bee's hum - ming, From the cho - ral throng, Know we thou art com - ing, Bring - ing life and song
Like a bird in fleet - ness, Sing - ing on her way, Fold me in thy sweet - ness, An - gel light of day!
Down the low - ly mead - ow, Up the ris - ing ground, Waves of light and shad - ow Chase each oth - er round.
Oh! thou gold - en morn - ing, Bright - est boon of earth, Mead and mount a - dorn - ing, Bless - ed be thy birth!

No. 57. DOWN BY THE RIVER-SIDE.

WORDS BY GEO. P. MORRIS. W.

1. Down by the riv - er-side I stray, As twilight shadows close, And the soft mu-sic of the spray Lulls na-ture to re - pose;
2. Down by the riv - er-side I own A treasure worth the sea, In one, to all the world unknown, Who's all the world to me;
Be - side the stream a maid-en dwells, My star of ev - en - tide! Pure as the wa-ter li - ly - bells, Down by the riv - er - side.
Soon, in her ear - ly bloom and glow, She is to be my bride, Where the sweet wa - ter - li - lies grow, Down by the riv - er - side.

No. 58. BY THE SEA.

WORDS BY ADELBERT OLDER.

W.

1. The wind up - on the sea Is whis - per - ing to me; The great waves rise and fall On the shore;
2. The cliff - tops, bare and brown, Up - on.. the sea look down, Where the rocks the wa - ters meet, Far be - low;
3. The mist - y shad-ows fall A - down the rock - y wall, And the tin - kling waves keep time, At my feet,
4. O wind! O moan-ing sea! A voice thou hast for me; As I list - en to.... thy strain, Wild - ly glad,
And I hear their sounding call, As they beat the rock - y wall,.... Ev - er more, Ev - er more, Ev - er more.
Or the waves, in whis - pers sweet, Come and mur - mur at my feet,.... Sad and slow, Sad and slow, Sad and slow.
Like some soft, me - lo - dious rhyme, Or the church-bells' dis - tant chime,.. Faint and sweet, Faint and sweet, Faint and sweet.
And a joy that's half a pain, Starts to be - ing in my brain. Sweet, yet sad, Sweet, yet sad...............

No. 59. THE HUNTING MORN.

WORDS BY CHAS. SWAIN.

1. Up! up! it is the hunt-ing morn, The woodland rings with mirth; The flowers in dew and light are born, And mer-ry wakes the earth.
2. The stag leaps by—a-way we fly— No cow-ard rein hangs back;... The bay-ing hounds, in cho-rus high, Close fol-low on the track:
3. The tar may boast his wing-ed ship, That sports mid wave and breeze; My flag and ship are horse and whip, And spreading plains my seas...
The deer are trooping down the glen To drink the waters clear, To drink the waters clear; Up! up again my greenwood men! To-day we hunt the deer.
Whilst echo, hid from human ken, Awakes each hollow near, A-wakes each hollow near— With "up a-gain, my greenwood men," To-day we hunt the deer.
clear
Can tars say when, from ocean's den, Such jovial strains they hear, Such jovial strains they hear, As "up a-gain, my greenwood men," To-day we hunt the deer.

Tally ho! tal-ly ho! tal-ly ho! tal-ly ho! To-day we hunt the deer. Tally ho! tal-ly ho! tal-ly ho! tal-ly ho! To-day we hunt the deer.
Tally ho! tal-ly ho! tal-ly ho! tal-ly ho! To-day we hunt the deer. Tally ho! tal-ly ho! tal-ly ho! tal-ly ho! To-day we hunt the deer.
Tally ho! tal-ly ho! tal-ly ho! tal-ly ho! To-day we hunt the deer. Tally ho! tal-ly ho! tal-ly ho! tal-ly ho! To-day we hunt the deer.
No. 60. SERENADE.
D. Words by H. W. LONGFELLOW.
SOLO. Tenor.
1. Stars of the sum-mer - night! Far in yon azure deeps, Hide, hide your gold - en light! She
2. Moon of the sum-mer - night! Far down yon western steeps, Sink, sink in sil - ver light! She
3. Wind of the sum-mer - night! Where yon-der woodbine creeps, Fold, fold thy pin - ions light! She
4. Dreams of the sum-mer - night! Tell her, her lover keeps Watch, while in slum-bers light She
PIANO FORTE.

CHORUS. Tenor. pp
1. Stars of the sum-mer night, Far in yon a - zure
Alto.
sleeps,...... my la - dy sleeps,............ sleeps.................... 2 Moon of the sum - mer night! Far down yon west - ern
Soprano. pp
3. Wind of the sum-mer night! Where yon - der wood-bine
4. Dreams of the sum-mer night! Tell her, her lov - er
Base.
pp ppp
deeps, Hide, hide your gold - en light. my la - dy sleeps, She sleeps, my la - dy sleeps, my la - dy sleeps.
steeps, Sink, sink in sil - ver light. She sleeps, my la - dy sleeps, my la - dy sleeps, my la - dy sleeps.
pp ppp
creeps, Fold, fold thy pin - ions light. She sleeps, my la - dy sleeps, my la - dy sleeps, my la - dy sleeps.
keeps Watch, while in slum - bers light. my la - dy sleeps, she sleeps, my la - dy sleeps, my la - dy sleeps.

No. 61. EVERY DAY HATH TOIL AND TROUBLE.

From BEETHOVEN.

1. Ev - ery day hath toil and trou - ble, Ev - ery heart hath care; Meek - ly bear thine own full bur - den, And thy broth-er's share.

2. Pa - tient - ly en - dur - ing ev - er Let thy spir - it be Bound, by links that can - not sev - er, To hu - man - i - ty.

3. La - bor! wait! tho' mid - night shad - ows Gath - er round thee here, And the storm a - bove thee lowering Fills thy heart with fear.

Fear not, shrink not, though the bur - den Heav - y to thee prove; God shall fill thy mouth with glad-ness, And thy heart with love.

La - bor! wait! thy mas - ter per - ished Ere his task was done; Count not lost the fleet - ing mo-ments, Life has but be - gun.

Wait in hope, the morn-ing dawn - eth, When the night is gone; And a peace - ful rest a - waits thee When thy work is done.

No. 62. FARE THEE WELL.

Words by G. P. Morris.

1. Fare thee well, but not for ev - er, Still we hope to meet a - gain; Fate de - crees that we must sev - er— May our hope be not in vain.
2. Like the shad-ows on the di - al, Lin-gers still our part-ing lay; Ev - ery true heart knows the tri - al Of this sad, un - welcome day.
Oth-er skies will bend a - bove thee, Oth-er scenes will claim their view; But re - mem-ber those who love thee, Far a - way, but ev - er true.
All the world is now be - fore thee, For thou art to roam at will; But with - in the land that bore thee True hearts e'er will love thee still.

No. 63. "IN MEMORIAM."

1. An - oth - er lit - tle form a-sleep, And a lit - tle spir - it gone; An - oth - er lit - tle voice is hushed, And a lit - tle an - gel born.
2. A pair of lit - tle ba - by shoes, And a lock of gold - en hair, The toy our lit - tle dar-ling loved, And the dress she used to wear.
3. The birds will sit on the branch a-bove, And sing a re - qui - em To the beautiful lit - tle sleep-ing form, That used to sing to them.
Two lit - tle feet are on the way To the home be-yond the skies; And our hearts are like the void that comes When a strain of mu - sic dies.
The lit - tle grave in the sha - dy nook, Where the flow-ers love to grow; And these are all of the lit - tle hope That came three years a - go.
But never again will the lit - tle lips To their songs of love re - ply; For that silvery voice is blend-ed with The min-strel-sy on high.

No. 64.—CHORAL. "Let all men praise the Lord." ARR. BY MENDELSSOHN.

ANDANTE CON MOTO.
Sopranos.
1. Let all men praise the Lord, In wor - ship low - ly bend - ing, On his most ho - ly word, Re - deemed from woe de -
Alto.
Tenors. mf
2. Glo - ry and praise to God The Fa - ther— Son be giv - en, And to the Ho - ly Ghost On high, enthroned in
Bass.
- pend - ing. He gra - cious is, and just; From child-hood us doth lead; On him we place our trust, And hope in time of need.
p
cres.
p
heav - en; Praise to the might-y God, With powerful arm and strong, He chang-eth night to day— Praise him with grate - ful song.

THE

PRAISE OF ZION.

LAUDAMUS. L. M.

W.

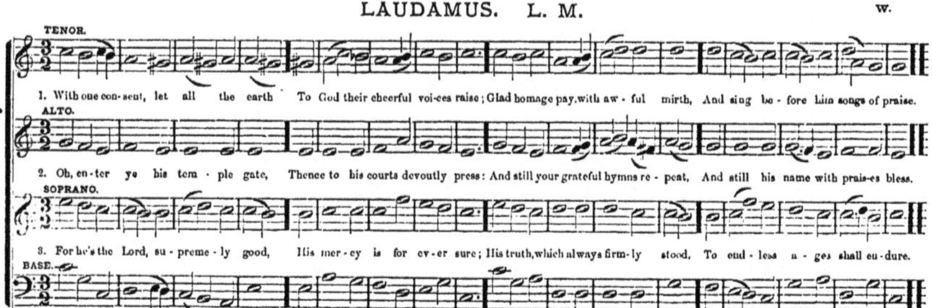
TENOR.
1. With one con-sent, let all the earth To God their cheerful voi-ces raise; Glad homage pay, with aw - ful mirth, And sing be - fore hiin songs of praise.
ALTO.
2. Oh, en-ter ye his tem - ple gate, Thence to his courts devoutly press: And still your grateful hymns re - peat, And still his name with prais-es bless.
SOPRANO.
3. For he's the Lord, su - preme - ly good, His mer - cy is for ev - er sure; His truth, which always firm - ly stood, To end - less a - ges shall en - dure.
BASE.

MENVILLE. L. M.

Arranged from MENDELSSOHN, Sym. No. 3, by Dr. L. MASON.

1. O thou that hear'st when sinners cry, Tho' all my crimes before thee lie, Be-hold me not with an - gry look, But blot their mem'ry from thy book.
2. Create my nature pure with - in, And form my soul a-verse to sin; Let thy good Spir-it ne'er de - part, Nor hide thy presence from my heart.
3. I can- not live without thy light, Cast out and banished from thy sight; Thy ho - ly joys, my God, re - store, And guard me that I fall no more.
BOYD. L. M.
A. D. JAY.
1. With one consent, let all the earth To God their cheerful voic- es raise; Glad homage pay, with aw-ful mirth, And sing be - fore him songs of praise.
2. Oh, en- ter ye his temple gate, Thence to his courts de - vout - ly press; And still your grateful hymns re-peat, And still his name with prais- es bless.
3. For he's the Lord, supremely good, His mer- cy is for - ev - er sure; His truth, which always firmly stood, To end- less a - ges shall en - dure.

MORTON. L. M.

CH. ZEUNER.

Awake, awake, each sluggish soul! Awake, and view the set- ting sun! See how the shades of death ad-vauce, Ere half the task of life is dove.
SOLI.
SOLI.
Awake, awake, each sluggish soul! Awake, and view the set- ting sun! See how the shades of death ad-vauce, Ere half the task of life is done.
LACY. L. M.
O. M. WYMAN.
1. Wait, O my soul, thy Maker's will! Tumultuous passions, all be still; Nor let a murmuring tho't a - rise: His ways are just, his counsels wise.
2. He in the thickest darkness dwells, Performs his work, the cause conceals; And, tho' his footsteps are uuknown, Judgment and truth support his throne.
3. In heaven, and earth, and air, and seas, He ex - e-cutes his firm de- crees; And by his saints it stands confessed, That what he does is ev - er best.

COMPASSION. L. M.
1. "Come hith - er, all ye weary souls; Ye heavy - lad-en sin - ners, come! I'll give you rest from all your toils, And raise you to my heaven - ly home.
2. "They shall find rest who learn of me: I'm of a meek and low - ly mind; But pas - sion rag-es like the sea, And pride is rest-less as the wind.
3. "Blest is the man whose shoulders take My yoke, and bear it with de - light: My yoke is ea - sy to his neck, My grace shall make the burden light."
STRONG. L. M.
C. H. P.
1. Come, let us sing the song of songs— The saints in heaven be - gan the strain— The homage which to Christ belongs: "Worthy the Lamb, for he was slain!"
2. Slain to re-deem us by his blood, To cleanse from ev - ery sin - ful stain, And make us kings and priests to God—"Worthy the Lamb, for he was slain!"
3. To him who suf - fered on the tree, Our souls, at his soul's price, to gain, Blessing, and praise, and glory be: "Worthy the Lamb, for he was slain!"

PATRIUS. L. M.
1. Come, wea-ry souls, with sin distressed, Come, and accept the prom-ised rest; The Sav-iour's gra - cious call o - bey, And cast your gloom-y fears a - way.
2. Op-pressed with guilt,—a painful load,—Oh, come and bow be-fore your God! Di - vine com-pas - sion, mighty love Will all the pain - ful load re move.
3. Here mercy's boundless ocean flows To cleanse your guilt and heal your woes; Par-don, and life, and end - less peace— How rich the gift, how free the grace!
ARMOR. L. M.
O. R. BARROWS.
Stand up, my soul! shake off thy fears, And gird the gospel ar-mor on; March to the gates.................. of endless joy, Where Je-sus, thy great Captain 's gone.
Stand up, my soul! shake off thy fears, And gird the gospel ar-mor on; March to the gates of endless joy, Where Je-sus, thy great Captain 's gone.
Stand up, my soul! shake off thy fears, And gird the gospel ar-mor on; March to the gates....... of end-less joy, Where Je-sus, thy great Captain 's gone.
March to the gates.................. &c.

SHENLEY. L. M.
1. Je - sus demands this heart of mine, Demands my love, my joy, my care; But ah! how dead to things di - vine, How cold my best af - fec - tions are.
2. 'Tis sin, a - las! with dread-ful power, Divides my Saviour from my sight; Oh, for one hap - py, cloudless hour Of sa - cred free-dom, sweet de - light!
3. Lord! let thy love shine forth and raise My captive powers from sin and death, And fill my heart and life with praise, And tune my last ex - pir - ing breath.
NORWAY. L. M.
1. My soul be - fore thee prostrate lies; To thee, her Source, my spir - it flies: My wants I mourn, my chains I see,— Oh, let thy presence set me free!
2. Un - done and lost, for aid I cry; In thy death, Saviour, let me die; Griev'd with thy grief, pained with thy pain, Ne'er let me live for self a - gain.
3. In life's short day let me yet more Of thine en - livening love implore; My mind must deep-er sink in thee, My foot stand firm, from wandering free.

WOODSTOCK. L. M.

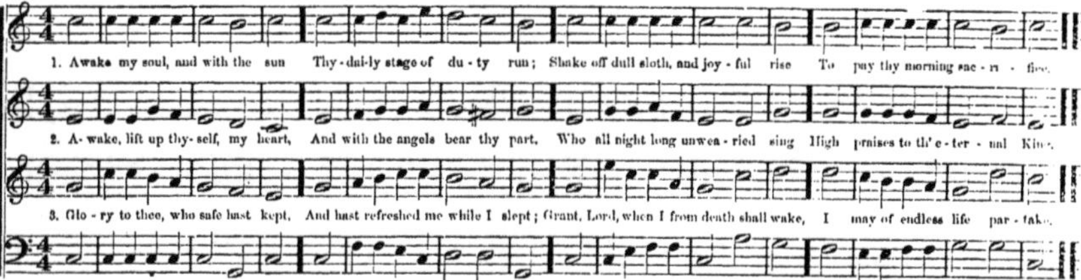
1. Awake my soul, and with the sun Thy-dai-ly stage of du - ty run; Shake off dull sloth, and joy - ful rise To pay thy morning sac - ri - fice.
2. A- wake, lift up thy- self, my heart, And with the angels bear thy part, Who all night long unwea - ried sing High praises to th' e - ter - nal Kin
3. Glo - ry to thee, who safe hast kept, And hast refreshed me while I slept; Grant, Lord, when I from death shall wake, I may of endless life par - tak

ENERGY. L. M.

W.

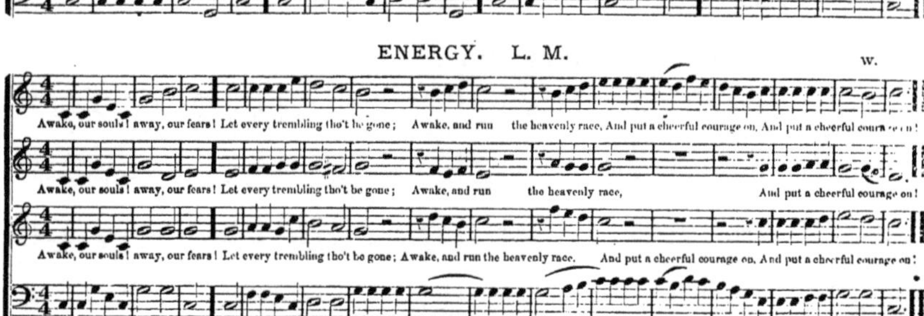
Awake, our souls! away, our fears! Let every trembling tho't be gone; Awake, and run the heavenly race, And put a cheerful courage on, And put a cheerful cour
Awake, our souls! away, our fears! Let every trembling tho't be gone; Awake, and run the heavenly race, And put a cheerful courage on!
Awake, our souls! away, our fears! Let every trembling tho't be gone; Awake, and run the heavenly race. And put a cheerful courage on, And put a cheerful courage on!

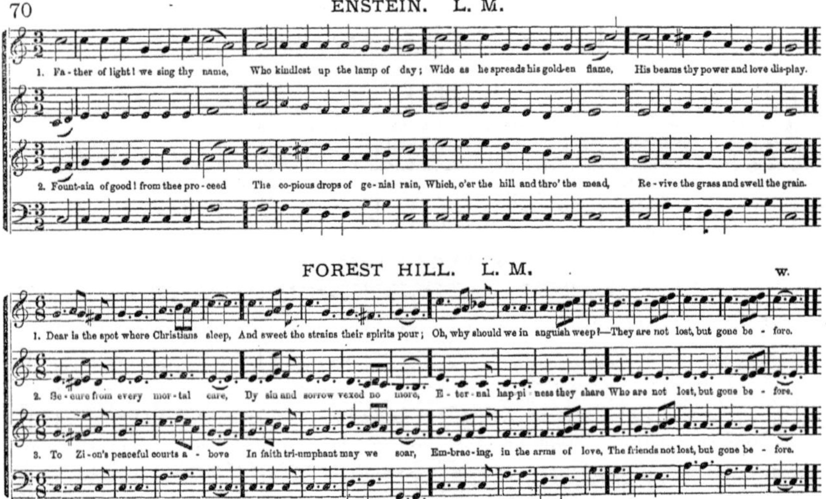
ENSTEIN. L. M.
1. Fa - ther of light! we sing thy name, Who kindlest up the lamp of day; Wide as he spreads his gold-en flame, His beams thy power and love dis-play.
2. Fount-ain of good! from thee pro - ceed The co-pious drops of ge - nial rain, Which, o'er the hill and thro' the mead, Re - vive the grass and swell the grain.
FOREST HILL. L. M.
W.
1. Dear is the spot where Christians sleep, And sweet the strains their spirits pour; Oh, why should we in anguish weep?—They are not lost, but gone be - fore.
2. Se - cure from every mor - tal care, By sin and sorrow vexed no more, E - ter - nal hap - pi - ness they share Who are not lost, but gone be - fore.
3. To Zi - on's peaceful courts a - bove In faith tri-umphant may we soar, Em-brac - ing, in the arms of love, The friends not lost, but gone be - fore.

GREENWOOD. L. M.

1. Sweet is the scene when Christians die, When ho-ly souls re - tire to rest; How mildly beams the clos-ing eye! How gently heaves th'ex-pir-ing breast!
2. So fades a sum-mer cloud a - way; So sinks the gale when storms are o'er; So gently shuts the eye of day; So dies a wave a - long the shore.
3. Triumphant smiles the vic - tor's brow, Fanned by some guardian an - gel's wing; O Grave! where is thy vic-tory now? And where, O Death! where is thy sting!

KIMBALL. L. M.

O. R. BARROWS.

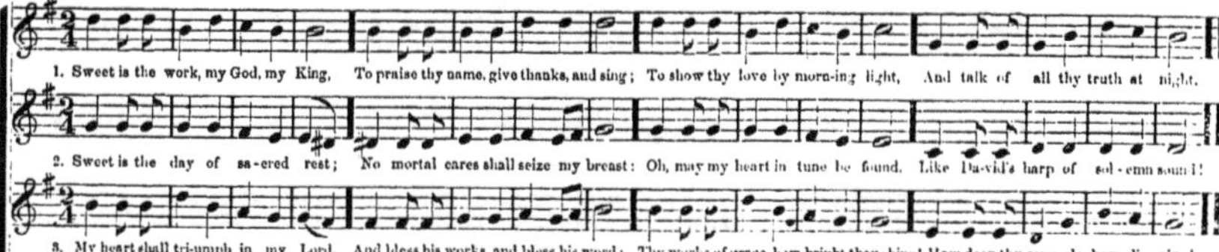
1. Sweet is the work, my God, my King, To praise thy name, give thanks, and sing; To show thy love by morn-ing light, And talk of all thy truth at night.
2. Sweet is the day of sa-cred rest; No mortal cares shall seize my breast: Oh, may my heart in tune be found, Like Da-vid's harp of sol - emn sound!
3. My heart shall tri-umph in my Lord, And bless his works, and bless his word; Thy works of grace, how bright they shine! How deep thy counsels, how di - vine!

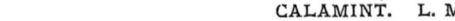

CALAMINT. L. M.

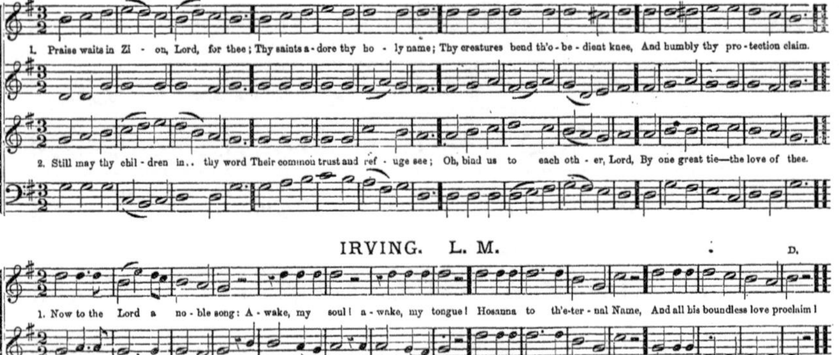
1. Praise waits in Zi - on, Lord, for thee; Thy saints a - dore thy ho - ly name; Thy creatures bend th'o - be - dient knee, And humbly thy pro - tection claim.
2. Still may thy chil - dren in.. thy word Their common trust and ref - uge see; Oh, bind us to each oth - er, Lord, By one great tie—the love of thee.

IRVING. L. M.

D.

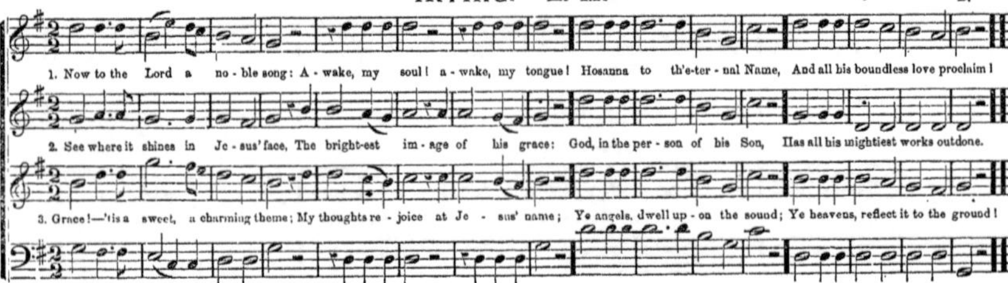
1. Now to the Lord a no - ble song: A - wake, my soul! a - wake, my tongue! Hosanna to th'e - ter - nal Name, And all his boundless love proclaim!
2. See where it shines in Je - sus' face, The bright-est im - age of his grace: God, in the per - son of his Son, Has all his mightiest works outdone.
3. Grace!—'tis a sweet, a charming theme; My thoughts re - joice at Je - sus' name; Ye angels, dwell up - on the sound; Ye heavens, reflect it to the ground!

VINTNER. L. M.

1. Thine earthly Sabbaths, Lord, we love,—But there's a nobler rest a - bove: To that our longing souls aspire, With cheerful hope and strong desire.
2. No more fatigue, no more dis-tress, Nor sin nor death shall reach the place; No groans shall mingle with the songs Which war-ble from im - mor - tal tongues.
3. No rude alarms of rag - ing foes; No cares to break the long re - pose; No midnight shade, no clouded sun; But sa - cred, high, e - ter - nal noon.
BUFFORD. L. M.
1. Awake, my soul! lift up thine eyes; See where thy foes against thee rise, In long array, in numerous host; Awake, my soul, or thou art lost! Awake, my soul, or thou art lost.
2. Thou tread'st upon enchanted ground; Perils and snares beset thee round; Beware of all; guard every part; But most, the traitor in thy heart. But most, the traitor in thy heart.
3. Come then, my soul! now learn to wield The weight of thine immortal shield; Put on the armor, from above, Of heavenly truth, and heavenly love, Of heavenly truth, &c.

TOWER. L. M.
W. D. R.
1. Rejoice, ye saints, rejoice and praise The blessings of re - deem- ing grace! Jesus, your ev- er - last - ing tower, Stands firm against the tempest's power.
2. He is a ref-uge ev - er nigh; His love endures as mountains high; His name 's a rock, which winds above, And waves below, can nev- er move.
3. While all things change, he changes not; He ne'er forgets, though oft for - got; His love will ev-er be the same; His word, enduring as his name.
MERNET. L. M.
*
1. Let one loud song of praise a- rise To God, whose goodness ceaseless flows, Who dwells enthroned above the skies, And life and breath on all bestows.
2. Great Source of life, our souls confess The va - rious rich-es of thy grace; Crowned with thy mercy, we rejoice, And in thy praise ex - alt our voice.

BAKER. L. M.

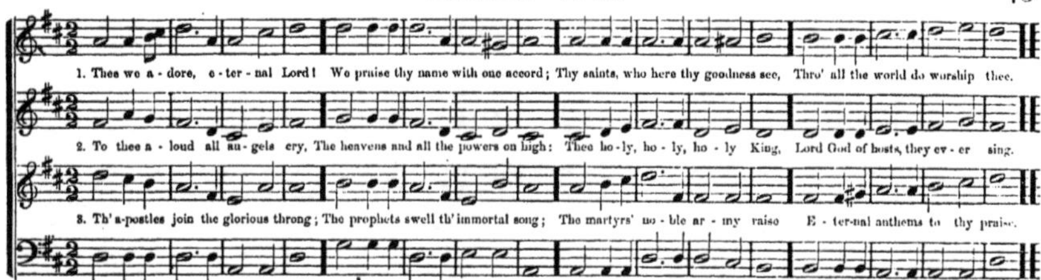
1. Thee we a - dore, e - ter - nal Lord! We praise thy name with one accord; Thy saints, who here thy goodness see, Thro' all the world do worship thee.
2. To thee a - loud all an - gels cry, The heavens and all the powers on high: Thee ho - ly, ho - ly, ho - ly King, Lord God of hosts, they ev - er sing.
3. Th' a-postles join the glorious throng; The prophets swell th' immortal song; The martyrs' no - ble ar - my raise E - ter-nal anthems to thy praise.

EMPIRE. L. M.

1. Jesus shall reign where'er the sun Does his suc-ces-sive journeys run; His kingdom stretch from shore to shore, Till moons shall wax and wane no more.
2. People and realms of ev - ery tongue Dwell on his love with sweetest song; And in-fant voi-ces shall proclaim Their early blessings on his name.
3. Blessings abound where'er he reigns; The prisoner leaps to loose his chains; The weary find e - ter - nal rest, And all the sons of want are

TWILIGHT. L. M.
1. Soft - ly the shade of evening falls, Sprinkling the earth with dew - y tears, While nature's voice to slumber calls, And silence reigns within the spheres.
2. How sweet the bour of clös - ing day, When all is peace - ful and se - rene, And when the sun with cloudless ray Sheds mellow lus - tre o'er the scene.
MANTON. L. M.
1. There is a stream, whose gentle flow Supplies the city of our God; Life, love, and joy still gliding thro', Life, love, and joy still gliding thro', And wat'ring our divine abode.
2. That sacred stream, thine holy word, Our grief allays, our fear controls; Sweet peace thy promises afford, Sweet peace thy promises afford, And give new strength to fainting souls.
3. Zion enjoys her Monarch's love, Secure against a threat'ning hour; Nor can her firm foundations move, Nor can her firm foundations move, Built on his truth and arm'd with pow'r.

NOONDAY. L. M.
W.
1. There is a re - gion love - lier far Than sa - ges tell or po - ets sing, Brighter than noonday glo - ries are, And softer than the tints of spring.
2. It is not fann'd by sum - mer's gale, 'Tis not refreshed by ver - nal showers, It never needs the moonbeams pale, For there are known no evening hours.
SABBATH. L. M.
O. R. BARROWS.
1. Thine earth - ly Sab - baths, Lord, we love,— But there's a no - bler rest a - bove: To that our long - ing
2. No more fa - tigue, no more.... dis - tress, Nor sin nor death shall reach the place; No groans.. shall min - gle
3. No rude.... a - larms of rag - ing foes; No cares.... to break the long.... re - pose; No mid - night shade,... no

SABBATH. (Concluded.)

BERNE. L. M.

From BEETHOVEN

souls a - spire, With cheer - ful hope and strong de - sire.
with the songs Which war - ble from im - mor - tal tongues.
cloud - ed sun; But sa - cred, high, e - ter - nal noon.
1. The flow - ery spring, at God's command, Perfumes the
2. His hand in au - tumn rich - ly pours, Through all her
3. The changing sea - sons, months, and days De - mand suc -
air, and paints the land: The sum - mer rays with vig - or shine, To raise the corn, and cheer the vine.
coasts, re - dun - dant stores; And win - ters, soft - ened by his care, No more the face of hor - ror wear.
- ces - sive songs of praise; And be the cheer - ful hom - age paid, With morn - ing light, and eve - ning shade.

CARRIE. L. M. 6 lines.

1. The Lord my pas - tore shall pre - pare, And feed me with a shep - herd's care; His pres - ence shall my wants sup - ply, And
2. When in the sul - try glebe I faint; Or on the thirst - y mountain pant, To fer - tile vales, and dew - y meads, My
3. Though in the paths of death I tread, With gloom - y hor - rors o - ver - spread, My stead - fast heart shall fear no ill, For
guard me with a watch - ful eye: My noon - day walks he shall at - tend, And all my mid - night hours de - fend.
wea - ry, wandering steps he leads; Where peace - ful riv - ers, soft and slow, A - mid the ver - dant land - scape flow.
thou, O Lord, art with me still: Thy friend - ly rod shall give me aid, And guide me through the dread - ful shade.

BELLEVILLE. L. M.

*
1. A - wake, my soul, and with the sun Thy dai - ly stage of du - ty run; Shake off dull sloth, and joyful rise To pay thy morn-ing sac-ri - fice.
2. A- wake, lift up thy - self, my heart, And with the an - gels bear thy part, Who all night long un-wea-ried sing High praises to th' e - ter-nal King.
3. Lord, I my vows to thee re - new; Scat - ter my sins like morn - ing dew; Guard my first springs of tho't and will, And with thyself my spir-it fill.
STANWOOD. L. M.
W.
1. Stand up, my soul! shake off thy fears, And gird the gos - pel ar - mor on; March to the gates of endless joy, Where Jesus, thy great Captain's gone.
2. Hell and thy sins re - sist thy course; But hell and sin are vanquish'd foes: Thy Je - sus nailed them to the cross, And sung the triumph when he rose.
3. There shall I wear a star - ry crown, And tri-umph in al - might-y grace, While all the ar - mies of the skies Join in my glorious Leader's praise.

VINELAND. L. M.
D.
1. Oh, come, loud anthems let us.... sing, Loud thanks to our al-might-y King! For we our voi - ces high should raise, When our sal-va-tion's Rock we... praise.
2. In - to his pres-ence let us haste, To thank him for his fav - ors past; To him ad - dress in joy - ful.... songs The praise that to his name be - longs.
3. Oh, let us to his courts re - pair, And bow with a - do - ra - tion there! Down on our knees, de-vout - ly,.... all Be - fore the Lord, our Mak-er, fall.
DEANE. L. M.
1. Our Helper, God! we bless thy name, The same thy pow'r, thy grace the same; The tokens of thy lov - ing care O - pen and crown and close the year.
2. A - mid ten thousand snares we stand, Sup-port-ed by thy guard-ian hand; And see, when we sur - vey our ways, Ten thousand mon - u - ments of praise.
3. Thus far thine arm hath led us on; Thus far we make thy mer - cy known; And, while we tread this des-ert land, New mercies shall new songs de - mand.

AYBOL. L. M.
D.
1. Thus far the Lord has led me on; Thus far his power prolongs my days; And every evening shall make known Some fresh me-mo- rial of his grace.
2. Much of my time has run to waste, And I, perhaps, am near my home; But he forgives my fol - lies past, And gives me strength for days to come.
3. I lay my bod - y down to sleep; Peace is the pil - low for my head; While well-ap-point-ed an - gels keep Their watchful stations round my bed.
SHERMAN. L. M.
G. S. CHENEY.
1. Oh, that my heart was right with thee, And loved thee with a perfect love; Oh, that my Lord would dwell in me, And nev - er from his seat re - move.
2. Oh, let my prayer acceptance find, And bring thy mighty blessing down; Eye-sight impart, for I am blind, And seal me thine a - dopt- ed son.

BATH. L. M. Double.

DECLAMANDO.
1. The heavens declare thy glo-ry, Lord; In ev-ery star thy wisdom shines; But when our eyes behold thy word, We read thy name in fair-er lines.
3. Sun, moon, and stars convey thy praise Round the whole earth, and never stand; So when thy truth began its race, It touched and glanced on every land.
5. Great Sun of Righteousness, a-rise! Bless the dark world with heavenly light: Thy gospel makes the simple wise, Thy laws are pure, thy judgments right.
2. The roll-ing sun, the changing light, And night, and day, thy power confess; But the blest volume thou hast writ, Reveals thy just-ice and thy grace.
4. Nor shall thy spreading gospel rest, Till thro' the world thy truth hath run; Till Christ hath all the nations blest That see the light, or feel the sun.
6. Thy noblest wonders here we view In souls renewed, and sins forgiven; Lord, cleanse my sins, my soul renew, And make thy word my guide to heaven.

EVANDALE. L. M.

*
1. Re - turn, my soul, un - to thy rest, From vain pursuits and maddening cares, From lonely woes that wring thy breast,—The world's alluring, fa-tal snares.
2. Re - turn un - to thy rest, my soul, From all the wanderings of thy thought,—From sickness unto death made whole, Safe through a thousand perils brought.
3. God is thy Rest;—with heart inclined To keep his word, that word believe: Christ is thy Rest; with lowly mind, His light and eas - y yoke re - ceive.
HALL. L. M.
W. D. R.
1. God calling yet!—shall I not hear? Earth's pleasures shall I still hold dear? Shall life's swift passing years all fly, And still my soul in slumbers lie?
2. God calling yet!—shall I not rise? Can I his loving voice de - spise, And basely his kind care re-pay? He calls me still: can I de - lay?
3. God calling yet!—I cannot stay; My heart I yield without de - lay: Vain world, farewell! from thee I part; The voice of God hath reached my heart!

LOWE. L. M.
W.
1. He that hath made his refuge, God, Shall find a most se-cure a - bode; Shall walk all day beneath his shade, And there, at night, shall rest his head.
1. From all that dwell be-low the skies, Let the Cre-a-tor's praise a-rise; Let the Redeemer's name be sung, Through every land, by ev - ery
2. E - ter - nal are thy mercies, Lord; E - ter - nal truth attends thy word: Thy praise shall sound from shore to shore, Till suns shall rise and set no
MASARDIS. L. M.
C. H. P.
1. With all my powers of heart and tongue, I'll praise my Ma - ker in my song; Angels shall hear the notes I raise, Approve the song, and join the
2. To God I cried when troubles rose; He heard me, and subdued my foes: He did my rising fears control, And strength diffused thro' all my
3. I'll sing thy truth and mercy, Lord, I'll sing the won - ders of thy word; Not all thy works and names below So much thy power and glory show.

MARGATE. L. M. Double.

1. The spacious fir - mament on high, With all the blue e-the-real sky, . And spangled heavens, a shining frame, Their great o - rig - in - al .pro - claim.
3. Soon as the eve - ning shades pre-vail, The moon takes up the wondrous tale, And nightly to the listening earth Repeats the sto - ry of her birth;—
5. What tho', in sol - emn si-lence, all Move round this dark ter-res-trial ball? What tho' nor real voice nor sound A-mid their ra - diant orbs be found?
2. Th'unwearied sun, from day to day, Does his Cre - a - tor's pow'r display, And publish - es to ev - ery land The work of an Almighty hand.
4. While all the stars that round her burn, And all the plan - ets in their turn, Confirm the tid - ings as they roll, And spread the truth from pole to pole.
6. In reason's ear they all re - joice, And ut-ter forth a glorious voice; For-ev - er sing - ing, as they shine, "The hand that made us is Di - vine."

FAIRSTAR. L. M.

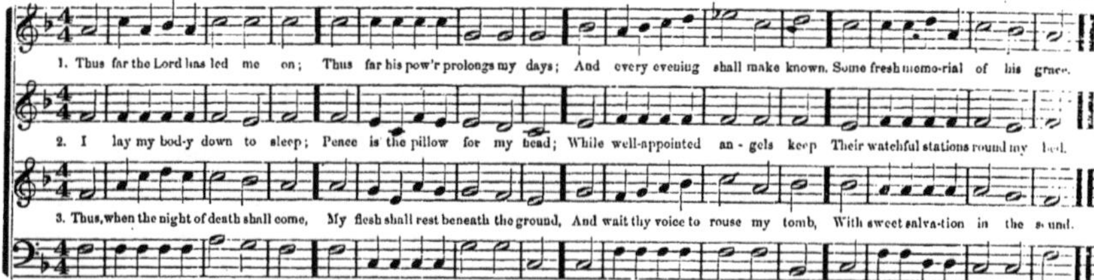
1. Thus far the Lord has led me on; Thus far his pow'r prolongs my days; And every evening shall make known. Some fresh memo-rial of his grace.
2. I lay my bod-y down to sleep; Peace is the pillow for my head; While well-appointed an - gels keep Their watchful stations round my
3. Thus, when the night of death shall come, My flesh shall rest beneath the ground, And wait thy voice to rouse my tomb, With sweet salva-tion in the

CONTRITION. L. M.

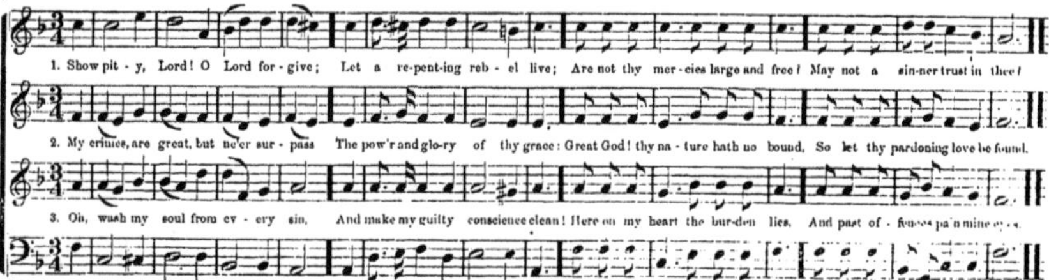
1. Show pit - y, Lord! O Lord for - give; Let a re-pent-ing reb - el live; Are not thy mer - cies large and free! May not a sin-ner trust in thee!
2. My crimes, are great, but ne'er sur - pass The pow'r and glo-ry of thy grace: Great God! thy na - ture hath no bound, So let thy pardoning love be found.
3. Oh, wash my soul from ev - ery sin, And make my guilty conscience clean! Here on my heart the bur-den lies, And past of -

CORRY. L. M.
H. A. B.
1. Come, O my soul! in sa-cred lays, Attempt thy great Cre-a-tor's praise; But oh, what tongues can speak his fame! What mor-tal verse can reach the theme!
2. Enthroned a-mid the ra-diant spheres, He glo-ry like a gar-ment wears; To form a robe of light di-vine, Ten thousand suns a-round him shine.
3. In all our Maker's grand de-signs, Almighty power, with wis-dom, shines; His works, thro' all this wondrous frame, Declare the glo-ry of his name.
FORESTER. L. M.
D.
1. See gentle pa-tience smile on pain, See dy-ing hope re-vive a-gain; Hope wipes the tear from sor-row's eye, While faith points up-ward to the sky.
2. Asleep in Je-sus! bless-ed sleep! From which none ever wake to weep;— A calm and un-dis-turbed re-pose, Un-broken by the last of foes.
3. Asleep in Je-sus! oh, for me May such a bliss-ful ref-uge be! Se-cure-ly shall my ash-es lie, And wait the sum-mons from on high.

PARMA. L. M.

D.
1. When I survey the wondrous cross, On which the Prince of Glory died, My rich-est gains I count for loss, And pour contempt on all my pride.
2. See from his head, his hands, his feet, Sor - row and love flow mingled down! Did e'er such love and sor-row meet, Or thorns compose so rich a crown.
3. Were the whole realm of nature mine, That were an offering far too small; Love so a-maz-ing, so di - vine, De-mands my soul, my life, my all.
REST. L. M.
O. R. BARROWS.
1. Re - turn, my soul, and sweetly rest On thy al-migh-ty Father's breast; The bounties of his grace a - dore, And count his wondrous mer-cies o'er.
2. Thy mer-cy, Lord, preserved my breath, And snatched my fainting soul from death; Removed my sorrows, dried my tears, And saved me from sur - round-ing snares.
3. What shall I ren - der to the Lord? Or how his wondrous grace re - cord? To him my grate-ful voice I'll raise, With just thanksgiv-ing to his praise.

ULM. L. M. 6 lines.

1. Loosed from my God, and far re - moved, Long have I wandered to and fro; O'er earth in end - less cir - cles roved,
2. Self - ish pur - suits, and na - ture's maze, The things of sense, for thee I leave: Put forth thy hand, thy hand of grace;
3. En - dow me with my Sa - viour's peace, Con - firm and keep my long - ing heart; In thee may all my wanderings cease;
Nor found where - on to rest be - low: But now, my God, to thee I fly, For, oh! es - tranged from thee, I die.
In - to the ark of love re - ceive; Take my poor, flut - tering soul to rest, And still it, Fa - ther, on thy breast.
From thee may I no more de - part: Nev - er a - gain from thee re - move, Loved with an ev - er - last - ing love!

RHEIMS. L. M.
1. As when the wea-ry traveler gains The height of some o'erlook-ing hill, His heart re-vives, if o'er the plains He sees his home, though distant still,—
2. So when the Christian pilgrim views, By faith, his mansi-e in the skies, The sight his fainting strength renews, And wings his speed to reach the prize.
3. "'Tis there, he says," "I am to dwell With Jesus in the realms of day; Then shall I bid my cares fare-well, And he will wipe my tears a-way."
LANZON. L. M.
1. Now to the Lord a no-ble song: Awake, my soul! awake, my tongue! Ho-san-na to th'e-ter-nal Name, And all his bound-less love proclaim!
2. See where it shines in Jesus' face, The brightest im-age of his grace: God, in the per-son of his Son, Has all his migh-tiest works outdone.
3. Grace! 'tis a sweet, a charming theme; My thoughts rejoice at Jesus' name: Ye angels, dwell up-on the sound: Ye heavens, re-flect it to the ground!

SANCTUS. L. M.

1. How rich the blessings, O my God, Which teach this grateful heart to glow; How kindly poured, and free bestowed, The riv - ers of thy mer-cy flow!
2. How calmly rolls the sea of life! Se - cure in thine im - mor-tal trust, The soul has hushed her secret strife, Nor long- er shud-ders at the dust.

DUNNING. L. M.

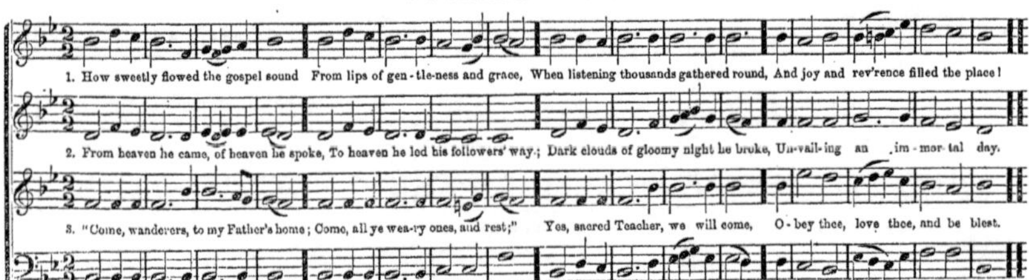
1. How sweetly flowed the gospel sound From lips of gen - tle-ness and grace, When listening thousands gathered round, And joy and rev'rence filled the place!
2. From heaven he came, of heaven he spoke, To heaven he led his followers' way; Dark clouds of gloomy night he broke, Un-vail-ing an im - mor- tal day.
3. "Come, wanderers, to my Father's home; Come, all ye wea-ry ones, and rest;" Yes, sacred Teacher, we will come, O - bey thee, love thee, and be blest.

MERCY-SEAT. L. M.
O. P. BARROWS.
1. From ev- ery storm-y wind that blows, From ev - ery swelling tide of woes, There is a calm, a sure re-treat; 'Tis found beneath the mer - cy - seat.
2. There, there, on ea- gle wings we soar, And sense and sin molest no more, And heaven comes down our souls to greet, And glory crowns the mer . cy . seat!
3. Oh! let my hand for- get her skill, My tongue be si - lent, cold, and still, This throbbing heart forget to beat, If I for - get the mer - cy - seat.
TARSUS. L. M.
D.
1. At anchor laid, re-mote from home, Toil - ing, I cry, sweet spirit, come! Ce - les-tial breeze, no long- er stay, But swell my sails, and speed my way.
2. Fain would I mount, fain would I glow, And loose my ca- ble from be-low; But I can only spread my sail,—Thou, thou must breathe th' auspicious gale.

ANNIE. L. M.
W.
1. Blest hour! when mortal man re - tires To hold communion with his God, To send to heav'n his warm de-sires, And lis - ten to the sa - cred word.
2. Blest hour! when earthly cares re - sign Their em-pire o'er his an-xious breast, While all around the calm di - vine Proclaims the ho - ly day of rest.
3. Blest hour! when God himself draws nigh, Well pleas'd his people's voice to hear, To hush the pen - i - ten - tial sigh, And wipe a-way the mourner's tear.
HOMEWELL. L. M.
*
1. As when the wea - ry traveler gains The height of some o'er-look - ing hill, His heart re-vives, if o'er the plains He sees his home, tho' dis - tant still,—
2. While he sur - veys the much-lov'd spot, He slights the space that lies between; His past fatigues are now for-got, Be - cause his journey's end is seen.
3. Thus, when the Christian pil-grim views, By faith, his man-sion in the skies, The sight his fainting strength re-news, And wings his speed to reach the prize.

GUEST. L. M.

1. Behold a Stran - ger at , the door: He gent-ly knocks, has knock'd be-fore; Has wait-ed long, is wait-ing still: You treat no oth - er friend so ill.
2. Oh, lovely at - ti - tude! he stands With melting heart and o - pen hands: Oh, matchless kindness!—and he shows This matchless kind - ness to his foes.
3. Oh, welcome him, the Prince of Peace! Now may his gen - tle reign in-crease! Throw wide the door, each will-ing mind; And be his em - pire all man - kind.

ATREM. L. M.

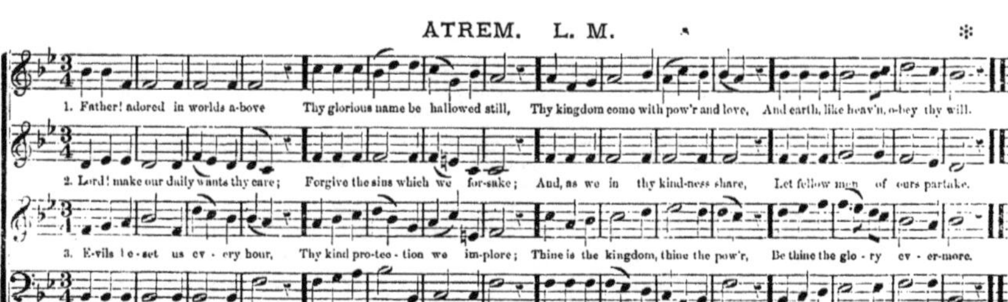
1. Father! adored in worlds a-bove Thy glorious name be hallowed still, Thy kingdom come with pow'r and love, And earth, like heav'n, o-bey thy will.
2. Lord! make our daily wants thy care; Forgive the sins which we for-sake; And, as we in thy kind-ness share, Let fellow men of ours partake.
3. E-vils be-set us ev - ery hour, Thy kind pro-tec - tion we im-plore; Thine is the kingdom, thine the pow'r, Be thine the glo - ry ev - er-more.

CARROLL. L. M.
From the German by *
1. Come, O my soul! in sa - cred lays, Attempt thy great Cre - a - tor's praise: But, oh, what tongue can speak his fame! What mortal verse can reach the theme!
2. Enthron'd a - mid the ra-diant spheres, He glo-ry, like a gar-ment, wears; To form a robe of light di-vine, Ten thousand suns a - round him shine.
3. In all our Mak - er's grand de - signs, Almighty power, with wis-dom, shines; His works, thro' all this wondrous frame, Declare the glo - ry of his name.
ARVILLE. L. M.
1. When I sur - vey the wondrous cross On which the Prince of Glo - ry died, My richest gain I count but loss, And pour contempt on all my pride.
2. For - bid it, Lord, that I should boast, Save in the death of Christ my God: All the vain things that charm me most—I sac-ri-fice them to his blood.
3. See, from his head, his hands, his feet, Sor - row and love flow min-gled down! Did e'er such love and sor-row meet, Or thorns compose so rich a crown?

FLORENCE. L. M.

1. Whither, oh, whith-er should I fly, But to thy lov - ing Father's breast! Se - cure within thine arms to lie, And safe be-neath thy wings to rest!
2. In all my ways thy hand I own, Thy rul-ing prov - i - dence I see: As - sist me still my course to run, And still di - rect my paths to thee.
3. I have no skill the snare to shun; But thou, O God, my wis-dom art; I ev - er in - to ru - in run; But thou art great-er than my heart.

FLORA. L. M.

1. Come, weary souls, with sin dis - tressed, Come, and ac-cept the promised rest; The Saviour's gracious call o - bey, And cast your gloomy fears a - way.
2. Oppress'd with guilt,—a painful load,— Oh, come and bow be-fore your God! Di - vine compassion, might-y love Will all the pain-ful load re - move.
3. Here mercy's boundless o - cean flows, To cleanse your guilt and heal your woes; Par-don, and life, and end-less peace—How rich the gift, how free the grace!

MONSON. L. M.

*

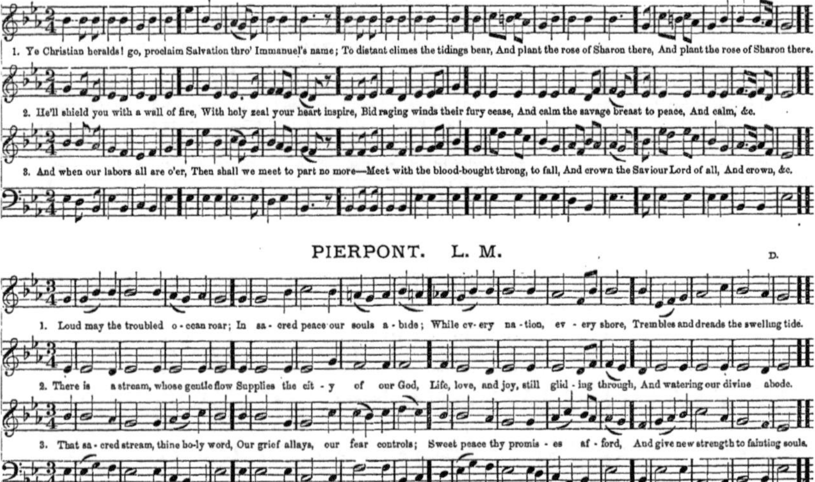
1. Ye Christian heralds! go, proclaim Salvation thro' Immanuel's name; To distant climes the tidings bear, And plant the rose of Sharon there, And plant the rose of Sharon there.
2. He'll shield you with a wall of fire, With holy zeal your heart inspire, Bid raging winds their fury cease, And calm the savage breast to peace, And calm, &c.
3. And when our labors all are o'er, Then shall we meet to part no more—Meet with the blood-bought throng, to fall, And crown the Saviour Lord of all, And crown, &c.
PIERPONT. L. M.
D.
1. Loud may the troubled o - cean roar; In sa - cred peace our souls a - bide; While ev - ery na - tion, ev - ery shore, Trembles and dreads the swelling tide.
2. There is a stream, whose gentle flow Supplies the cit - y of our God, Life, love, and joy, still glid - ing through, And watering our divine abode.
3. That sa - cred stream, thine ho-ly word, Our grief allays, our fear controls; Sweet peace thy promis - es af - ford, And give new strength to fainting souls.

ARNIM. L. M.

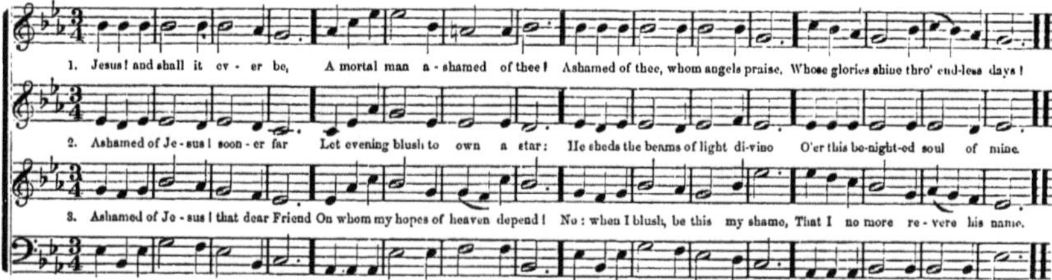
1. Jesus! and shall it ev - er be, A mortal man a - shamed of thee! Ashamed of thee, whom angels praise, Whose glories shine thro' end-less days!
2. Ashamed of Je - sus! soon - er far Let evening blush to own a star: He sheds the beams of light di-vine O'er this be-night-ed soul of mine.
3. Ashamed of Je - sus! that dear Friend On whom my hopes of heaven depend! No: when I blush, be this my shame, That I no more re - vere his name.

HARTLAND. L. M.

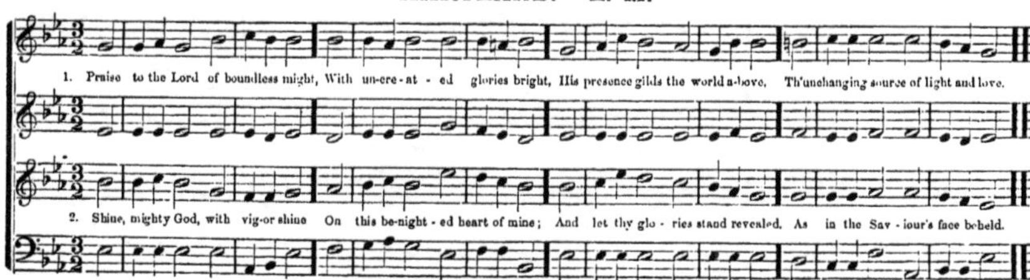
1. Praise to the Lord of boundless might, With un-cre - at - ed glories bright, His presence gilds the world a-bove, Th'unchanging source of light and love.
2. Shine, mighty God, with vig-or shine On this be-night - ed heart of mine; And let thy glo - ries stand revealed, As in the Sav - iour's face beheld.

HARRINGTON. L. M.

J. D. CONLEY.

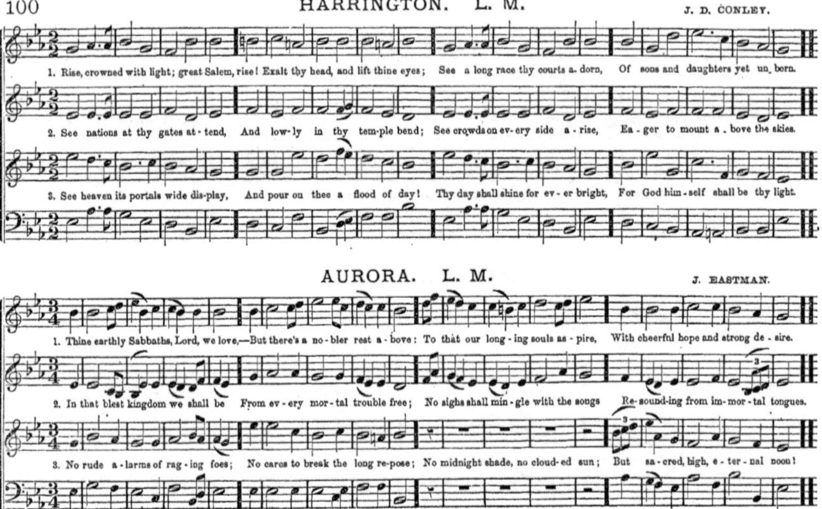
1. Rise, crowned with light; great Salem, rise! Exalt thy head, and lift thine eyes; See a long race thy courts a- dorn, Of sons and daughters yet un_born.
2. See nations at thy gates at- tend, And low- ly in thy tem-ple bend; See crowds on ev- ery side a - rise, Ea - ger to mount a - bove the skies.
3. See heaven its portals wide dis-play, And pour on thee a flood of day! Thy day shall shine for ev - er bright, For God him - self shall be thy light.
AURORA. L. M.
J. EASTMAN.
1. Thine earthly Sabbaths, Lord, we love,—But there's a no - bler rest a - bove: To that our long - ing souls as - pire, With cheerful hope and strong de - sire.
2. In that blest kingdom we shall be From ev - ery mor - tal trouble free; No sighs shall min - gle with the songs Re- sound-ing from im - mor - tal tongues.
3. No rude a - larms of rag - ing foes; No cares to break the long re-pose; No midnight shade, no cloud- ed sun; But sa - cred, high, e - ter - nal noon!

NELLIE. L. M.

W.

1. How blest the sacred tie that binds, In union sweet, ac - cord- ing minds! How swift the heavenly course they run, Whose hearts and faith and hopes are one!
2. To each the soul of each how dear! What jealous care, what ho- ly fear! How doth the generous flame with - in Refine from earth and cleanse from sin!
3. Their streaming tears together flow For human guilt and hu - man woe; Their ardent prayers u-nit - ed rise, Like mingling flames in sac-ri - fice.
GEORGIA. L. M.
1. Sweet is the work, my God, my King, To praise thy name, give thanks, and sing; To show thy love by morning light, And talk of all thy truth at night.
2. Sweet is the day of sa-cred rest; No mortal cares shall seize my breast: Oh, may my heart in tune be found, Like David's harp of solemn sound.
3. My heart shall triumph in the Lord, And bless his works, and bless his word; Thy works of grace, how bright they shine! How deep thy counsels, how divine!

BERLIN. L. M.
1. Be-fore Je - ho - vah's aw - ful throne, Ye na-tions bow with sa-cred joy: Know that the Lord is God a - lone; He can cre-ate, and he destroy.
2. His sovereign pow'r, without our aid, Made us of clay, and form'd us men; And when, like wand'ring sheep we stray'd, He brought us to his fold a - gain.
3. We are his peo - ple, we his care, Our souls, and all our mor - tal frame: What lasting hon-ors shall we rear, Almight-y Mak - er, to thy name!
LINCOLN. L. M.
C. E. MESSER.
1. In vain my roving thoughts would find, A portion worthy of the mind; On earth the soul can nev-er rest, For earth can nev - er make me blest.
2. Can last-ing hap - pi - ness be found Where seasons roll their has - ty round! And days and hours with rapid flight Sweep cares and pleasures out of sight!

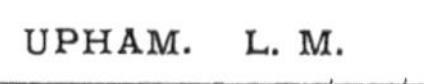

UPHAM. L. M.

D.

1. Wake, O my soul, and hail the morn, For un-to us a Saviour's born; See, how the an-gels wing their way, To usher in the glo-rious day.

2. Hark! what sweet music, what a song, Sounds from the bright ce-les-tial throng! Sweet song, whose melting sounds impart Joy to each raptured, listening heart.

PATTEN. L. M.

W.

1. Sweet is the light of Sabbath eve, And soft the sunbeams ling'ring there; For these blest hours the world I leave, Wafted on wings of faith and prayer.

2. Season of rest! the tran-quil soul Feels the sweet calm and melts in love; And while these sacred mo-ments roll, Faith sees a smil-ing heav'n a-bove.

3. Nor will our days of toil be long: Our pilgrimage will soon be trod; And we shall join the cease-less song, The end-less Sab-bath of our God.

POPE. L. M. Double.

W.

1. An-oth-er six day's work is done; An-oth-er Sab-bath is be - gun: Re-turn, my soul, un-to thy rest; En-joy the day thy God hath blest.
3. That heavenly calm within the breast! It is the pledge of that dear rest Which for the church of God re-mains,—The end of cares, the end of pains.
2. Oh, that our thoughts and thanks may rise, As grateful in-cense to the skies! And draw from heaven that calm re-pose, Which none but he that feels it knows;
4. In ho - ly du-ties let the day, In ho - ly pleasures, pass a - way. How sweet a Sab-bath thus to spend, In hope of one that ne'er shall end!

STOWELL. L. M.

W.

SOPRANO SOLO
1. From ev - ery storm - y wind that blows, From ev - ery swell - ing tide of woes, There is a calm, a sure re - treat; 'Tis found be - neath the mer - cy - seat.
CHORUS.
2. There is a place where Je - sus sheds The oil of glad - ness on our heads,— A place, than all be - sides, more sweet; It is the blood - bought mer - cy - seat.

3.

There is a scene where spirits blend,
Where friend holds fellowship with friend:
Though sundered far, by faith they meet
Around one common mercy-seat!

4.

There, there on eagle's wings we soar,
And sense and sin molest no more;
And heaven comes down our souls to greet,
While glory crowns the mercy-seat.

5.

Oh! let my hand forget her skill,
My tongue be silent, cold and still,
This throbbing heart forget to beat,
If I forget the mercy-seat.

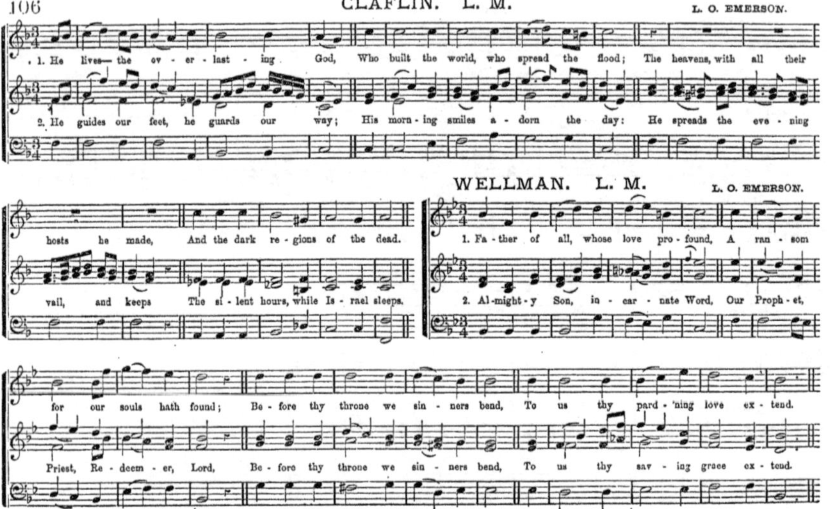
CLAFLIN. L. M.
L. O. EMERSON.
1. He lives— the ev - er - last - ing God, Who built the world, who spread the flood; The heavens, with all their hosts he made, And the dark re - gions of the dead.
2. He guides our feet, he guards our way; His morn - ing smiles a - dorn the day: He spreads the eve - ning vail, and keeps The si - lent hours, while Is - rael sleeps.
WELLMAN. L. M.
L. O. EMERSON.
1. Fa - ther of all, whose love pro - found, A ran - som for our souls hath found; Be - fore thy throne we sin - ners bend, To us thy pard - 'ning love ex - tend.
2. Al - might - y Son, in - car - nate Word, Our Proph - et, Priest, Re - deem - er, Lord, Be - fore thy throne we sin - ners bend, To us thy sav - ing grace ex - tend.

TOPSFIELD. L. M.
H. F. HANSON.
1. High in the heavens, eter - nal God! Thy goodness in full glo - ry shines; Thy truth shall break thro' every cloud That vails and darkens thy de - signs.
2. For ev - er firm thy just - ice stands, As mountains their founda - tions keep: Wise are the won - ders of thy hands; Thy judgments are a might - y deep.
3. Life, like a foun-tain, rich and free, Springs from the presence of my Lord; And in thy light our souls shall see The glories promised in thy word.
BARROWS. L. M.
J. H. FOSTER.
1. Great God! to thee my evening song With hum-ble grat - i - tude I raise: Oh, let thy mer-cy tune my tongue, And fill my heart with live - ly praise.
2. My days, unclouded as they pass, And ev - ery gen-tly roll-ing hour, Are monuments of wondrous grace, And wit - ness to thy love and power.
3. And yet this thoughtless, wretched heart, Too oft re-gardless of thy love, Un - grateful, can from thee de-part, And, fond of tri - fles, vain - ly rove.

THE OLD HUNDRED. L. M. From Marot and Beza's Psalms, Geneva, 1543.
With one con- sent, let all the earth To God their cheerful voi - ces raise; Glad hom- age pay, with aw- ful mirth, And sing be - fore him songs of praise.
HAMBURG. L. M. Arr. from a Gregorian Chant, by Dr. L. Mason.
Thou great In - structor, lest I stray, Oh, teach my err - ing feet thy way! Thy truth, with ever fresh de - light, Shall guide my doubtful steps a - right.
MISSIONARY CHANT. L. M. C. Zeuner.
1. Ye Christian heralds! go, proclaim Sal - vation thro' Im - manuel's name; To distant climes the tidings bear, And plant the rose of Sharon there.
WARD. L. M. Arr. from a Scotch tune by Dr. L. Mason.
There is a stream, whose gentle flow Supplies the ci - ty of our God; Life, love, and joy still gliding through, And wat'ring our di - vine a - bode.

☞ *These, and the following well known tunes, may, perhaps, be regarded as the standards in this metre.*

DUKE STREET. L. M.
J. Hatton.
1. Un - to the Lord, un - to the Lord, Oh, sing a new and joy - ful song! De-clare his glo - ry, tell a - broad The wonders that to him be - long.
UXBRIDGE. L. M.
Dr L. Mason.
1. Who shall the Lord's elect con- demn? 'T is God who jus- ti - fies their souls; And mer- cy, like a might - y stream, O'er all their sins di - vine - ly rolls.
STONEFIELD. L. M.
Stanley.
1. God of the seas, thine aw - ful voice, Bids all the rolling waves re- joice; And one soft voice of thy command, Can sink them si - lent on the sand.
ROCKINGHAM. L. M.
From "Carmina Sacra."
1. Prais- es to him who built the hills; Prais- es to him the stream who fills; Prais- es to him who lights each star That sparkles in the blue a - far.

HEBRON. L. M.
Dr. L. Mason.
Far from my tnoughts, vain world, be gone. Let my re - li - gious hours a-lone: Fain would my eyes my Saviour see, I wait a vis - it, Lord, from thee.
FEDERAL STREET. L. M.
H. K. Oliver.
God in his tem - ple let us meet; Low on our knees be - fore him bend; Here hath he fixed his mer - cy - seat, Here, on his Sab-bath we at - tend.
WINDHAM. L. M.
Daniel Read.
Broad is the road that leads to death, And thousands walk to - geth-er there; But wisdom shows a nar-row path, With here and there a trav - el - er.
ROSEDALE. L. M.
G. F. Root. 1843.
Great God, to thee my evening song With hum-ble grat - i - tude I raise; Oh, let thy mer - cy tune my tongue, And fill my heart with live - ly praise.

SACRIFICE. C. M.

D 111

1. E - ter - nal Fa - ther, God of love, To thee our hearts we raise; Thy all - sus - tain - ing pow'r we prove, And gladly sing thy praise.
2. Thine, whol-ly thine, oh, let us be! Our sac - ri - fice re - ceive; Made and preserved and saved by thee, To thee ourselves we give.
3. Come, Ho - ly Ghost! the Sa - viour's love Shed in our hearts a - broad; So shall we ev - er live and move, And be, with Christ, in God.

STILL WATERS. C. M.

W.

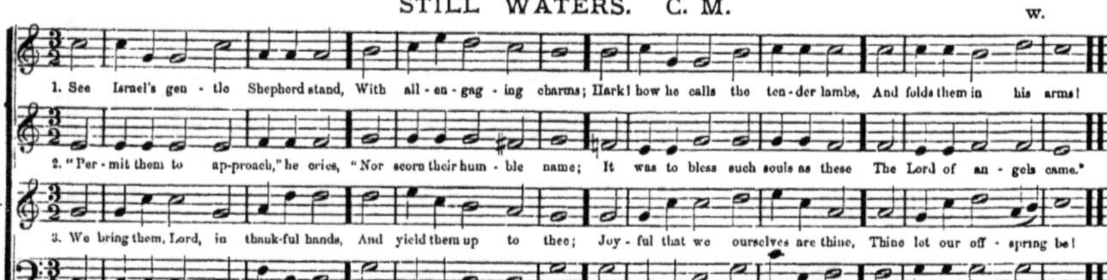
1. See Israel's gen - tle Shepherd stand, With all - en - gag - ing charms; Hark! how he calls the ten - der lambs, And folds them in his arms!
2. "Per - mit them to ap-proach," he cries, "Nor scorn their hum - ble name; It was to bless such souls as these The Lord of an - gels came."
3. We bring them, Lord, in thank-ful hands, And yield them up to thee; Joy - ful that we ourselves are thine, Thine let our off - spring be!

JOSQUIN. C. M.*

From a Collection of Music, by
C. F. BECKER, Organist, Leipzig.

1. From thee, my God, my joys shall rise, And run e - ter - nal rounds, Be - yond the lim - its of the skies, And all cre - a - ted bounds.
2. The ho - ly tri-umphs of my soul Shall death it - self out - brave, Leave dull mor - tal - i - ty be hind, And fly be-yond the grave.
3. There, where my bless - ed Je - sus reigns, In heaven's un - measured space, I'll spend a long e - ter - ni - ty In pleasure and in praise.
MYRTLE. C. M.
W.
1. When brighter suns and mild-er skies Pro - claim the ope - ning year, What various sounds of joy a - rise! What prospects bright ap - pear!
2. Earth and her thou - sand voic-es give Their thousand notes of praise; And all, that by his mer - cy live, To God their off - 'ring raise.
3. Thus, like the morn - ing, calm and clear, That saw the Sav - iour rise, The spring of heaven's e - ter - nal year Shall dawn on earth and skies.

* "Josquin," said Luther, after having heard one of his masses, "is master of his notes; they must do as he chooses; other composers must do as their notes choose." He lived in the fifteenth century.—*Encyclopædia Americana.*

ELSDALE. C. M.
1. Lord, thou wilt hear me when I pray; I am for - ev - er thine; I fear be - fore thee all the day, Nor would I dare to sin.
2. And while I rest my wea - ry head, From cares and busi - ness free, 'Tis sweet con-vers - ing on my bed With my own heart and thee.
3. I pay this eve - ning sac - ri - fice; And when my work is done, Great God! my faith and hope re - lies Up - on thy grace a - lone.
DANTE. C. M.
D.
1. As pants the hart for cool - ing streams, When heat-ed in the chase, So longs my soul, O God, for thee, And thy re - fresh- ing grace.
2. For thee, my God, the liv - ing God, My thirst - y soul doth pine; Oh! when shall I be - hold thy face, Thou Maj - es - ty di - vine.
3. Why rest - less, why cast down, my soul? Trust God; and he'll em - ploy His aid for thee, and change these sighs To thankful hymns of joy.

ENGELHART. C. M.
W.
1. Our Father, God, who art in heaven, All hal - lowed be thy name! Thy king-dom come; thy will be done, In earth and heaven the same!
2. Give us, this day, our dai - ly bread; And, as we those for-give Who sin a - gainst us, so may we For - giv - ing grace re - ceive.
3. In - to temp - ta - tion lead us not; From e - vil set us free; And thine the king-dom, thine the power And glo - ry, ev - er be.
WACHUSETT. C. M.
W.
1. 'Tis by thy strength the mountains stand, God of e - ter - nal power! The sea grows calm at thy com - mand, And tem - pests cease to roar.
2. Thy morn-ing light and eve - ning shade Suc - ces - sive com-forts bring; Thy plen-teous fruits make har - vest glad; Thy flowers a - dorn the spring.
3. Sea - sons and times, and moons and hours, Heaven, earth, and air are thine; When clouds dis - till in fruit - ful showers, The au - thor is di - vine!

HAPPY HOME. C. M.

1. Happy the home, when God is there, And love fills ev - ery breast; Where one their wish, and one their prayer, And one their heavenly rest.
2. Hap-py the home where Je - sus' name Is sweet to ev - ery ear; Where children ear - ly lisp his fame, And parents hold him dear.
3. Hap-py the home where prayer is heard, And praise is wont to rise; Where parents love the sa - cred word, And live but for the skies.
KATAHDIN. C. M.
W.
1. Oh! could our thoughts and wishes fly A - bove these gloomy shades, To those bright worlds beyond the sky Which sorrow ne'er in - vades!
2. There joys un - seen by mortal eyes, Or rea - son's feeble ray, In ev - er - bloom - ing prospect rise, Un-conscious of de - cay.
3. Lord! send a beam of light di - vine To guide our upward aim; With one re - viv - ing touch of thine Our languid hearts in - flame.

EBENE. C. M.

W.

1. Whence those triumphant bursts of joy, Whose sound thro' heaven rings? They welcome Jesus to the throne, And crown him King of kings, And crown him, crown him, crown him King of kings.
2. Look up, ye saints, and while you gaze Forget all earth - - ly things; Unite to sing the Saviour's praise, And crown him King of kings, And crown him, crown him, crown him King of kings.

ROCKLAND. C. M.

D.

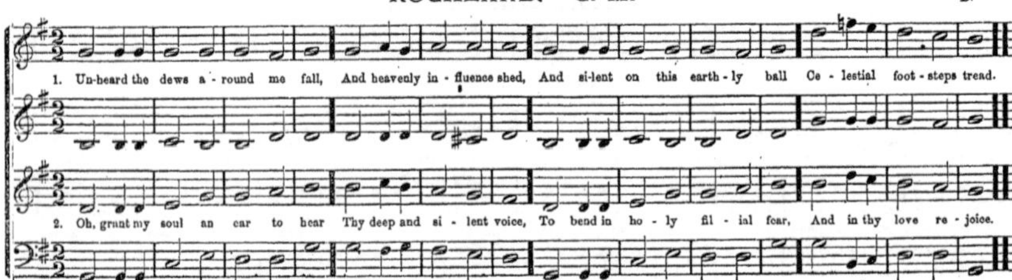
1. Un-heard the dews a - round me fall, And heavenly in - fluence shed, And si-lent on this earth - ly ball Ce - lestial foot - steps tread.
2. Oh, grant my soul an ear to hear Thy deep and si - lent voice, To bend in ho - ly fil - ial fear, And in thy love re - joice.

JONES. C. M. Peculiar.

1. There is an hour of peaceful rest, To mourning wand'rers given; There is a tear for souls distressed, A balm for every wounded breast: 'Tis found above—in heaven.
2. There is a home for weary souls, By sin and sorrow driv'n,—When toss'd on life's tempestuous shoals, Where storms arise, and ocean rolls, And all is drear—but heav'n.
3. There faith lifts up her cheerful eye To brighter prospects given; And views the tempest passing by, The evening shadows quickly fly, And all serene—in heaven.
SPOHR. C. M.
Arranged from SPOHR.
1. As pants the hart for cool - ing streams, When heat - ed in the chase; So longs my soul, O God, for thee, And thy re - fresh - ing grace.
2. For thee, my God, the liv - ing God, My thirst - y soul doth pine; Oh! when shall I be - hold thy face, Thou Maj - es - ty di - vine!
3. Why rest - less, why cast down, my soul? Trust God; and he'll em - ploy His aid for thee, and change these sighs To thank - ful hymns of joy.

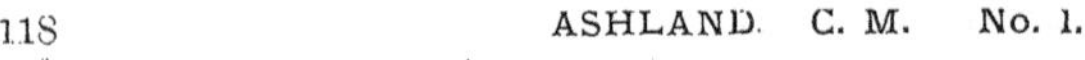

ASHLAND. C. M. No. 1.

1. Plunged in a gulf of dark de - spair, We wretched sin - ners lay, Without one cheerful beam of hope, Or spark of glimmering day.
1. Plunged in a gulf of dark de - spair, We wretched sin - ners lay, Without one cheerful beam of hope, Or spark of glimmering day.

ASHLAND. C. M. No. 2.

2. With pitying eyes the Prince of Grace Be - held our help - less grief: He saw, and, oh, a-maz-ing love!— He ran to our re - lief.
2. With pitying eyes the Prince of Grace Be - held our help - less grief: He saw, and, oh, a-maz-ing love!— He ran to our re - lief.

ASHLAND. C. M. No. 3.

3. Down from the shining seats a - bove, With joy- ful haste he fled, En- tered the grave in mor - tal flesh, And dwelt a - mong the dead.
3. Down from the shining seats a - bove, With joy- ful haste he fled, En- tered the grave in mor - tal flesh, And dwelt a - mong the dead.
ASHLAND. C. M. No. 4.
4. Oh, for this love let rocks and hills Their lasting silence break; And all harmonious human tongues The Saviour's praises speak, The Saviour's praises speak!
4. Oh, for this love let rocks and hills Their lasting silence break; And all harmonious human tongues, And all harmonious human tongues The Saviour's praises speak!
4. Oh, for this love let rocks and hills Their lasting silence break; And all harmonious human tongues The Saviour's praises speak!

ONGE. C. M.
W.
Come, let us join our cheerful songs With angels round the throne; Ten thousand thousand are their tongues, But all their joys are one, But all their joys are one.
Come, let us join our cheerful songs With angels round the throne; Ten thousand thousand are their tongues, But all their joys are one, But all their joys are one.
Ten thousand thousand are their tongues,
Come, let us join our cheerful songs With angels round the throne; Ten thousand thousand are their tongues, But all their joys are one, But all their joys are one.
JANVRIN. C. M.
D.
1. I sing th' al-might-y power of God, That made the mountains rise, That spread the flow - ing seas a - broad, And built the loft - y skies.
2. I sing the wis - dom that ordained The sun to rule the day; The moon shines full at his com-mand, And all the stars o - bey.
3. I sing the goodness of the Lord, That filled the earth with food; He formed the crea - tures with his word, And then pronounced them good.

RESTORATION. C. M.
D
121
1. Al - might-y grace, thy heal-ing power, How glorious, how di - vine! That can to life and bliss re - store A heart so vile as mine.
2. Thy pard'ning love, so free, so sweet, Dear Saviour, I a - dore; Oh, keep me at thy sa - cred feet, And let me rove no more!
EMMA. C. M.
W.
To thee be-fore the dawning light, My gra-cious God, I pray: I med - i - tate thy name by night, And keep thy law by day.
To thee be-fore the dawning light, My gra-cious God, I pray: I med - i - tate thy name by night, And keep thy law by day.

PEMBROKE. C. M.
* Arranged from the "Tonus Peregrinus."
1. Oh, for that ten - der - ness of heart Which bows be - fore the Lord! Own ing how just and good thou art, And trembling at thy word.
2. Oh, for those hum - ble, con - trite tears Which from re - pent - ance flow! Oh, for that sense of guilt which fears The long - sus-pend - ed blow!
3. Sav - iour. to me in pit - y give, For sin, the deep dis - tress— The pledge thou wilt at last re - ceive; And bid me die in peace.
LAUDATE. C. M.
D.
1. O God! our help in a - ges past, Our hope for years to come, Our shel - ter from the storm - y blast, And our e - ter - nal home.
2. Be - fore the hills in or - der stood, Or earth re-ceived her frame, From ev - er - last - ing thou art God, To end - less years the same.
3. A thou-sand a - ges in thy sight Are like an eve - ning gone— Short as the watch that ends the night Be - fore the ris - ing sun.

CROSBY. C. M.

1. Our God, our help in a - ges past, Our hope for years to come, Our shelter from the storm-y blast, And our e - ter - nal home!
2. Under the shad - ow of thy throne, Thy saints have dwelt se - cure; Suf - ficient is thine arm a - lone, And our de - fense is sure.
3. Before the hills in or - der stood, Or earth received her frame, From ever - last - ing thou art God, To end - less years the same.
MEDITATION. C. M.
D.
1. When all thy mercies, O my God, My ris - ing soul surveys, Transport - ed with the view, I'm lost In wond - er, love, and praise!
2. Un-numbered com - forts on my soul Thy tend-er care bestowed, Be - fore my in - fant heart conceived From whom those com - forts flowed.
3. When, in the slip-pery paths of youth, With heedless step I ran, Thine arm, un - seen, conveyed me safe, And led me up to man.

CANTOR. C. M. Double.

D.

1. The bird let loose in East-ern skies, Re - turn - ing fond - ly home, Ne'er stoops to earth her wing, nor flies Where i - dler warblers roam.
3. So grant me, Lord, from ev - ery snare Of sin - ful pas - sion free, A - loft, through faith's se - ren - er air, To hold my course to thee.
2. But high she shoots thro' air and light, A - bove all low de - lay, Where nothing earth-ly bounds her flight, Nor shad - ow dims her way.
4. No sin to cloud, no lure to stay My soul, as home she springs; Thy sun - shine on her joy - ful way, Thy free - dom in her wings.

SUNSET. C. M.
1. Soon will our fleet - ing hours be past; And as the set - ting sun Sinks downward in the ra - diant west, Our part - ing beams be gone.
2. May He, from whom all bless - ings flow, Our sa - cred rites at - tend, U - nit - ing all in wis-dom's ways, Till life's short jour - ney end;
3. And as the rap - id sands run down, Our vir - tue still im - prove, Till each re - ceive the glo - rious crown Of nev - er - fad - ing love.
BRADFORD. C. M.
T. K. WILSON.
1. How sweet up - on this hal - - lowed day, The best of all the seven, To cast our earth-ly thoughts a - way, And think of God and heav'n.
2. How sweet to be al - lowed to pray, Our sins to be for-giv'n, With fil - ial con - fi - dence to say, "Fa - ther, who art in heav'n."

WATKINS. C. M.
W.
1. Why should our tears in sor - row flow, When God re-calls his own, And bids them leave a world of woe For an im - mor - tal crown!
2. Is not e'en death a gain to those Whose life to God is given! Glad - ly to earth their eyes they close, To o - pen them in heaven.
3. Their toils are past, their work is done, And they are ful - ly blest: They fought the fight, the vic - t'ry won, And en - tered in - to rest.
WIEN. C. M.
D.
Joy to the world! the Lord is come! Let earth receive her King; Let every heart prepare him room, And heav'n and nature sing.
Joy to the world! the Lord is come! Let earth receive her King; Let every heart prepare him room, And heav'n and nature sing.
Joy to the world, the Lord is come! Let earth re-ceive her King; Let ev - ery heart pre-pare him room, And heav'n, And heav'n and na - ture sing.

STAR C. M.
O. R. BARROWS.
1. Bright was the guiding star that led, With mild, be-nig - nant ray, The Gentiles to the low - ly shed Where the Re-deem - er lay.
2. But, lo! the Scripture's clearer light Now points to his a - bode; It shines thro' sin and sor - row's night, To guide us to our God.
3. Oh, let us tread the nar - row path, While light and grace are given; And thus escape the com - ing wrath, And reign with him in heaven.
TRANSPORT. C. M.
D.
1. When all thy mer-cies, O my God, My ris - ing soul sur - veys, Trans-port-ed with the view, I'm lost In won-der, love, and praise!
2. Un - numbered comforts on my soul Thy ten - der care be - stowed, Be - fore my in-fant heart con-ceived From whom those comforts flowed.
3. When, in the slippery paths of youth, With heedless steps I ran, Thine arm, unseen, conveyed me safe, And led me up to man.

REDEEMER. C. M.
D.
1. Thou dear Re - deem-er, dy - ing Lamb, I love to hear of thee; No mu - sic like thy charm-ing name, Nor half so sweet can be.
2. Oh, may I ev - er hear thy voice In mer - cy to me speak; In thee, my Priest, will I re - joice, And thy sal - va - tion seek.
3. My Je - sus shall be still my theme, While on this earth I stay; I'll sing my Je - sus' love - ly name, When all things else de - cay.
PARKER. C. M.
IRVING EMERSON.
1. My God, my Fa - ther, bliss - ful name! Oh, may I call thee mine? May I with sweet as - sur - ance claim A por - tion so di - vine?
2. What-e'er thy prov - i - dence de - nies I calm - ly would re - sign; For thou art good and just and wise: Oh, bend my will to thine!
3. What-e'er thy sa - cred will or - dains, Oh, give me strength to bear! And let me know my Fa - ther reigns, And trust his ten - der care.

STANTON. C. M.
1. Awake, my soul! stretch every nerve, And press with vigor on: A heavenly race demands thy zeal, A bright, immortal crown, A bright, immor - - tal crown.
2. A cloud of witness-es a-round Hold thee in full survey: Forget the steps al-read-y trod, And onward urge thy way, And onward urge........... thy way.
3. 'Tis God's all an - i-mating voice, That calls thee from on high; 'Tis his own hand presents the prize To thine aspiring eye, To thine as - pir - - ing eye.
FINLAND. C. M.
D.
1. Oh, praise the Lord! for he is good; In him we rest ob - tain: His mer - cy has through a - ges stood, And ev - er shall re - main.
2. Let all the peo - ple of the Lord His prais - es spread a - round; Let them his grace and love re - cord, Who have sal - va - tion found.
3. Now let the east in him re - joice, The west its trib - ute bring, The north and south lift up their voice In hon - or of their King.

BACON. C. M.

W.

1. Sweet was the time when first I felt The Saviour's pard - 'ning blood Applied to cleanse my soul from guilt, And bring me home to God.
2. Soon as the morn the light re - vealed. His prais-es tuned my tongue; And, when the evening shade pre-vailed, His love was all my song.
3. In prayer, my soul drew near the Lord, And saw his glo - ry shine; And when I read his ho - ly word, I called each prom - ise mine.
DALE. C. M.
D.
1. Mere human power shall fast de - cay, And youth-ful vig - or cease; But they who wait up - on the Lord In strength shall still in - crease.
2. They with un - wea - ried feet will tread The path of life di - vine; With growing ar - dor on - ward move, With grow-ing brightness shine.
3. On ea-gles' wings they mount, they soar— The wings of faith and love; Till, past the cloud - y re - gions here, They rise to heaven a - bove.

MILLINOKET. C. M.
D.
1. Je - sus! the very thought of thee With gladness fills my breast; But dear - er far thy face to see, And in thy presence rest.
2. Nor voice can sing, nor heart can frame, Nor can the memory find A sweeter sound than thy blest name, O Sav - iour of man- kind!
3. O Hope of ev - ery contrite heart, O Joy of all the meek! To those who fall, how kind thou art, How good to those who seek!
ADVENT. C. M.
*
1. Hark, the glad sound! the Saviour comes, The Saviour promised long; Let ev - ery heart prepare a throne, And every voice a song, And ev - ery voice a song.
2. He comes, the prisoner to release, In Sa- tan's bondage held; The gates of brass before him burst, The i - ron fetters yield, The i - ron fet-ters yield.
3. Our glad hosannas, Prince of Peace, Thy welcome shall pro- claim, And heaven's eter-nal arches ring With thy beloved name, With thy be - lov- ed name.

BRADBURY. C. M.
W. From "Harp of Judah."
By permission.
1. And can mine eyes, with- out a tear, A weeping Sav - iour see! Shall I not weep his groans to hear Who groaned and died for me!
2. Blest Jesus! let those tears of thine Sub - due each stubborn foe; Come, fill my heart with love di- vine, And bid my sor - rows flow.
WINNER. C. M.
*
1. To thee, my Shepherd and my Lord, A grateful song I'll raise; Oh, let the feeblest of thy flock At- tempt to speak thy praise!
2. But how shall mortal tongue express A subject so di - vine! Do jus - tice to so vast a theme, Or praise a love like thine!
3. My life, my joy, my hope, I owe To thine a - maz - ing love; Ten thousand thousand comforts here, And nobler bliss a - bove.

JUSTIN. C. M.
D. 133
1. Oh, help us, Lord!—each hour of need Thy heavenly suc - cor give; Help us in thought and word and deed, Each hour on earth we live.
2. Oh, help us when our spir - its bleed, With contrite an - guish sore; And when our hearts are cold and dead, Oh, help us, Lord, the more!
3. Oh, help us, Je - sus! from on high; We know no help but thee; Oh, help us so to live and die, As thine in heaven to be!
LIME STREET. C. M.
Z. S. PATTEN.
1. How dread are thine e - ter - nal years, O ev - er - last - ing Lord! By prostrate spir - its day and night In - ces-sant - ly a - dored!
2. Yet I may love thee too, O Lord! Al - might - y as thou art, For thou hast stooped to ask of me The love of my poor heart.
3. No earthly fa - ther loves like thee; No mother half so mild Bears and for-bears, as thou hast done With me, thy sin - ful child.

134
CHAMPNEY. C. M. Peculiar.
D.
1. There is an hour of peaceful rest, To mourning wanderers given; There is a tear for souls distressed, A balm for every wounded breast: 'Tis found above—in heaven.
2. There is a home for weary souls, By sin and sorrow driven,—When toss'd on life's tempestuous shoals, Where storms arise, and ocean rolls, And all is drear—but heaven,
3. There faith lifts up her cheerful eye To brighter prospects given; And views the tempest passing by, The evening shadows quickly fly, And all se-rene— in heaven.
ORLAND. C. M.
CH. ZEUNER.
1. Let chil - dren hear the might - y deeds, Which God per-formed of old,— Which in our young-er years we saw, And which our fa - thers told.
2. He bids us make his glo - ries known, His works of power and grace; And we'll con - vey his won-ders down Through ev - ery ris - ing race.
3. Our lips shall tell them to our sons, And they a - gain to theirs, That gen - e - ra - tions yet un - born May teach them to their heirs.

AUBURN. C. M.

L. O. EMERSON.

1. I sing th' al - might - y power of God, That made the mount - ains rise, That spread the flow - ing seas a - broad,
2. I sing the wis - dom that or - dained The sun to rule the day; The moon shines full at his com - mand,
And built the loft - y skies.
And all the stars o - bey.
BERREAN. C. M.
L. O. EMERSON.
1. Thou art the Way: to thee a - lone From sin and death we flee; And he.... who would the
2. Thou art the Truth: thy word a - lone True wis - dom can im - part; Thou on - ly canst in -
Fa - ther seek, Must seek him, Lord, by thee, Must seek him, Lord, by thee.
- struct the mind, And pu - ri - fy the heart, And pu - ri - fy the heart.
CODA. f ff
Hal - le - lu - jah! Hal - le - lu - jah! Thou art the Way!
Hal - le - lu - jah! Hal - le - lu - jah! Thou art the Truth!

KINEO. C. M.
W.
1. Great God! the na - tions of the earth Are by cre - a - tion thine; And in.... thy works, by all be - held, Thy power and glo - ry shine.
2. But, Lord, thy great - er love hath sent Thy gos - pel to mankind, Un - vail - ing what rich stores of grace Are treas - ured in thy mind.
3. Oh, when shall these glad ti - dings spread The spa - cious earth a - round, Till ev - ery tribe and ev - ery soul Shall hear the joy - ful sound!
STILLWELL. C. M.
D.
1. Oh, for that ten - der - ness of heart Which bows be - fore the Lord! Own - ing how just and good thou art, And trembling at thy word.
2. Oh, for those hum - ble, con - trite tears Which from re - pent-ance flow! Oh, for that sense of guilt which fears The long-sus - pend - ed blow!
3. Sav - iour, to me in pit - y give, For sin, the deep dis - tress— The pledge thou wilt at last re - ceive; And bid me die in peace.

SYMPATHY. C. M.
D.
1. Lord, hear the voice of my complaint; Ac - cept my se - cret prayer; To thee a - lone, my God, my King, Will I for help re - pair.
2. Thou, in the morn, my voice shalt hear; And with the dawning day, To thee de - vout - ly I'll look up, To thee de - vout - ly pray.
GROVER. C. M.
W.
1. Great God! how in - fi-nite art thou! What worth-less worms are we! Let the whole race of crea - tures bow, And pay their praise to thee.
2. Thy throne e - ter - nal a - ges stood, Ere seas or stars were made; Thou art the ev - er - liv - ing God, Were all the na - tions dead.
3. E - ter - ni - ty, with all its years, Stands pres - ent in thy view; To thee there's no - thing old ap - pears, Great God! there's no - thing new.

BRIERY. C. M.
W.
1. There is a land, a hap-py land, Where tears are wiped a - way From ev - ery eye by God's own hand, And night is turned to day.
2. There is a home, a hap-py home, Where way-worn travelers rest; Where toil and lan - guor nev - er come, And ev - ery mourn-er's blest.
3. There is a crown, a dazzling crown, Bedecked with jew - els fair; And priests and kings of high re-nown That crown of glo - ry wear.
VERANTA. C. M.
O. R. BARROWS.
1. A - las! and did my Saviour bleed? And did my Sovereign die? Would he de - vote that sa - cred head For such a worm as I?
2. Was it for crimes that I had done, He groaned up - on the tree? A - maz - ing pi - ty! grace un - known! And love be-yond de - gree!
3. Well might the sun in darkness hide, And shut his glo - ries in, When God, the migh-ty Mak - er, died For man the creature's sin.

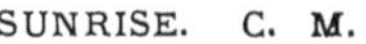
SUNRISE. C. M.

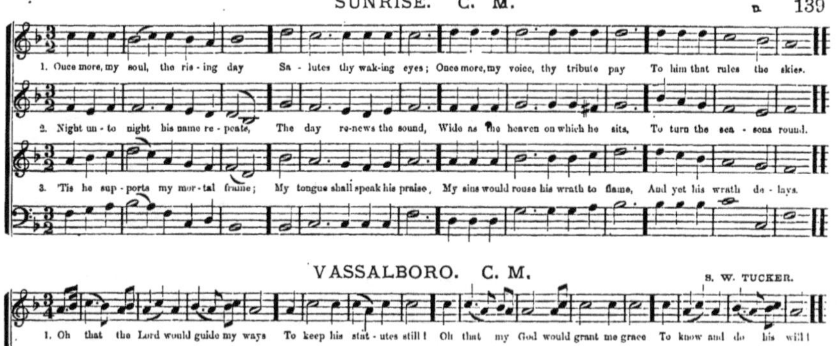
1. Once more, my soul, the ris - ing day Sa - lutes thy wak-ing eyes; Once more, my voice, thy tribute pay To him that rules the skies.
2. Night un - to night his name re - peats, The day re-news the sound, Wide as the heaven on which he sits, To turn the sea - sons round.
3. 'Tis he sup - ports my mor - tal frame; My tongue shall speak his praise, My sins would rouse his wrath to flame, And yet his wrath de - lays.

VASSALBORO. C. M.

S. W. TUCKER.

1. Oh that the Lord would guide my ways To keep his stat - utes still! Oh that my God would grant me grace To know and do his will!
2. Oh, send thy Spir - it down, to write Thy law up - on my heart; Nor let my tongue in - dulge de - ceit, Nor act the li - ar's part.
3. Or - der my foot - steps by thy word, And make my heart sin - cere; Let sin have no do - min - ion, Lord, But keep my

PRINCETON. C. M.

1. To thee. my Shep - herd and my Lord, A grate-ful song I'll raise; Oh, let the fee - blest of thy flock At - tempt to speak thy praise!
2. But how shall mor - tal tongue ex-press A sub-ject so di - vine! Do jus-tice to so vast a theme, Or praise a love like thine!
3. My life, my joy, my hope, I owe To thine a - maz - ing love; Ten thousand thous-and com-forts here, And no-bler bliss a - bove.

AGNUS. C. M.

D. W. BARTLETT.

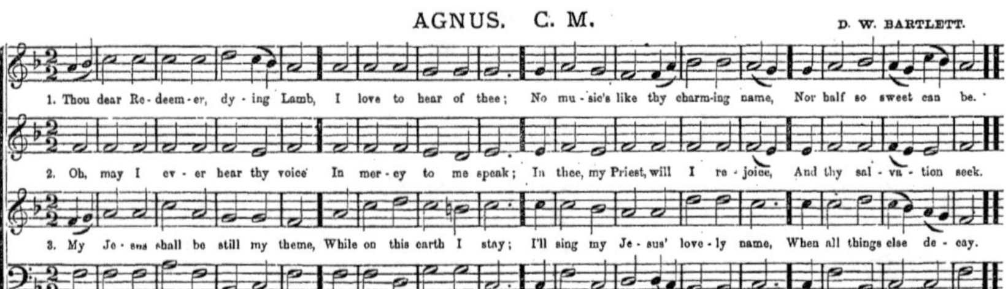
1. Thou dear Re - deem - er, dy - ing Lamb, I love to hear of thee; No mu - sic's like thy charm-ing name, Nor half so sweet can be.
2. Oh, may I ev - er hear thy voice In mer - cy to me speak; In thee, my Priest, will I re - joice, And thy sal - va - tion seek.
3. My Je - sus shall be still my theme, While on this earth I stay; I'll sing my Je - sus' love - ly name, When all things else de - cay.

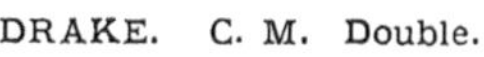
DRAKE. C. M. Double.

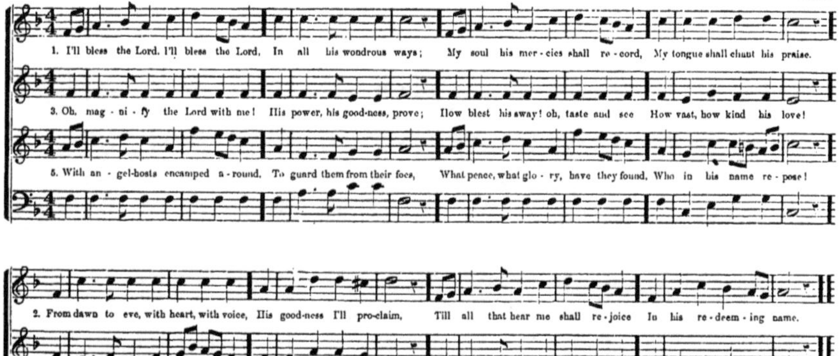
1. I'll bless the Lord. I'll bless the Lord, In all his wondrous ways; My soul his mer - cies shall re - cord, My tongue shall chant his praise.
3. Oh, mag - ni - fy the Lord with me! His power, his good-ness, prove; How blest his sway! oh, taste and see How vast, how kind his love!
5. With an - gel-hosts encamped a - round, To guard them from their foes, What peace, what glo - ry, have they found, Who in his name re - pose!

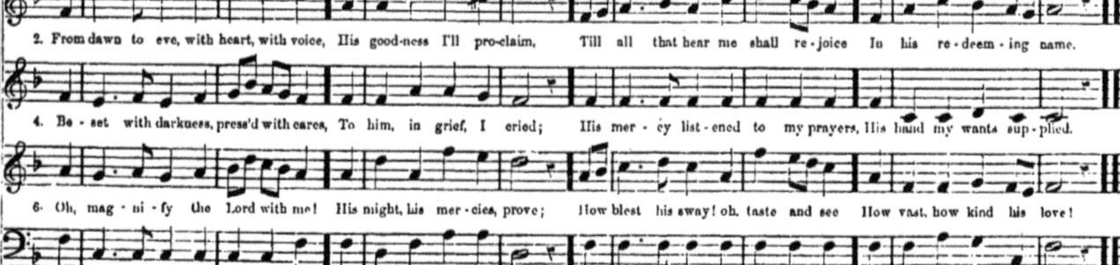
2. From dawn to eve, with heart, with voice, His good-ness I'll pro-claim, Till all that hear me shall re - joice In his re - deem - ing name.
4. Be - set with darkness, press'd with cares, To him, in grief, I cried; His mer - cy list - ened to my prayers, His hand my wants sup - plied.
6. Oh, mag - ni - fy the Lord with me! His might, his mer - cies, prove; How blest his sway! oh, taste and see How vast, how kind his love!

PERTH. C. M. Double. *

1. With songs and hon - ors sound-ing loud, Ad - dress the Lord on high; O - ver the heav'ns he spreads his cloud, And wa - ters vail the sky.
3. His stead - y coun - sels change the face Of the de - clin - ing year; He bids the sun cut short his race, And win - t'ry days ap - pear.
5. He sends his word, and melts the snow, The fields no long - er mourn; He calls the warm - er gales to blow, And bids the spring re - turn.
2. He sends his show'rs of bless - ing down To cheer the plains be - low; He makes the grass the mountains crown, And corn in val - leys grow.
4. His hoar - y frost, his flee - cy snow, De - scend and clothe the ground; The liq - uid streams forbear to flow, In i - cy fet - ters bound.
6. The chang-ing wind, the fly - ing cloud, O - bey his might - y word; With songs and hon - ors sound - ing loud, Praise ye the sov - ereign Lord!

ALARD. C. M.

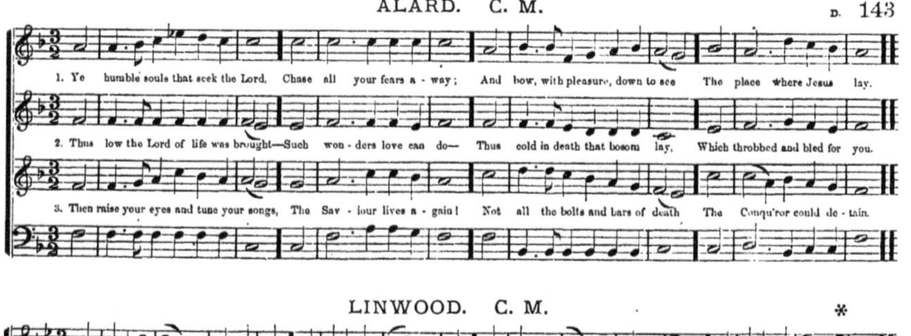
1. Ye humble souls that seek the Lord, Chase all your fears a - way; And bow, with pleasure, down to see The place where Jesus lay.
2. Thus low the Lord of life was brought—Such won - ders love can do— Thus cold in death that bosom lay, Which throbbed and bled for you.
3. Then raise your eyes and tune your songs, The Sav - iour lives a - gain! Not all the bolts and bars of death The Conqu'ror could de - tain.

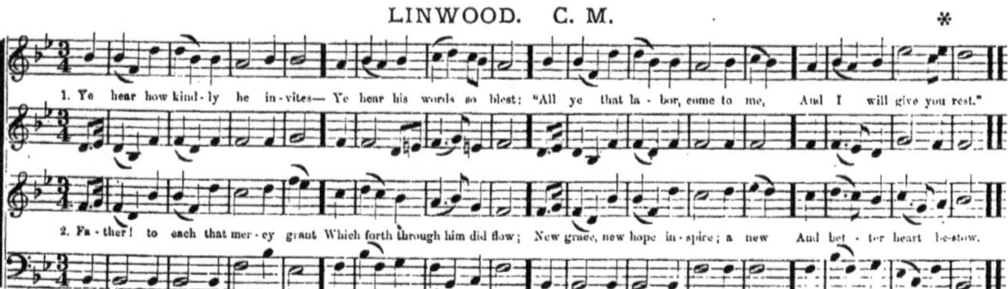
LINWOOD. C. M.
*
1. Ye hear how kind - ly he in - vites— Ye hear his words so blest: "All ye that la - bor, come to me, And I will give you rest."
2. Fa - ther! to each that mer - cy grant Which forth through him did flow; New grace, new hope in - spire; a new And bet - ter heart be-stow.

TRUMAN. C. M. *

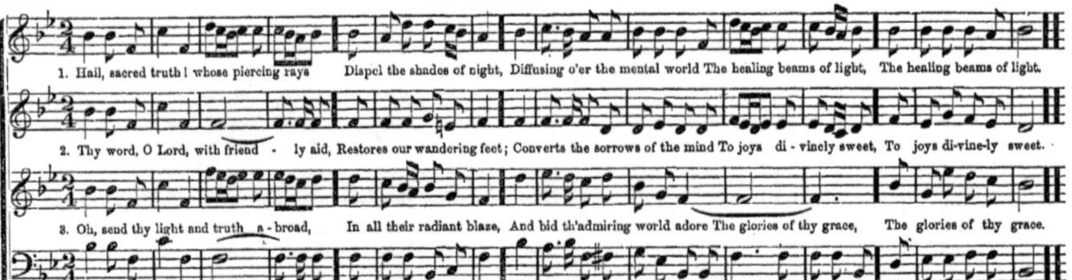

1. Hail, sacred truth! whose piercing rays Dispel the shades of night, Diffusing o'er the mental world The healing beams of light, The healing beams of light.
2. Thy word, O Lord, with friend - ly aid, Restores our wandering feet; Converts the sorrows of the mind To joys di - vinely sweet, To joys di-vine-ly sweet.
3. Oh, send thy light and truth a - broad, In all their radiant blaze, And bid th'admiring world adore The glories of thy grace, The glories of thy grace.

ROSELAND. C. M.

J. P. M.

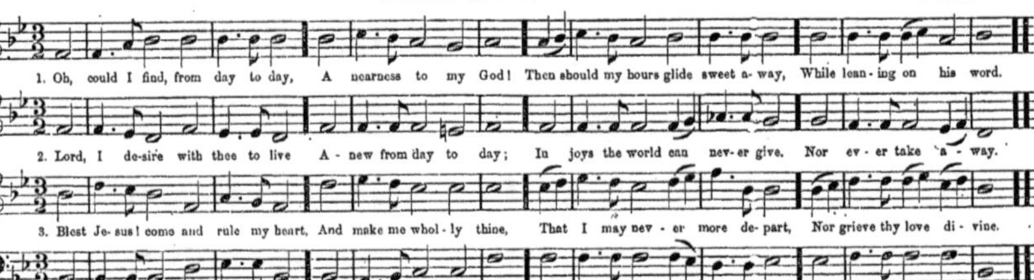

1. Oh, could I find, from day to day, A nearness to my God! Then should my hours glide sweet a- way, While lean - ing on his word.
2. Lord, I de-sire with thee to live A - new from day to day; In joys the world can nev- er give. Nor ev - er take a - way.
3. Blest Je- sus! come and rule my heart, And make me whol - ly thine, That I may nev - er more de- part, Nor grieve thy love di - vine.

EMERSON. C. M.

1. Lord, I ap-proach the mer - cy - seat, Where thou dost an - swer prayer; There hum - bly fall be - fore thy feet, For none can per - ish there.
2. Thy prom-ise is my on - ly plea; With this I ven - ture nigh: Thou call - est burd-ened souls to thee, And such, O Lord, am I.
VINCENT. C. M.
1. My God, how wonder- ful thou art, Thy maj - es - ty how bright! How glo - ri - ous thy mer-cy - seat, In depths of burn - ing light.
2. My God, how wonder- ful thou art, Thou ev - er- last-ing Friend! On thee I stay my trusting heart, Till faith in vis - ion end.

CHESUNCOOK. C. M.
1. As pants the hart for cool - ing streams, When heat-ed in the chase; So longs my soul, O God, for thee, And thy re - fresh - ing grace.
2. For thee, my God, the liv - ing God, My thirst - y soul doth pine; Oh! when shall I be - hold thy face, Thou maj - es - ty di - vine?
3. Why rest - less, why cast down, my soul? Trust God; and he'll em - ploy His aid for thee, and change these sighs To thank-ful hymns of joy.
FISHER. C. M.
1. When mus-ing sor - row weeps the past, And mourns the pres - ent pain, 'Tis sweet to think of peace at last, And feel that death is gain.
2. 'Tis not that murmuring thoughts arise, And dread a Fa - ther's will; 'Tis not that meek sub - mis-sion flies, And would not suf - fer still:
3. It is that heaven-born faith sur-veys The path that leads to light, And longs her ea - gle plumes to raise, And lose her - self in sight.

CAVARE. C. M.

1. Thou dear Re-deem-er, dy - ing Lamb, I love to hear of thee; No mu-sic's like thy charming name, Nor half so sweet can be.
2. Oh, may I ev - er hear thy voice In mer - cy to me speak; In thee, my Priest, will I re - joice, And thy sal - va - tion seek.
3. My Je - sus shall be still my theme, While on this earth I stay; I'll sing my Je - sus' love-ly name, When all things else de - cay.
GOODWIN. C. M.
D. From "Harp of Judah."
By permission.
1. See Israel's gen - tle Shep - herd stand With all - en - gag - ing charms; Hark, how he calls the ten - der lambs, And folds them in his arms.
2. "Per - mit them to approach," he cries, "Nor scorn their hum - ble name; For 'twas to bless such souls as these, The Lord of an - gels came."
3. We bring them, Lord, in thank - ful hands, And yield them up to thee; Joy - ful that we our-selves are thine,— Thine let our off-spring be.

148
SPENCER. C. M.
*
1. Oh, speed thee, Christian! on thy way, And to thine ar - mor cling; With gird - ed loins the call o - bey Which grace and mer - cy bring.
2. There is a bat - tle to be fought, An up - ward race to run, A crown of glo - ry to be sought, A vic - t'ry to be won.
3. Oh, faint not, Christian! for thy sighs Are heard be - fore the throne; The race must come be - fore the prize, The cross be - fore the crown.
FRIBOURG. C. M.
D.
1. Je - sus, in thy transport - ing name What bliss - ful glo - ries rise! Je - sus—the an - gels' sweetest theme! The won - der of the skies.
2. Well might the skies with won - der view A love so strange as thine! No thought of an - gels ev - er knew Com - pas - sion so di - vine!
3. Je - sus, and didst thou leave the sky To hear our sins and woes? And didst thou bleed, and groan, and die For vile, re - bel - lious foes?

CREDO. C. M.
D.
1. Lord, I be-lieve; thy pow'r I own, Thy word I would o-bey; I wan-der com-fort-less and lone, When from thy truth I stray.
2. Lord, I be-lieve; but gloom-y fears Sometimes be-dim my sight; I look to thee with pray'rs and tears, And cry for strength and light.
3. Lord, I be-lieve; but oft, I know, My faith is cold and weak: My weak-ness strengthen, and be-stow The con-fi-dence I seek.
QUAIN. C. M.
1. My God, how won-der-ful thou art, Thy maj-es-ty how bright! How glorious is thy mer-cy-seat, In depths of burn-ing light!
2. Yet I may love thee too, O Lord, Al-might-y as thou art; For thou hast stoop'd to ask of me The love of my poor heart.
3. No earthly fa-ther loves like thee, No moth-er half so mild Bears and forbears, as thou hast done With me, thy sin-ful child.

HOWLAND. C. M.

CRONSTADT. C. M.

J. S. BROOKS.

1. To whom, my Sav - iour, shall I go, If I de - part from thee, My guide thro' all this vale of woe, And more than all to me.
2. Lord, I have felt thy dy - ing love Breathe gent - ly thro' my heart, To whis - per hope of joys a - bove, And can we ev - er part?
1. Be thou, O God, by night, by day, My guide, my guard from sin; My life, my trust, my light di - vine, To keep me pure from sin.
2. So may my soul up - on the wings Of faith, un - wea - ried rise, Till at the gate of heav'n it sings, 'Midst light from par - a - dise.

WIEMAR. C. M.

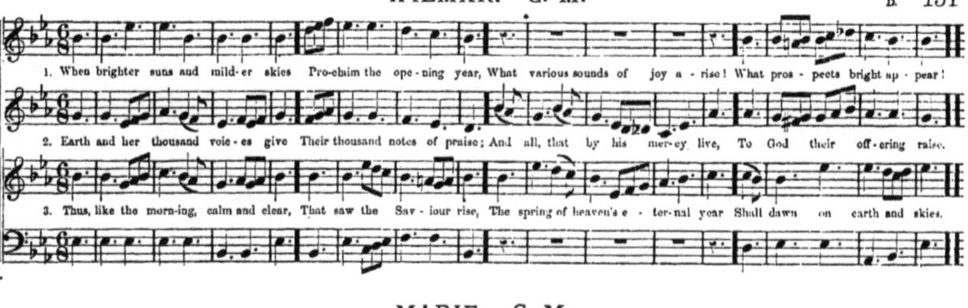
1. When brighter suns and mild-er skies Pro-claim the ope-ning year, What various sounds of joy a-rise! What pros-pects bright ap-pear!
2. Earth and her thousand voic-es give Their thousand notes of praise; And all, that by his mer-cy live, To God their off-ering raise.
3. Thus, like the morn-ing, calm and clear, That saw the Sav-iour rise, The spring of heaven's e-ter-nal year Shall dawn on earth and skies.

MARIE. C. M.

Miss S. SPOFFORD.

1. Oh for a heart to praise my God! A heart from sin set free; A heart that's sprinkled with the blood So free-ly shed for me;—
2. A heart re-signed, sub-mis-sive, meek, My dear Re-deem-er's throne; Where on-ly Christ is heard to speak, Where Je-sus reigns a-lone.
3. Oh for a low-ly, con-trite heart, Be-liev-ing, true, and clean; Which nei-ther life nor death can part From him that dwells with-in!

Treble and Tenor may be inverted.

BENEDICTUS. C. M.

D.

1. Je - sus! the ver-y thought of thee With glad-ness fills my breast; But dear-er far thy face to see, And in thy pres-ence rest.
2. Nor voice can sing, nor heart can frame, Nor can the memory find A sweeter sound than thy blest name, O Sav-iour of man-kind!
3. O Hope of ev-ery con-trite heart, O Joy of all the meek! To those who fall, how kind thou art, How good to those who seek!
SHIELD. C. M.
O. R. BARROWS.
1. See Is - rael's gen - tle Shep-herd stand With all - en - gag - ing charms; Hark, how he calls the ten - der lambs, And folds them in his arms!
2. "Per mit them to approach," he cries, "Nor scorn their hum-ble name; For 'twas to bless such souls as these, The Lord of an - gels came."
3. We bring them Lord, in thank-ful bands, And yield them up to thee; Joy - ful that we our - selves are thine,—Thine let our off-spring be.

HALLE. C. M.

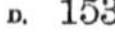
D. 153

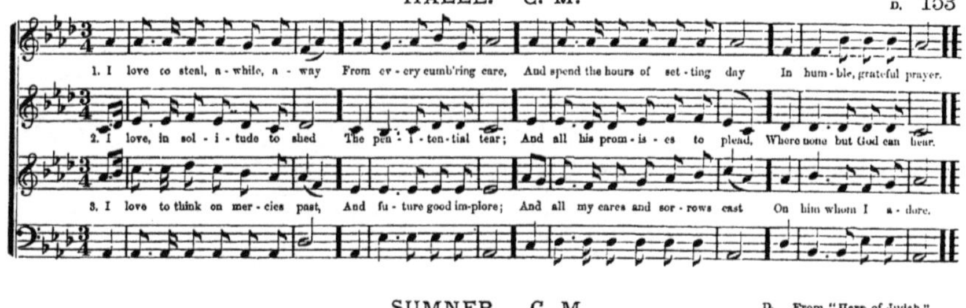
1. I love to steal, a - while, a - way From ev - ery cumb'ring care, And spend the hours of set - ting day In hum - ble, grateful prayer.
2. I love, in sol - i - tude to shed The pen - i - ten - tial tear; And all his prom - is - es to plead, Where none but God can hear.
3. I love to think on mer - cies past, And fu - ture good im-plore; And all my cares and sor - rows cast On him whom I a - dore.

SUMNER. C. M.

D. From "Harp of Judah." *By Permission.*

1. With sa - cred joy we lift our eyes To those bright realms a - bove—That glorious tem - ple in the skies, Where dwells e - ter - nal love.
2. While in the house of prayer we kneel, With trust and ho - ly fear, Thy mer - cy and thy truth re - veal, And lend a gra-cious ear.

CHAUNCEY STREET. C. M.
1. O all ye lands, re - joice in God! Sing prais - es to his name; Let all the earth, with one ac-cord, His wondrous acts pro-claim;
2. And let his faith - ful serv - ants tell How, by re-deem-ing love, Their souls are saved from death and hell, To share the joys a - bove.
3. Oh, then, re - joice, and shout for joy, Ye ran-somed of the Lord! Be grate - ful praise your sweet employ, His pres - ence your re - ward.
Soprano and Tenor may be inverted.
SHARON. C. M.
D.
1. By cool Si - lo - am's sha - dy rill How fair the lil - y grows! How sweet the breath, be - neath the hill, Of Sha - ron's dew - y rose!
2. Lo! such the child, whose ear - ly feet The paths of peace have trod, Whose se - cret heart, with influence sweet, Is up - ward drawn to God.
3. By cool Si - lo - am's sha - dy rill The lil - y must de - cay; The rose that blooms be-neath the hill Must short - ly fade a - way.

THORNBURN. C. M.
CH. ZEUNER.
1. To God ad - dress the joy - ful psalm, Who won-drous things hath done; Whose own right hand, and ho - ly arm, The vic - to - ry have won.
2. He, to the Gen - tile na - tions round, Hath made his mer - cy known; And, to the world's re - mot - est bound, His just - ice shall be shown.
3. The prom-ised Sav - iour meek-ly came, And man's full ran - som paid; A - gain he comes, his own to claim, In aw - ful pomp ar-rayed.
SPARTAS. C. M.
SALEM WILDER.
1. Hear me, O God, nor hide thy face, But an - swer, lest I die! Hast thou not built a throne of grace, To hear when sin - ners cry!
2. As on some lone - ly build-ing's top The spar - row tells her moan, Far from the tents of joy and hope, I sit and grieve a - lone.
3. But thou for ev - er art the same, O my E - ter - nal God! A - ges to come shall know thy name, And spread thy works a - broad.

LOCKE. C. M.

M. L. LAWRENCE.

1. When musing sor - row weeps the past, And mourns the pres- ent pain, 'Tis sweet to think of peace at last, And feel that death is gain.
2. 'Tis not that murmuring thoughts a - rise, And dread a Fa - ther's will; 'Tis not that meek sub - mis - sion flies, And would not suf - fer still:
3. It is that heaven-born faith sur - veys The path that leads to light, And longs her ea - gle plumes to raise, And lose her - self in sight.
HUDSON. C. M.
CH. ZEUNER.
1. How sweet, how heavenly is the sight, When those who love the Lord In one an - oth - er's peace de - light, And so ful - fill his word!
SOLO.
TUTTI.
2. When each can feel his brother's sigh, And with him bear a part! When sor - row flows from eye to eye, And joy from heart to heart!
SOLO.
TUTTI.
3. When, free from en - vy, scorn, and pride, Our wish - es all a - bove, Each can his broth-er's fail - ings hide, And show a broth-er's love!

BUCKMINSTER. C. M.
C. M. WYMAN.
1. Thou art my por - tion, O my God; Soon as I know thy way, My heart makes haste t' o - bey thy word, And suffers no de - lay.
2. I choose the path of heavenly truth, And glory in my choice; Not all the rich - es of the earth Could make me so re - joice.
3. The tes - ti - mon - ies of thy grace I set be - fore mine eyes; Thence I de - rive my dai - ly strength, And there my com - fort lies.
FLETCHER. C. M.
M. D. F.
1. How sweet, how heavenly is the sight, When those who love the Lord In one an - other's peace de - light, And so ful - fill his word!
2. When each can feel his brother's sigh, And with him bear a part! When sor - row flows from eye to eye, And joy from heart to heart!
3. When, free from envy, scorn, and pride, Our wish - es all a - bove, Each can his brother's fail - ings hide, And show a brother's love!

JASPER. C. M. Double.

mp Allegretto.
Dim.
mp
Dim.
1. There is a ci - ty fair and bright, That eye hath nev - er seen, Where ev - er dwell-eth pure de - light, And heavenly peace se - rene.
3. There liv - ing wa - ters cease-less flow From out the heaven-ly throne; There fair - est fruits per - ren - nial grow, And want is nev - er known,
5. Nor sin nor sor - row com - eth there, Nor ev - er death nor pain, In love a - bid - ing, free from care, There saints for - ev - er reign.
mf
mp
f
2. High walls of pre - cious gems and gold Se - cure from ev' - ry ill; Un - heard of bliss and joys un - told With - in its bor - ders dwell:
4. Nor sun by day nor moon by night This heaven-ly ci - ty needs; But glo - ry sheds a crys - tal light That nev - er wanes nor fades.
6. A - mong the ma - ny man-sions there, Oh! is there one for me? Dear Lord, an hum - ble place pre-pare, That I may dwell with thee.
ILBA. C. M.
Arranged from Gregorian Tone V.
1. The Lord is wise, the Lord is just, The Lord is good and true; And they who in his prom-ise trust Will find it bear them through.
2. His word will stay their sink - ing hearts, Their feet shall nev - er slide: Tho' heav'ns dissolve and earth de - parts; In God they safe a - bide.

ST. ANNS. C. M.
Dr. Wm. Croft.
Thro' all the chang-ing scenes of life, In trou-ble and in joy, The prais-es of my God shall still My heart and tongue em-ploy.
MARLOW. C. M.
Arranged by Dr. L. Mason.
Lord, how se-cure my conscience was, And felt no in-ward dread! I was a-live with-out the law, And thought my sins were dead.
DUNDEE. C. M.
"Scotch Psalter."
O Je-sus, thou the beau-ty art Of an-gel-worlds a-bove; Thy name is mu-sic to the heart, En-chant-ing it with love.
DEDHAM. C. M.
Arranged by Dr. L. Mason.
Thou art the Way: to thee a-lone From sin and death we flee; And he who would the Fa-ther seek, Must seek him, Lord, by thee.

ORTONVILLE. C. M.
Dr. Thos. Hastings.
We'll sing the power of him who died His peo - ple to re - deem; He is our Saviour, true and tried, And he shall be our theme, And he shall be our theme.
STEPHENS. C. M.
W. Jones.
To our Al - might - y Ma - ker, God, New hon - ors be ad - dressed; His great sal - va - tion shines a - broad, And makes the na - tions blest.
DOWNS. C. M.
Dr. L. Mason.
Au - thor of good! to thee we turn: Thine ev - er - wake - ful eye A - lone can all our wants dis - cern— Thy hand a - lone sup - ply.
BALERMA. C. M.
H. Wilson.
Lo! what a glo - rious sight ap - pears To our be - liev - ing eyes! The earth and seas are passed a - way, And the old roll - ing skies.

COWPER. C. M.
Dr. L. Mason.
1. There is a fountain filled with blood, Drawn from Immanuel's veins · And sinners plunged beneath that flood, Lose all their guilty stains, Lose all their guilty stains.
EVAN. C. M.
From "The Hallelujah."
1. In mer - cy, Lord, re - mem- ber me, Through all the hours of night; And grant to me most gra-cious - ly The safeguard of thy might.
DENFIELD. C. M.
Arr. from C. G. Glaser, by Dr. L. Mason.
1. Lord, may our sym - pa - thiz-ing breasts Thy generous pleas - ure know, Kind - ly to share in oth- ers' joys, And weep for oth - ers' woe!
NAOMI. C. M.
Dr. L. Mason.
1. Father! whate'er of earth-ly bliss Thy sov- ereign will de - nies Ac - cept- ed at thy throne of grace, Let this pe - ti - tion rise:

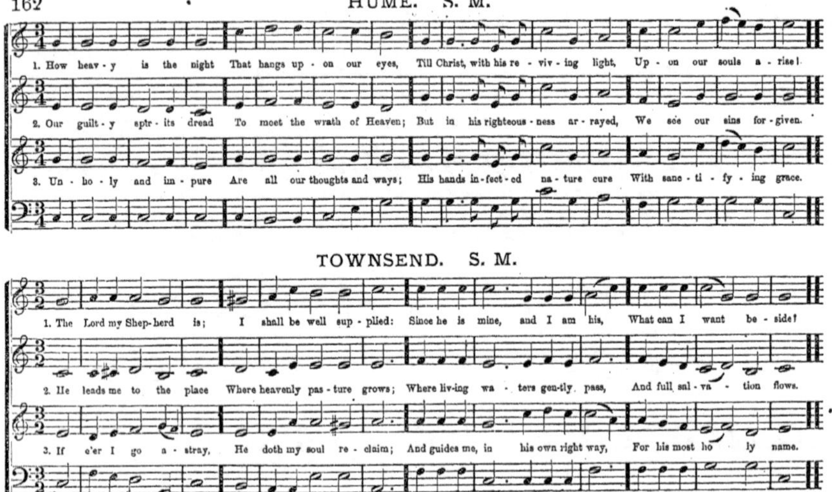
HUME. S. M.
1. How heav - y is the night That hangs up - on our eyes, Till Christ, with his re - viv - ing light, Up - on our souls a - rise!
2. Our guilt - y spir - its dread To meet the wrath of Heaven; But in his righteous - ness ar - rayed, We see our sins for - given.
3. Un - ho - ly and im - pure Are all our thoughts and ways; His hands in - fect - ed na - ture cure With sanc - ti - fy - ing grace.
TOWNSEND. S. M.
1. The Lord my Shep-herd is; I shall be well sup - plied: Since he is mine, and I am his, What can I want be - side?
2. He leads me to the place Where heavenly pas - ture grows; Where liv-ing wa - ters gen-tly pass, And full sal - va - tion flows.
3. If e'er I go a - stray, He doth my soul re - claim; And guides me, in his own right way, For his most ho - ly name.

PUTNEY. S. M.

1. Let songs of end - less praise, From ev - ery na - tion rise, Let all the lands their trib - ute raise To him who rules the
2. His mer - cy and his love Are bound - less as his name; And all e - ter - ni - ty shall prove, His truth re - mains the same.

QUITO. S. M.

1. A - rise, ye saints, a - rise! The Lord our Leader is; The foe be - fore his ban - ner flies, For vic - - to - ry is his.
2. Lead on, al - mighty Lord, Lead on to vic - to - ry! En - couraged by the bright re - ward, With joy we'll fol - low thee.
3. We'll fol - low thee, our Guide, Our Saviour and our King; We'll fol - low thee, thro' grace sup - plied From heaven's e - ter - nal spring.

ABBIE. S. M.

W.

1. Come to the land of peace; From shadows come a - way; There all the sounds of weep-ing cease, And storms no more have sway.
2. Fear hath no dwell-ing here; But pure re - pose and love Breathe thro' the bright, ce - les - tial air The spir - it of the dove.
3. Come to the bright and blest, Gathered from ev - ery land; For here thy soul shall find its rest, A - mid the shin - ing band.
DUREN. S. M.
D.
1. The Lord my Shep-herd is: I shall be well sup-plied: Since he is mine, and I am his, What can I want be - side?
2. He leads me to the place Where heavenly pas-ture grows; Where liv - ing wa - ters gen - tly pass, And full sal - va - tion flows.
3. If e'er I go a - stray, He doth my soul re - claim; And guides me, in his own right way, For his most ho - ly name.

MUNICH. S. M.

D. From "Harp of Judah." *By permission.*

SOPRANO SOLO
1. Oh, cease, my wandering soul, On rest-less wing to roam; All this wide world, to ei-ther pole, Has not for thee a home.
2. Be-hold the ark of God! Be-hold the o-pen door! Oh, haste to gain that dear a-bode, And roam, my soul, no more.
LYNNE. S. M.
1. My soul! be on thy guard; Ten thousand foes a-rise; The hosts of sin are pressing hard To draw thee from the skies.
2. Oh, watch, and fight, and pray! The bat-tle ne'er give o'er; Re-new it bold-ly ev-ery day, And help di-vine im-plore.
3. Ne'er think the vic-t'ry won, Nor once at ease sit down; Thy arduous work will not be done Till thou ob-tain thy crown.

166
HART. S. M.
*
1. My soul, it is thy God Who calls thee by his grace; Now loose thee from each cumbering load, And bend thee to........ the race.
2. Make thy sal-va-tion sure; All sloth and slumber shun; Nor dare a moment rest se-cure, Till thou the goal...... hast won.
3. Thy crown of life hold fast; Thy heart with courage stay; Nor let one trembling glance be cast A-long the back - - ward way.
ALPHA. S. M.
J. EASTMAN.
1. Thy name, Almight-y Lord, Shall sound through distant lands; Great is thy grace, and sure thy word; Thy truth for - ev - er stands.
2. Far be thine hon - or spread, And long thy praise en - dure, Till morning light and evening shade Shall be exchanged no - more.

BEAMES. S. M.
1. Behold, the morning sun Begins his glorious way; His beams thro' all the nations run, And life and light convey; His beams thro' all the nations run, And life and light convey.
2. But where the Gospel comes, It spreads diviner light; It calls dead sinners from their tombs, And gives the blind their sight; It calls dead sinners from their tombs, And, &c.
3. Thy laws are just and pure, Thy truth without deceit; Thy promises forever sure, And thy rewards are great; Thy promises forever sure, And thy rewards are great.
FARMINGTON. S. M.
D.
1. How gen - tle God's commands! How kind his pre - cepts are! Come, cast your bur - dens on the Lord, And trust his con - stant care.
2. Be - neath his watch - ful eye His saints se - cure - ly dwell; That hand which bears all na - ture up, Shall guard his chil - dren well.
3. Why should this anx - ious load Press down your wea - ry mind? Haste to your heaven - ly Fa - ther's throne, And sweet re - freshment find.

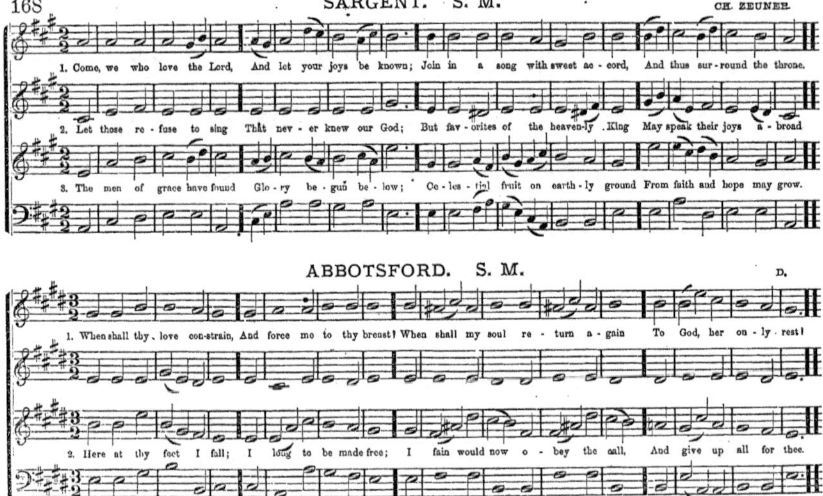
SARGENT. S. M.
CH. ZEUNER.
1. Come, we who love the Lord, And let your joys be known; Join in a song with sweet ac - cord, And thus sur - round the throne.
2. Let those re - fuse to sing That nev - er knew our God; But fav - orites of the heaven-ly King May speak their joys a - broad
3. The men of grace have found Glo - ry be - gun be - low; Ce - les - tial fruit on earth - ly ground From faith and hope may grow.
ABBOTSFORD. S. M.
D.
1. When shall thy love con-strain, And force me to thy breast? When shall my soul re - turn a - gain To God, her on - ly rest!
2. Here at thy feet I fall; I long to be made free; I fain would now o - bey the call, And give up all for thee.

GASCONY. S. M.

D.

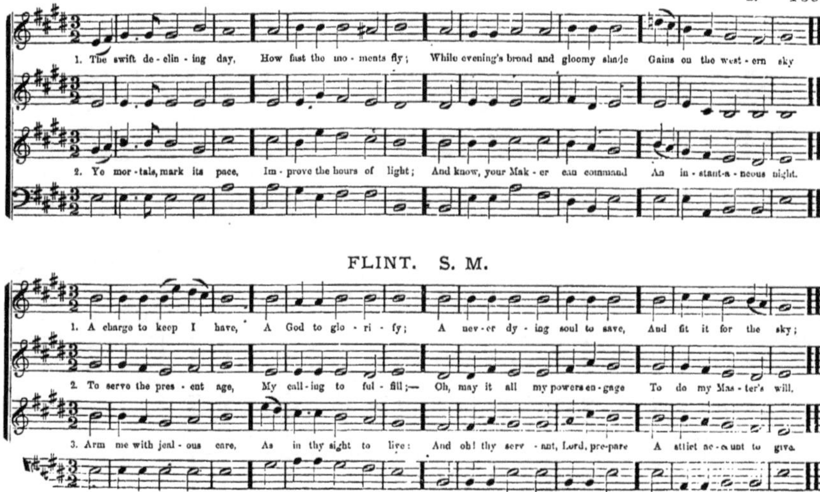
1. The swift de - clin - ing day, How fast the mo - ments fly; While evening's broad and gloomy shade Gains on the west - ern sky
2. Ye mor - tals, mark its pace, Im - prove the hours of light; And know, your Mak - er can command An in - stant-a - neous night.
FLINT. S. M.
1. A charge to keep I have, A God to glo - ri - fy; A nev - er dy - ing soul to save, And fit it for the sky;
2. To serve the pres - ent age, My call - ing to ful - fill;— Oh, may it all my powers en - gage To do my Mas - ter's will.
3. Arm me with jeal - ous care, As in thy sight to live: And oh! thy serv - ant, Lord, pre-pare A strict ac - count to give.

SERENE. S. M.
J. E. GOULD. By permission.
ANDANTE. DOLCE.
Second Ending.
1. Se - rene I lay me down Be-neath his guardian care; I slept, and I a-woke, and found My kind pre - serv - er near.
cres.
2. Thus does thine arm sup-port This weak de-fence-less frame; But whence these fav-ors Lord, to me, All worth - less as I am?
REFLECTION. S. M.
W. From "Harp of Judah."
By permission.
1. And must this bod - y die? This mor - tal frame de - cay? And must these ac - tive limbs of mine Lie moldering in the clay?
2. God, my Re - deem - er, lives, And ev - er from the skies Looks down and watches all my dust, Till he shall bid it rise.
3. Ar-rayed in glo - rious grace, Shall these vile bod - ies shine, And ev - ery shape, and ev - ery face Look heavenly and di - vine

NEWTONVILLE. S. M. Double.

L. O. EMERSON.

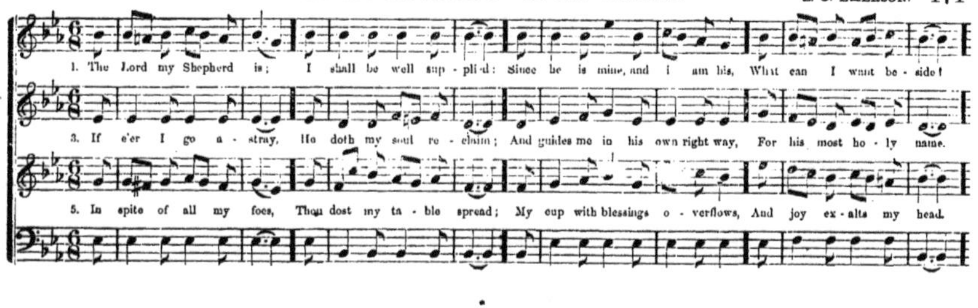
1. The Lord my Shepherd is; I shall be well sup - pli'd: Since he is mine, and I am his, What can I want be - side!
3. If e'er I go a - stray, He doth my soul re - claim; And guides me in his own right way, For his most ho - ly name.
5. In spite of all my foes, Thou dost my ta - ble spread; My cup with blessings o - verflows, And joy ex - alts my head.

2. He leads.... me to the place Where heaven - ly pas - ture grows; Where liv - ing wa - ters gent - ly pass, And full sal - va - tion flows.
4. While he ..... af - fords his aid, I can - - not yield to fear; Though I should walk thro' death's dark shade, My Shepherd's with me there.
6. The boun - ties of thy love Shall crown.... my fu - ture days; Nor from thy house will I re - move, Nor cease to speak thy praise.

BONDEE. S. M.

1. Far from these scenes of night Un - bound - ed glo - ries rise, And realms of in - fin - ite de - light, Un - known to mor - tal eyes.
2. There sick - ness nev - er comes, There grief no more com - plains: Health tri - umphs in im - mor - tal bloom, And pur - est pleas - ure reigns.
3. No strife nor en - vy there The sons of peace mo - lest: But har - mo - ny, and love sin - cere, Fill ev - ery hap - py breast.
HALSEY. S. M.
CH. ZEUNER.
1. Sing prais - es to our God, And bless his sa - cred name; His great sal - va - tion, all a - broad, From day to day pro - claim.
2. 'Midst hea - then na - tions place The glo - ries of his throne; And let the won - ders of his grace Thro' all the earth be known.
3. The gods, the heathen boasts, Nor hear—nor see—nor move; Je - ho - vah is the Lord of hosts, Who spread the heavens a - bove!

CAROLUS. S. M.

J. P. M.

1. Did Christ o'er sin - ners weep, And shall our cheeks be dry? Let floods of pen - i - ten - tial grief Burst forth from ev - ery eye.
2. The Son of God in tears The wondering an - gels see! Be thou as - ton - ished, O my soul! He shed those tears for thee.
3. He wept that we might weep; Each sin de-mands a tear; In heaven a - lone no sin is found, And weeping is not there.

KINDNESS. S. M.

O. B. BARROWS.

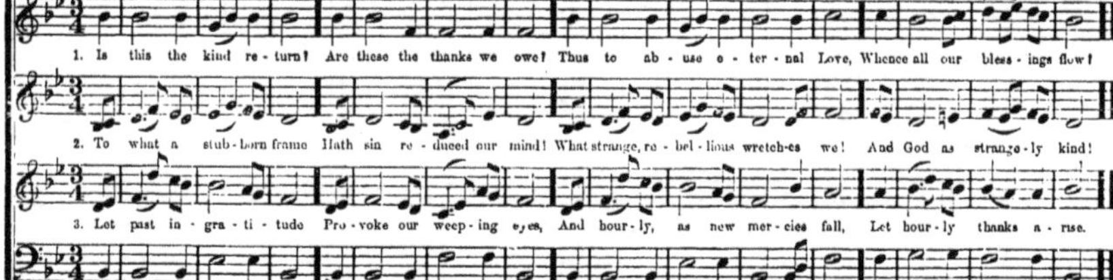
1. Is this the kind re - turn? Are these the thanks we owe? Thus to ab - use e - ter - nal Love, Whence all our bless - ings flow!
2. To what a stub - born frame Hath sin re - duced our mind! What strange, re - bel - lious wretch-es we! And God as strange - ly kind!
3. Let past in - gra - ti - tude Pro - voke our weep - ing eyes, And hour - ly, as new mer - cies fall, Let hour - ly thanks a - rise.

DENNETT. S. M. *

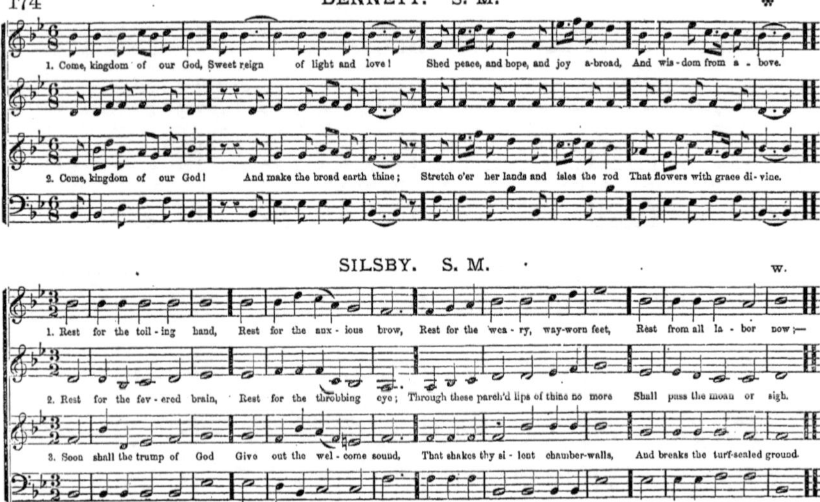
1. Come, kingdom of our God, Sweet reign of light and love! Shed peace, and hope, and joy a-broad, And wis-dom from a - bove.
2. Come, kingdom of our God! And make the broad earth thine; Stretch o'er her lands and isles the rod That flowers with grace di-vine.
SILSBY. S. M.
W.
1. Rest for the toil-ing hand, Rest for the anx-ious brow, Rest for the wea-ry, way-worn feet, Rest from all la-bor now;—
2. Rest for the fev-ered brain, Rest for the throbbing eye; Through these parch'd lips of thine no more Shall pass the moan or sigh.
3. Soon shall the trump of God Give out the wel-come sound, That shakes thy si-lent chamber-walls, And breaks the turf-sealed ground.

HEIMWEH. S. M.
D.
Melody in Tenor. Soprano and Tenor may be inverted.
1. Oh, where shall rest be found— Rest for the wea - ry soul! 'Twere vain the o - cean depths to sound, Or pierce to ei - ther pole.
2. The world can nev - er give The bliss for which we sigh: 'Tis not the whole of life to live, Nor all of death to die.
3. Be - yond this vale of tears There is a life a - bove, Un - measured by the flight of years; And all that life is love.
ROWLAND. S. M.
D.
1. While my Re - deemer's near, My shepherd and my guide, I bid fare - well to anx - ious fear; My wants are all sup - plied.
2. To ev - er fra - grant meads, Where rich a - bun - dance grows, His gracious hand in - dul - gent leads, And guards my sweet re - pose.
3. Dear Shepherd, if I stray, My wand'ring feet re - store; To thy fair pastures guide my way, And let me rove no more.

176
CANBY. S. M.
CH. ZEUNER.
1. Have mer - cy, Lord, on me, As thou wert ev - er kind; Let me, op-pressed with loads of guilt, Thy wont - ed par - don find.
2. A - gainst thee, Lord, a - lone, And on - ly in thy sight, Have I transgress'd; and, though condemned, Must own thy judg-ments right.
3. Blot ou my cry - ing sins, Nor me in an - ger view; Cre - ate in me a heart that's clean, An up - right mind re - new.
WOODARD. S. M.
*
1. How glo - rious is the hour When first our souls a - wake, And thro' the Spir - it's quick'ning power Of the new life par - take.
2. With rich - er beau-ty glows The world, be - fore so fair; Her ho - ly light re - lig - ion throws, Re - flect-ed ev - ery - where.

BEMIS. S. M.
C. M. WYMAN.
1. Come, Ho - ly Spir - it, come! Let thy bright beams a - rise: Dis - pel the sor - row from our minds, The dark - ness from our eyes.
2. Con - vince us of our sin; Then lead to Je - sus' blood, And to our wondering view re - veal The se - cret love of God.
3. Re - vive our droop - ing faith, Our doubts and fears re - move, And kin - dle in our breasts the flame Of nev - er - dy - ing love.
MOORE. S. M.
W.
1. The day is past and gone, The eve - ning shades ap - pear; O may I ev - er keep in mind, The night of death draws near.
2. Lord, keep me safe this night, Se - cure from all my fears; May an - gels guard me while I sleep, Till morn - ing light ap - pears.
3. Lord, when my days are past, And I from time re - move, Oh, may I in thy bo - som rest, The bo - som of thy love.

WARDWELL. S. M. Double.

D.

Come, sound his praise a - broad, And hymns of glory sing: Je - hovah is the sovereign God, The u- ni -ver- sal King.
1. Come, sound his praise a - broad, And hymns of glo - ry sing: Je - ho-vah is the sovereign God, The u - ni - ver - sal King.
Come, sound his praise a - broad, And hymns of glory sing: Je - hovah is the sovereign God, The u- ni -ver- sal King.
He gave the seas their bound; The watery worlds are all his own, And all the solid ground.
2. He formed the deeps un - known; He gave the seas their bound; The watery worlds are all his own, And all the sol - id ground.
The watery worlds are all his own, And all the solid ground.

ELDEN. S. M.
H. L. M.
1. Sol - diers of Christ! a - rise, And put your ar - mor on,— Strong in the strength which God sup-plies Through his e - ter - nal Son,—
2. Strong in the Lord of hosts, And in his might - y power: Who in the strength of Je - sus trusts, Is more than con - quer - or.
3. Stand, then, in his great might, With all his strength en - dued; But take, to arm you for the fight, The pan - o - p'y of God;
NUT-BUSH. S. M.
W.
SOPRANO SOLO.
1. A - wake, and sing the song Of Mo - ses and the Lamb! Wake, ev - ery heart, and ev - ery tongue, To praise the Saviour's name!
2. Sing, till we feel our hearts As - cend - ing with our tongues; Sing, till the love of sin de - parts, And grace in - spires our songs.
3. Soon shall we hear him say, "Ye bless - ed chil - dren, come!" Soon will he call us hence a - way To our e - ter - nal home.

HARTWELL. S. M.

1. Oh, where shall rest be found— Rest for the wea - ry soul! 'Twere vain the o - cean's depths to sound, Or pierce to ei - ther pole.
2. The world can nev - er give The bliss for which we sigh: 'Tis not the whole of life to live, Nor all of death to die.
3. Be - yond this vale of tears There is a life a - bove, Un - meas-ured by the flight of years; And all that life is love.
BAYONNE. S. M.
D.
1. Thy name, Al - might - y Lord, Shall sound through dis-tant lands: Great is thy grace, and sure thy word; Thy truth for - ev - er stands.
2. Far be thine hon - or spread, And long thy praise en - dure; Till morn - ing light and eve - ning shade, Shall be ex-changed no more.

HOOPER. S. M.
W. From "Harp of Judah." By permission.
181
SOPRANO SOLO.
1. And is.... there, Lord, a rest, For wea-ry souls de-signed, Where not a care shall stir the breast, Or sor-row en-trance find?
2. Is there a bliss-ful home, Where kin-dred minds shall meet, And live and love, nor ev-er roam From that se-rene re-treat!
WESLEY. S. M.
1. Sol-diers of Christ! a-rise, And gird your ar-mor on,— Strong in the strength which God sup-plies, Through his e-ter-nal Son,—
2. Strong in the Lord of hosts, And in his might-y power: Who in the strength of Je-sus trusts, Is more than con-quer-or.
3. Stand, then, in his great might, With all his strength en-dued; But take, to arm you for the fight, The pan-o-ply of God.

EIDDA. S. M.

D.

1. Oh, where shall rest be found—Rest for the wea - ry soul? 'Twere vain the o - cean depths to sound, Or pierce to ei - ther pole.
2. The world can nev - er give The bliss for which we sigh: 'Tis not the whole of life to live, Nor all of death to die.
3. Be - yond this vale of tears There is a life a - bove, Un - measured by the flight of years; And all that life is love.
HULLAH. S. M.
D. From "Harp of Judah."
By Permission.
1. While my Re-deem - er's near, My shepherd and my guide, I bid fare - well to anx - ious fear: My wants are all.... sup-plied.
2. To ev - er fragrant meads, Where rich a - bun-dance grows, His gra - cious hand in - dul - gent leads, And guards my sweet re - pose.
3. Dear Shepherd, if I stray, My wand'ring feet re - store; To thy fair pas - tures guide my way, And let me rove no more.

HEDGE. S. M.

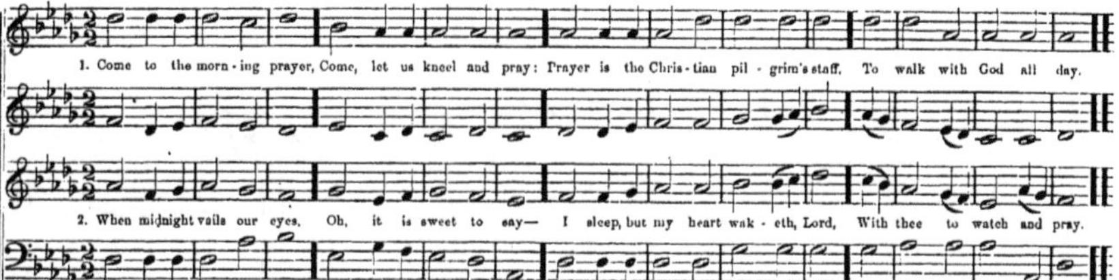
1. Come to the morn - ing prayer, Come, let us kneel and pray: Prayer is the Chris - tian pil - grim's staff, To walk with God all day.
2. When midnight vails our eyes, Oh, it is sweet to say— I sleep, but my heart wak - eth, Lord, With thee to watch and pray.

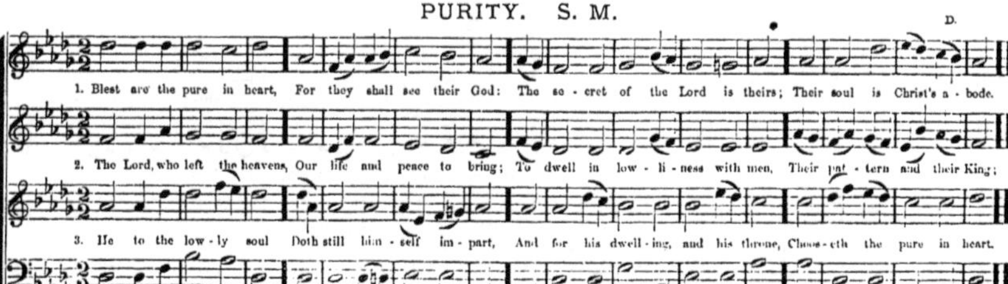
PURITY. S. M.
D.
1. Blest are the pure in heart, For they shall see their God: The se - cret of the Lord is theirs; Their soul is Christ's a - bode.
2. The Lord, who left the heavens, Our life and peace to bring; To dwell in low - li - ness with men, Their pat - tern and their King;
3. He to the low - ly soul Doth still him - self im - part, And for his dwell - ing, and his throne, Choos - eth the pure in heart.

LILLY COVE. S. M.
W.
1. If through un - ruf - fled seas, Toward heaven we calm - ly sail, With grate-ful hearts, O God, to thee We'll own the fos - tering gale.
2. But should the surg - es rise, And rest de - lay to come, Blest be the sor - row, kind the storm, Which drives us near - er home.
3. Soon shall our doubts and fears All yield to thy con-trol; Thy ten - der mer - cies shall il-lume The mid-night of the soul.
HIMMEL. S. M.
D.
1. Oh! bless the Lord, my soul! His grace to thee pro - claim; And all that is with - in me join To bless his ho - ly name.
2. Oh, bless the Lord, my soul! His mer-cies bear in mind; For - get not all his ben - e - fits; The Lord to thee is kind.
3. He will not al - ways chide; He will with pa - tience wait; His wrath is ev - er slow to rise, And rea - dy to a - bate.

BOYLSTON. S. M.
Dr. L. Mason.
I love thy king - dom, Lord— The house of thine a - bode, The church our blest Re - deem - er saved With his own pre - cious blood.
ST. THOMAS. S. M.
A. Williams.
To God, the on - ly wise, Our Sa - viour and our King; Let all the saints be - low the skies Their hum - ble prais - es bring.
OLMUTZ. S. M.
Arr. from a Gregorian Chant, by Dr. L. Mason.
To praise our Shepherd's care, His wis - dom, love, and might, Your loud - est, lof - tiest songs pre - pare, And bid the world u - nite.
STATE STREET. S. M.
J. C. Woodman.
Come to the land of peace; From sha - dows come a - way; Where all the sounds of weep - ing cease, And storms no more have sway.

LABAN. S. M.
Dr. L. Mason.
1. My soul, be on thy guard, Ten thousand foes a - rise; The hosts of sin are press - ing hard To draw thee from the skies.
BADEA. S. M.
German.
1. Oh! bless -ed souls are they, Whose sins are cov-ered o'er; Di - vine - ly blest, to whom the Lord Im-putes their guilt no more.
GORTON. S. M.
From Beethoven, by Dr. L. Mason.
1. While my Re- deem- er's near, My Shepherd and my Guide, I bid fare- well to ev - ery fear, My wants are all sup - plied.
DENNIS. S. M.
From Nageli, by Dr. L. Mason.
1. How gen - tle God's commands! How kind his pre - cepts are! Come, cast your bur - dens on the Lord, And trust his con - stant care.

DRUMMOND. S. M. (For Male Voices.)
W.
Serv - ant of God, well done! Rest from thy loved em - ploy! The bat-tle fought, the vic - t'ry won, En - ter thy Mas - ter's joy.
BOWMAN. C. M. (For Male Voices.)
D.
Re - turn, O wand - 'rer, now re - turn, And seek thy Father's face; Those new de - sires which in thee burn Were kin - dled by his grace.
PEARSON. C. M. (For Male Voices.)
W.
Hear what the voice from Heaven pro - claims For all the pi-ous dead; Sweet is the sa-vor of their names, And soft their sleep - ing bed.
FIELD. C. M. (Trio.)
D.
TENOR.
1. Thou dear Re - deem - er, dy - ing Lamb, I love to hear of thee; No mu-sic's like thy charm-ing name, Nor half so sweet can be.
SOPRANO.
2. Oh, may I ev - er hear thy voice In mer - cy to me speak; In thee, my Priest, will I re - joice, And thy sal - va - tion seek.

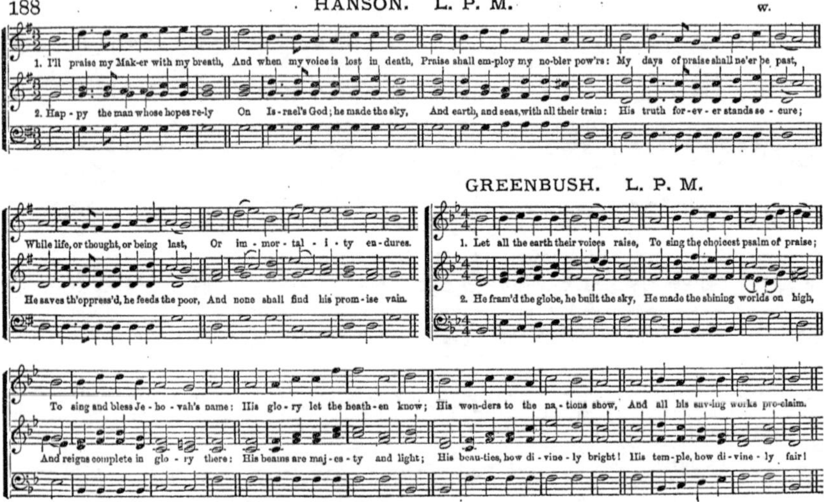
HANSON. L. P. M.
W.
1. I'll praise my Mak-er with my breath, And when my voice is lost in death, Praise shall em-ploy my no-bler pow'rs: My days of praise shall ne'er be past,
2. Hap - py the man whose hopes re-ly On Is - rael's God; he made the sky, And earth, and seas, with all their train: His truth for - ev - er stands se - cure;
While life, or thought, or being last, Or im - mor - tal - i - ty en - dures.
He saves th'oppress'd, he feeds the poor, And none shall find his prom - ise vain.
GREENBUSH. L. P. M.
1. Let all the earth their voices raise, To sing the choicest psalm of praise;
2. He fram'd the globe, he built the sky, He made the shining worlds on high,
To sing and bless Je - ho - vah's name: His glo - ry let the heath - en know; His won-ders to the na - tions show, And all his sav-ing works pro-claim.
And reigns complete in glo - ry there: His beams are maj - es - ty and light; His beau-ties, how di - vine - ly bright! His tem-ple, how di - vine - ly fair!

1. I love the vol - ume of thy word; What light and joy those leaves af - ford To souls be-nighted and distressed! Thy precepts guide my doubtful way,
2. Thy threatenings wake my slumb'ring eyes, And warn me where my danger lies; But 'tis thy blessed gos - pel, Lord, That makes my guilty conscience clean,
Thy fear forbids my feet to stray, Thy promise leads my heart to rest.
Converts my soul, subdues my sin, And gives a free, but large re - ward.
WILLOW. L. P. M.
1. Let all the earth their voices raise, To sing the choicest psalm of praise;
2. He framed the globe,-he built the sky, He made the shining worlds on high,
To sing and bless Je - ho-vah's name: His glory let the heathen know; His wonders to the nations show; And all his sav - ing works pro- claim.
And reigns complete in glo - ry there: His beams are majes- ty and light; His beauties, how divinely bright! His tem - ples, how di - vine - ly fair!

FREEMAN. C. P. M.

1. When thou, my righteous Judge, shalt come To take thy ransomed peo-ple home, Shall I among them stand? Shall such a worthless worm as I,
2. I love to meet among them now, Be - fore thy gracious feet to bow, Though vil - est of them all; But— can I bear the piercing thought?
Who sometimes am afraid to die, Be found at thy right hand!
What if my name should be left out, When thou for them shalt call!
ROLLISTON. C. P. M.
W.
1. The fes - tal morn, my God, is come, That calls me to thy sa - cred dome,
2. With ho - ly joy I hail the day That warns my thirst- ing soul a - way
Thy pres - ence to a - dore: My feet the sum - mons shall at - tend, With will - ing steps thy courts as - cend, And tread the hal - lowed floor.
To dwell a - mongst the blest! For, lo! my great Re - deem - er's power Un - folds the ev - er - last - ing door, And leads me to his rest!

LEIRA. C. P. M.

1. Oh, could I speak the match - less worth, Oh, could I sound the glo - ries forth Which in my Sav - iour shine!
2. I'd sing the pre - cious blood he spilt, My ran - som from the dread - ful guilt Of sin and wrath.. di - vine.
3. I'd sing the char - ac - ters he bears, And all the forms of love he wears, Ex-alt-ed on...... his throne:
I'd soar, and touch the heavenly strings, And vie with Gabriel, while he sings, In notes al-most di - vine, In notes al - most di - vine.
I'd sing his glorious righteousness, In which all-per-fect, heavenly dress My soul shall ev - er shine, My soul shall ev - er shine.
In loftiest songs of sweetest praise, I would to ev - er - last - ing days Make all his glo-ries known, Make all his glo - ries known.

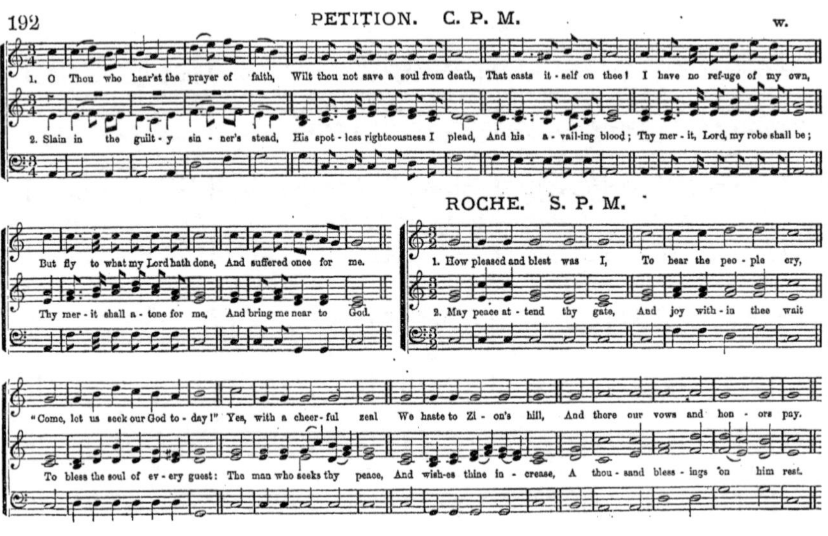
PETITION. C. P. M.
W.
1. O Thou who hear'st the prayer of faith, Wilt thou not save a soul from death, That casts it - self on thee! I have no ref-uge of my own,
2. Slain in the guilt - y sin - ner's stead, His spot - less righteousness I plead, And his a - vail-ing blood; Thy mer - it, Lord, my robe shall be;
But fly to what my Lord hath done, And suffered once for me.
Thy mer - it shall a - tone for me, And bring me near to God.
ROCHE. S. P. M.
1. How pleased and blest was I, To hear the peo - ple cry,
2. May peace at - tend thy gate, And joy with - in thee wait
"Come, let us seek our God to - day!" Yes, with a cheer - ful zeal We haste to Zi - on's hill, And there our vows and hon - ors pay.
To bless the soul of ev - ery guest: The man who seeks thy peace, And wish-es thine in - crease, A thou - sand bless - ings on him rest.

DALSTON. S. P. M.

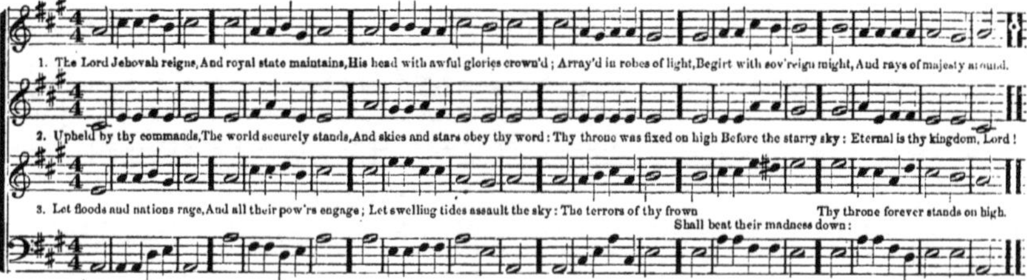
1. The Lord Jehovah reigns, And royal state maintains, His head with awful glories crown'd; Array'd in robes of light, Begirt with sov'reign might, And rays of majesty around.
2. Upheld by thy commands, The world securely stands, And skies and stars obey thy word: Thy throne was fixed on high Before the starry sky: Eternal is thy kingdom, Lord!
3. Let floods and nations rage, And all their pow'rs engage; Let swelling tides assault the sky: The terrors of thy frown Shall beat their madness down: Thy throne forever stands on high.

MONTVILLE. S. P. M.

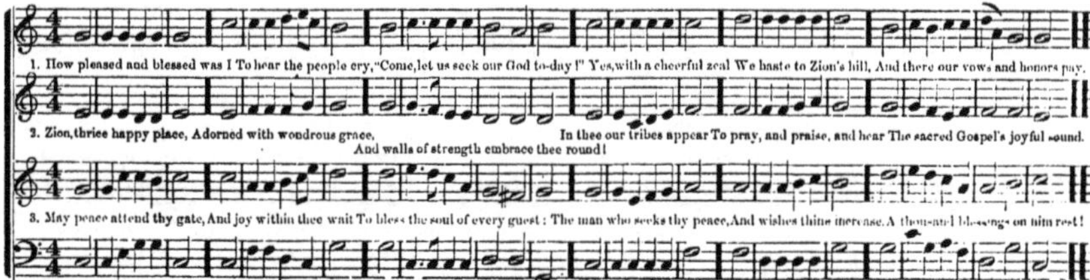
1. How pleased and blessed was I To hear the people cry, "Come, let us seek our God to-day!" Yes, with a cheerful zeal We haste to Zion's hill, And there our vows and honors pay.
2. Zion, thrice happy place, Adorned with wondrous grace, And walls of strength embrace thee round! In thee our tribes appear To pray, and praise, and hear The sacred Gospel's joyful sound.
3. May peace attend thy gate, And joy within thee wait To bless the soul of every guest: The man who seeks thy peace, And wishes thine increase, A thousand blessings on him rest!

TODD. H. M.

TODD. H. M.
1. Yes, the Re - deem - er rose; The Sav-iour left the dead; And o'er our hell - ish foes High raised his conqu'ring head: In wild dis-
2. Lo! the an - gel - ic bands In full as - sem - bly meet, To wait his high com - mands, And wor - ship at his feet; Joy - ful they
- may, The guards a - round Fall to the ground, And sink a - way.
come, And wing their way From realms of day To Je - sus' tomb.
MARSHFIELD. H. M.
D.
1. Lord of the worlds a - bove, How pleas-ant and how fair
2. Oh, hap-py souls that pray Where God ap - points to hear!
The dwellings of thy love, Thine earth - ly tem - ples are! To thine a - bode My heart as - pires, With warm de - sires, To see my God.
Oh, hap - py men that pay Their con - stant ser - vice there! They praise thee still; And hap - py they Who love the way To Zi - on's hill.

MESSER. H. M.
1. A - wake, ye saints, a - wake! And hail this sa - cred day; In lof - tiest songs of praise Your joy - ful hom - age pay:
2. On this au - spi - cious morn The Lord of life a - rose; He burst the bars of death, And vanquish'd all our foes;
Come, bless the day that God hath blest, The type of heaven's e - ter - nal rest.
And now he pleads our cause a - bove, And reaps the fruit of all his love.
WHITTAKER. H. M.
1. Hark! hark! the notes of joy Roll o'er the heaven-ly plains,
2. Hark! hark! the sound draws nigh, The joyful host de - scends;
And seraphs find em-ploy For their sublim - est strains: Some new de - light.... in heav'n is known; Loud sound the harps around the throne.
Je - sus forsakes the sky, To earth his footsteps bend: He comes to bless our fal - len race;.... He comes with messag es of grace.

MERLIN. H. M.
*
1. { Wel-come, de-light-ful morn, Thou day of sa-cred rest! I hail thy kind re-turn:—Lord, make these moments blest! } From low de-lights and mor-tal toys, I soar to reach im-mor-tal joys.
2. { Now may the King de-scend And fill his throne of grace; Thy scep-ter, Lord! ex-tend, While saints ad-dress thy face; } Let sin-ners feel thy quickening word, And learn to know and fear the Lord.
ROBERTS. H. M.
W.
1. O thou that hearest prayer! Attend our humble cry; And let thy servants share Thy blessing from on high: We plead the promise of thy word; Grant us thy Holy Spirit, Lord.
2. If earthly parents hear Their children when they cry; If they, with love sincere, Their children's wants supply; Much more wilt thou thy love display, And answer when thy children pray.

GRATITUDE. H. M.

1. Give thanks to God most high, The universal Lord, The sovereign King of kings, And be his grace adored; Thy mercy, Lord, Shall still endure, And ever sure A-bides thy word.
2. How mighty is his hand! What wonders hath he done! He formed the earth and seas, And spread the heavens alone; His power and grace Are still the same, And let his name Have endless praise.
WATERVILLE. H. M.
1. Ye boundless realms of joy, Ex - alt your Maker's fame; His praise your song em-ploy A - bove the star - ry frame. Your voi-ces raise, Ye che - ru - bim, And se - ra - phim, To sing his praise.
2. Thou moon, that rul'st the night, And sun, that guid'st the day, Ye glittering stars of night, To Him your homage pay; His praise de - clare, Ye heavens a - bove, And clouds that move in li - quid air.

REIGN. H. M.

O. R. B.

1. Ye boundless realms of joy, Ex - alt your Mak - er's fame; His praise your song em - ploy A - bove the star - ry frame: Your voi - ces raise, ye che - ru - bim, And ser - a - phim, to sing his praise.

2. Thou moon that rul'st the night, And sun that guid'st the day, Ye glittering stars of light, To him your homage pay: His praise de - clare, ye heav'ns a - bove, And clouds that move in liq - uid air.

PRAISE. H. M.

A - wake our drow - sy souls, And break each sloth - ful band; The wonders of this day Our noblest songs de - mand! Au - spi - - cious morn thy bliss - - ful rays Bright ser - aphs hail in songs of praise.

A - wake our drow - sy souls, And break each sloth - ful band; The wonders of this day Our noblest songs de-mand! Auspicious morn, thy blissful rays Bright seraphs hail in songs of praise. Bright seraphs hail in songs of praise.

Au - spi - - cious morn, thy bliss - - ful rays

MINDEN. H. M.

1. Lord of the worlds a - bove, How pleasant and how fair The dwellings of thy love, Thine earthly tem - ples are! To thine a -
2. Oh, hap - py souls that pray Where God ap - points to hear! Oh, hap - py men that pay Their constant ser - vice there! They praise thee

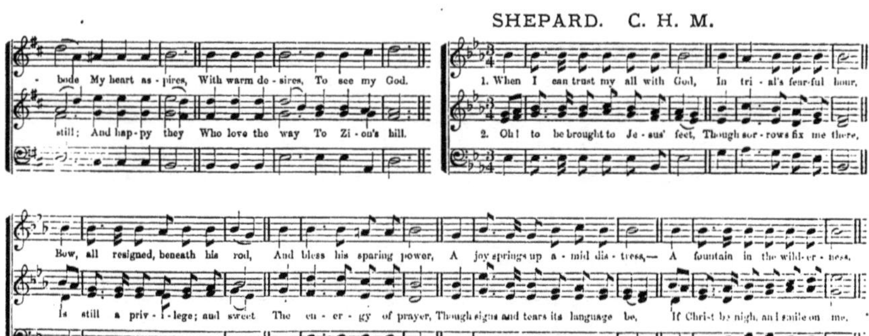
- bode My heart as - pires, With warm de - sires, To see my God.
still; And hap - py they Who love the way To Zi - on's hill.
SHEPARD. C. H. M.
1. When I can trust my all with God, In tri - al's fear-ful hour,
2. Oh! to be brought to Je - sus' feet, Though sor - rows fix me there,
Bow, all resigned, beneath his rod, And bless his sparing power, A joy springs up a - mid dis - tress,— A fountain in the wild-er - ness.
Is still a priv - i - lege; and sweet The en - er - gy of prayer, Though sighs and tears its language be, If Christ be nigh, and smile on me.

RESIGNATION. S. H. M.
1. Friend aft - er friend de - parts: Who hath not lost a friend? There is no u - nion here of hearts That finds not here an end:
2. Be - yond the flight of time, Be - yond this vale of death, There surely is some bless - ed clime Where life is not a breath,—
Were this frail world our fi - nal rest Liv - ing or dy - ing, none were blest.
Nor life's af - fec - tions transient fire, Whose sparks fly up - ward to ex - pire.
VINING. S. H. M.
1. Friend aft - er friend de - parts: Who hath not lost a friend?
2. Be - yond the flight of time, Be - yond this vale of death,
There is no u - nion here of hearts That finds not here an end: Where this frail world our fi - nal rest, Liv - ing or dy - ing, none were blest.
There surely is some bless - ed clime Where life is not a breath,—Nor life's af - fec - tions transient fire, Whose sparks fly up - ward to ex - pire.

OAKLAND. 7s. 6 lines.

1. Sav-iour! hap - py would I be, If I could but trust in thee; Trust thy wis - dom me to guide; Trust thy good-ness to pro - vide;
2. Trust thee on - ly as the light In the dark-est hour of night; Trust in sick - ness, trust in health; Trust in pov - er - ty and wealth;
Trust thy sav - ing love and power; Trust thee ev - ery day and hour.
Trust in joy, and trust in grief; Trust thy promise for re - lief.
GLADE. 7s. 6 lines.
J. EASTMAN.
1. Safe-ly through an - oth - er week God has brought us on our way;
2. While we pray for pard'ning grace, Thro' the dear Re-deem-er's name,
Let us now a bless-ing seek, Wait-ing in his courts to - day: Day of all the week the best, Em - blem of e - ter - nal rest.
Show thy rec - on - cil - ing face; Take a - way our sin and shame: From our worldly cares set free, May we rest this day in thee.

LIZZIE. 7s. 6 lines.

W.

SOPRANO SOLO.
1. Rock of A - ges! cleft for me; Let me hide my-self in thee! Let the wa - ter and the blood,
2. Could my zeal no re - spite know, Could my tears for - ev - er flow— All for sin could not a - tone;
3. While I draw this fleet - ing breath, When my eye-lids close in death. When I soar to worlds un - known,
From thy riv - en side that flowed, Be of sin the dou - ble cure— Cleanse me from its guilt and power.
Thou must save, and thou a - lone! No - thing in my hand I bring; Sim - ply to thy cross I cling.
See thee on thy judg - ment throne,— Rock of A - ges! cleft for me, Let me hide my - self in thee!

VALE. 7s.
1. Soft - ly fades the twi - light ray Of the ho - ly Sab - bath day; Gen - tly as life's set - ting sun, When the Chris - tian's course is run.
2. Peace is on the world a - broad; 'Tis the ho - ly peace of God,— Sym - bol of the peace with - in, When the spir - it rests from sin.
3. Still the Spirit lin - gers near, Where the evening wor - ship - er Seeks communion with the skies, Pressing on - ward to the prize.
EVERETT. 7s.
D.
1. Blest in - struct - or, from thy ways, Who can tell how oft he strays? Purge me from the guilt that lies Wrapt with - in my heart's dis - guise.
2. Let my tongue from er - ror free, Speak the words ap - proved by thee: To thine all - ob - serv - ing eyes, Let my thoughts pro - pi - tious rise.

GLADNESS. 7s.

W.

1. Praise the Lord, his glories show, Saints with - in his courts be - low, Angels round his throne a - bove, All that see and share his love.
2. Earth to heav'n, and heav'n to earth, Tell his won - ders, sing his worth; Age to age, and shore to shore, Praise him, praise him ev - er - more!
3. Praise the Lord, his mercies trace; Praise his prov - i - dence and grace— All that he for man hath done, All he sends us thro' his Son.
PLEYEL. 7s.
From PLEYEL.
1. To thy pas - tures fair and large, Heavenly Shepherd, lead thy charge; And my couch, with tend-'rest care, 'Mid the spring - ing grass pre - pare.
2. When I faint with summer's heat, Thou shalt guide my wea - ry feet To the streams that, still and slow, Through the ver - dant meadows flow.
3. Safe the drear - y vale I tread, By the shades of death o'erspread, With thy rod and staff sup - plied— This my guard, and that my guide.

IDA. 7s.
D.
1. Soft - ly, now, the light of day Fades up - on my sight a - way; Free from care, from la - bor free, Lord, I would commune with thee.
2. Soon, for me, the light of day Shall for - ev - er pass a - way; Then, from sin and sor - row free, Take me, Lord, to dwell with thee.
MORTLAND. 7s.
W.
1. Joy - ful be the hours to - day; Joy - ful let the sea - son be; Let us sing, for well we may; Je - sus! we will sing of thee.
2. Should thy peo - ple, si - lent be, Then the ver - y stones would sing: What a debt we owe to thee, Thee, our Sav - iour, thee, our King!
3. Joy - ful are we now to own, Rap - ture thrills us as we trace, All the deeds thy love hath done, All the rich - es of thy grace.

JEWETT. 7s.
W.
1. Come, said Je - sus' sa - cred voice, Come, and make my paths your choice; I will guide you to your home; Wea - ry wanderer, hith - er come!
2. Thou who, homeless and for- lorn, Long hast borne the proud world's scorn, Long hast roamed the barren waste, Wea - ry wanderer, hith - er haste.
3. Hith - er come! for here is found Balm that flows for ev - ery wound; Peace that ev - er shall en - dure, Rest e - ter - nal, sa - cred, sure.
FRANKLIN. 7s.
*
1. Cast thy bur - den on the Lord; Lean thou on - ly on his word: Ev - er will he be thy stay, Though the heavens shall melt a- way.
2. Ev - er in the rag - ing storm, Thou shalt see his cheering form, Hear his pledge of coming aid: "It is I, be not a - fraid."
3. Cast thy bur - den at his feet; Lin - ger near the mer - cy - seat: He will lead thee by the hand Gen - tly to the bet - ter land.

MILTON. 7s.

1. Let us, with a gladsome mind, Praise the Lord, for he is kind: For his mercies shall en - dure, Ev - er faith- ful, ev - er sure.
2. He, with all-commanding might, Filled the new made world with light: For his mercies shall en - dure, Ev - er faith- ful, ev - er sure.
3. All his creatures he doth feed; His full hand supplies their need: Let us, therefore, war-ble forth His high maj - es- ty and worth.

GRACE. 7s.

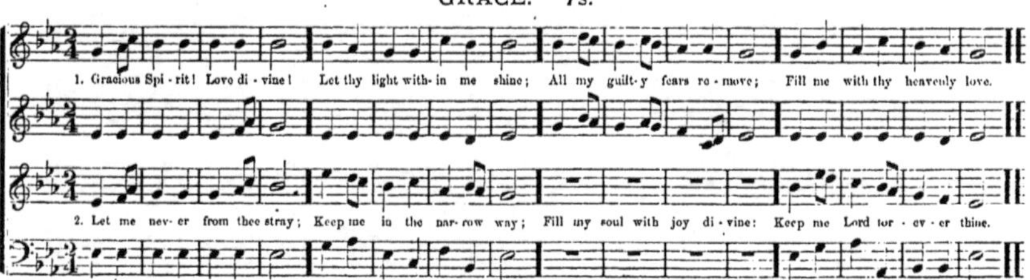
1. Gracious Spi - rit! Love di - vine! Let thy light with- in me shine; All my guilt- y fears re - move; Fill me with thy heavenly love.
2. Let me nev- er from thee stray; Keep me in the nar- row way; Fill my soul with joy di - vine: Keep me Lord for - ev - er thine.

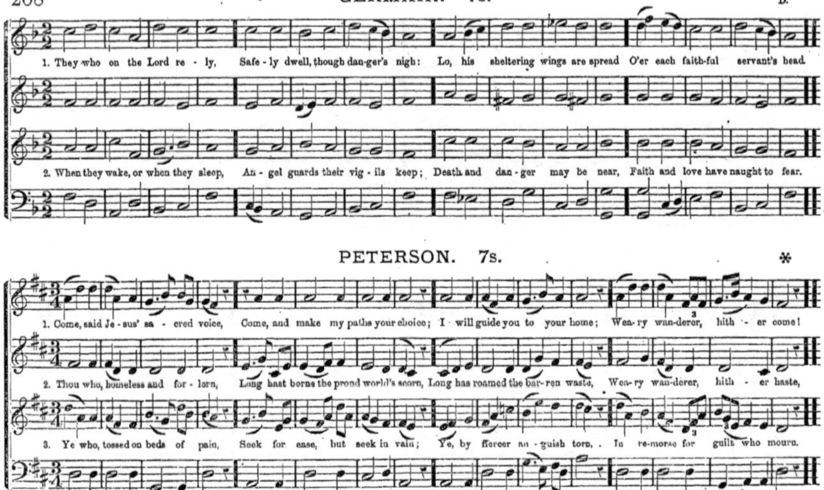
GERMAIN. 7s.
D.
1. They who on the Lord re - ly, Safe - ly dwell, though dan-ger's nigh: Lo, his sheltering wings are spread O'er each faith-ful servant's head.
2. When they wake, or when they sleep, An - gel guards their vig - ils keep; Death and dan - ger may be near, Faith and love have naught to fear.
PETERSON. 7s.
1. Come, said Je - sus' sa - cred voice, Come, and make my paths your choice; I will guide you to your home; Wea - ry wan-derer, hith - er come!
2. Thou who, homeless and for - lorn, Long hast borne the proud world's scorn, Long has roamed the bar - ren waste, Wea - ry wan-derer, hith - er haste,
3. Ye who, tossed on beds of pain, Seek for ease, but seek in vain; Ye, by fiercer an - guish torn, In re-morse for guilt who mourn.

HEAVENLY REST. 7s.

D. 209

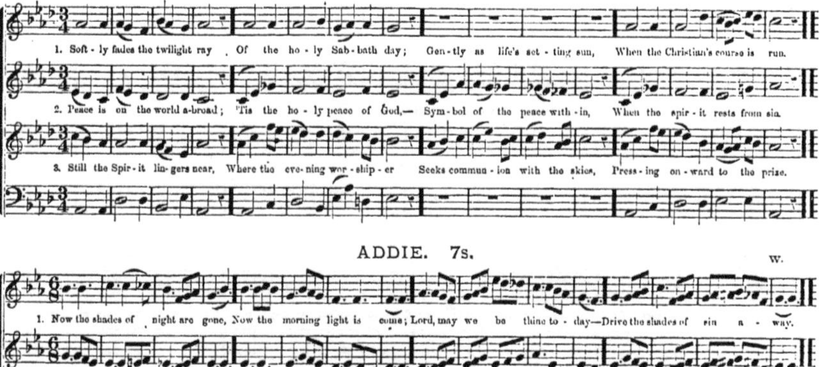
1. Soft - ly fades the twilight ray Of the ho - ly Sab - bath day; Gen - tly as life's set - ting sun, When the Christian's course is run.
2. Peace is on the world a-broad; 'Tis the ho - ly peace of God,— Sym - bol of the peace with - in, When the spir - it rests from sin.
3. Still the Spir - it lin - gers near, Where the eve - ning wor - ship - er Seeks commun - ion with the skies, Press - ing on - ward to the prize.
ADDIE. 7s.
W.
1. Now the shades of night are gone, Now the morning light is come; Lord, may we be thine to - day—Drive the shades of sin a - way.
2. When our life of work is past, Oh, re - ceive us, then at last; Night and sin will be no more, When we reach the heaven - ly shore.

INVITATION. 7s.
O. R. BARROWS.
1. Come, said Je - sus' sa - cred voice, Come, and make my paths your choice; I will guide you to your home; Wea - ry wan - derer, hith - er come!
2. Thou who, homeless and for - lorn, Long hast borne the proud world's scorn, Long hast roamed the bar-ren waste, Wea - ry wan - derer, hith - er haste.
3. Hith - er come! for here is found Balm that flows for ev - ery wound; Peace that ev - er shall en-dure, Rest e - ter - nal, sa - cred, sure.
LILLE. 7s.
D.
1. Chil - dren of the heavenly King, As ye jour - ney, sweet-ly sing; Sing your Sav-iour's worth - y praise, Glo - rious in his works and ways.
2. Ye are traveling home to God, In the way the fa - thers trod; They are hap - py now—and ye Soon their hap - pi - ness shall see.
3. Shout, ye lit - tle flock, and blest; You on Je - sus' throne shall rest: There your seat is now pre - pared—There your king-dom and re - ward.

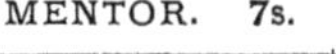
MENTOR. 7s.

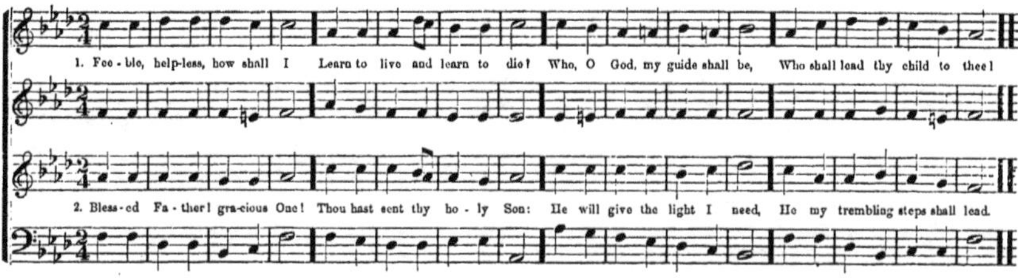
1. Fee - ble, help-less, how shall I Learn to live and learn to die? Who, O God, my guide shall be, Who shall lead thy child to thee!
2. Bless - ed Fa - ther! gra-cious One! Thou hast sent thy ho - ly Son: He will give the light I need, He my trembling steps shall lead.

PORTER. 7s.

C. M. WYMAN.

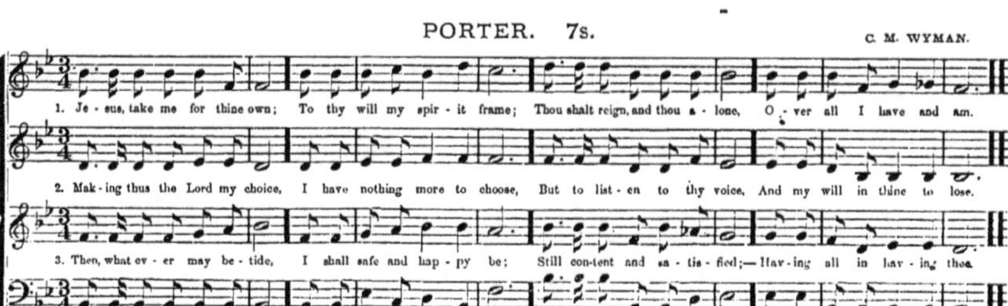
1. Je - sus, take me for thine own; To thy will my spir - it frame; Thou shalt reign, and thou a - lone, O - ver all I have and am.
2. Mak - ing thus the Lord my choice, I have nothing more to choose, But to list - en to thy voice, And my will in thine to lose.
3. Then, what ev - er may be - tide, I shall safe and hap - py be; Still con-tent and sa - tis - fied;— Hav - ing all in hav - ing thee.

MERRILL. 7s.
D.
1. Hark, my soul! it is the Lord; 'Tis thy Sav-iour; hear his word; Je-sus speaks, and speaks to thee; "Say, poor sin-ner, lov'st thou me
2. "Mine is an un-changing love, High-er than the heights a-bove, Deep-er than the depths be-neath, Free and faith-ful, strong as death."
3. Lord! it is my chief com-plaint That my love is cold and faint; Yet I love thee, and a-dore: Oh for grace to love thee more!
CURRIER. 7s.
S. A. WARD.
1. Now the shades of night are gone, Now the morn-ing light is come; Lord, may we be thine to-day— Drive the shades of sin a-way.
2. When our work of life is past, Oh, re-ceive us, then, at last; Night and sin will be no more, When we reach the heavenly shore.

CALAIS. 7s.

1. When be - fore thy throne we kneel, Fill'd with awe and ho - ly fear, Teach us, O our God, to feel, All thy sa - cred pres - ence near.
2. Oh, re - ceive the praise that dares Seek thy heaven-ex - alt - ed throne; Bless our off - 'ring, hear our prayer, In - fin - ite and ho - ly One.

TEMPLE GROVE. 7s.

M. L. LAWRENCE.

1. Go, ye mes - sen - gers of God, Like the beams of morn - ing fly; Take the won - der - work - ing rod, Wave the ban - ner-cross on high.
2. Where the loft - y min - a - ret Gleams a - long the morn-ing skies, Wave it till the cres - cent set, And the star of Ja - cob rise.
3. Go to many a trop - ic isle In the bo - som of the deep, Where the skies for - ev - er smile, And th'oppress'd for - ev - er weep.

COMPANIONSHIP. 7s.

1. Sweet the time, ex- ceed-ing sweet! When the saints to- geth- er meet, When the Saviour is the theme, When they join to sing of him.
2. Sing we, then, e - ter - nal love, Such as did the Fa- ther move: He be - held the world un - done, Loved the world, and gave his Son.
3. Sweet the place, ex- ceed-ing sweet! Where the saints in glo- ry meet; Where the Saviour's still the theme, Where they see and sing of him.
BENHAM. 7s.
1. Joy - ful be the hours to - day; Joy - ful let the sea - son be; Let us sing, for well we may: Je - sus! we will sing of thee.
2. Should thy peo- ple si - lent be, Then the ver - y stones would sing: What a debt we owe to thee, Thee, our Sav - iour, thee, our King!
3. Joy - ful are we now to own, Rap-ture thrills us as we trace All the deeds thy love hath done, All the rich - es of thy grace.

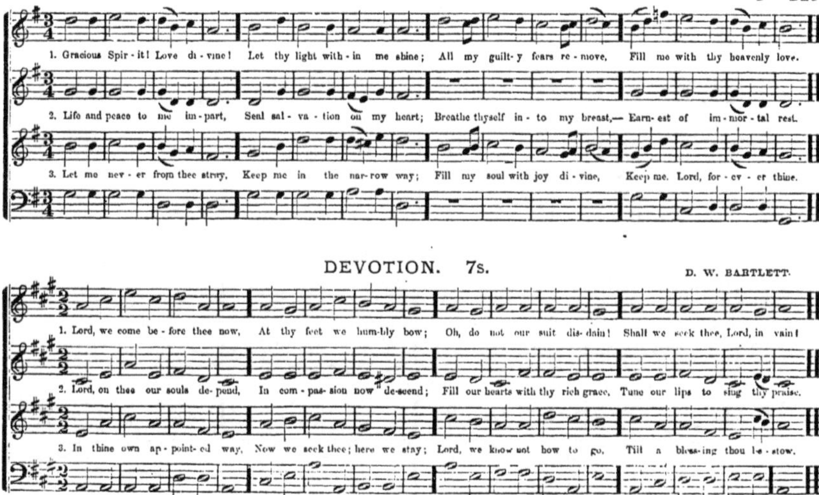
MINNIE. 7s.
D.
1. Gracious Spir - it! Love di - vine! Let thy light with - in me shine; All my guilt - y fears re - move, Fill me with thy heavenly love.
2. Life and peace to me im - part, Seal sal - va - tion on my heart; Breathe thyself in - to my breast,— Earn - est of im - mor - tal rest.
3. Let me nev - er from thee stray, Keep me in the nar - row way; Fill my soul with joy di - vine, Keep me, Lord, for - ev - er thine.
DEVOTION. 7s.
D. W. BARTLETT.
1. Lord, we come be - fore thee now, At thy feet we hum - bly bow; Oh, do not our suit dis - dain! Shall we seek thee, Lord, in vain!
2. Lord, on thee our souls de - pend, In com - pas - sion now de - scend; Fill our hearts with thy rich grace, Tune our lips to sing thy praise.
3. In thine own ap - point - ed way, Now we seek thee; here we stay; Lord, we know not how to go, Till a bless - ing thou be - stow.

GOODRICH. 7s.

D. G. M.

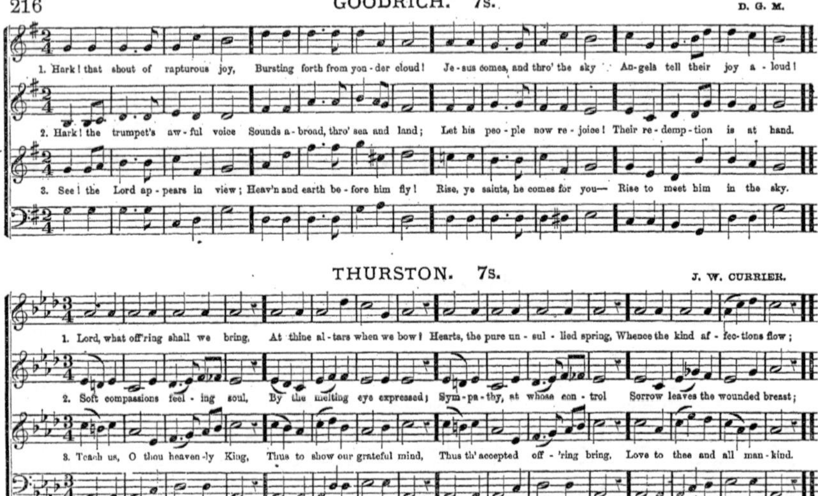
1. Hark! that shout of rapturous joy, Bursting forth from yon - der cloud! Je - sus comes, and thro' the sky An - gels tell their joy a - loud!
2. Hark! the trumpet's aw - ful voice Sounds a - broad, thro' sea and land; Let his peo - ple now re - joice! Their re - demp - tion is at hand.
3. See! the Lord ap - pears in view; Heav'n and earth be - fore him fly! Rise, ye saints, he comes for you— Rise to meet him in the sky.
THURSTON. 7s.
J. W. CURRIER.
1. Lord, what off'ring shall we bring, At thine al - tars when we bow? Hearts, the pure un - sul - lied spring, Whence the kind af - fec- tions flow;
2. Soft compassions feel - ing soul, By the melting eye expressed; Sym - pa - thy, at whose con - trol Sorrow leaves the wounded breast;
3. Teach us, O thou heaven - ly King, Thus to show our grateful mind, Thus th' accepted off - 'ring bring, Love to thee and all man - kind.

217
NUREMBERG. 7s.
German.
1. Praise to God, im - mor - tal praise, For the love that crowns our days; Bounteous Source of ev - ery joy, Let thy praise our tongues em - ploy.
PLEYEL'S HYMN. 7s.
Pleyel.
1. Chil- dren of the heavenly King, As ye jour- ney, sweet-ly sing; Sing your Saviour's wor - thy praise, Glorious in his works and ways.
MARTYN. 7s.
S. B. Marsh.
Fine.
1. Ma - ry to the Saviour's tomb Hast-ed at the ear - ly dawn,
Spice she bro't, and sweet perfume, But the Lord she loved had gone,
For a- while, she lingering stood, Filled with sorrow and sur - prise, D. C.
D. C. Trembling, while a crystal flood Issued from her weep - ing eyes.
Fine.
BENEVENTO. 7s.
S. Webbe.
Fine.
D. S.
1. While with ceaseless course, the sun Hasted thro' the former year, Many souls their race have run, Never more to meet us here; Fixed in an e - ter - nal state, They have done with all below;
D. S. We a lit - tle long - er wait, But how lit-tle, none can know.
Fine.

VIENNA 8s & 7s.
From MOZART.
1. Saviour, source of ev - ery bless-ing, Tune my heart to grate - ful lays; Streams of mer - cy, never ceasing, Call for ceaseless songs of praise.
2. Teach me some me - lo - dious measure, Sung by raptured saints a - bove; Fill my soul with sacred pleasure, While I sing re - deeming love.
3. Thou didst seek me when a stranger, Wandering from the fold of God; Thou, to save my soul from danger, Didst re - deem me with thy blood
CUTLER. 8s & 7s.
D.
1. On the dew - y breath of ev - en, Thousand o - dors mingling rise, Borne like in-cense up to heav - en,— Nature's eve - ning sac - ri - fice.
2. Thou, whose favors with-out number All our days of gladness bless, Let thine eye that knows no slumber, Guard our hours of helpless - ness.
Ritard.
3. Then, though conscious we are sleeping In the out - er courts of death; Safe beneath a Father's keep-ing, Calm we rest in per - fect faith.

LINDNER. 8s & 7s.

SADIE. 8s & 7s.

1. Saviour, source of ev - ery bless-ing, Tune my heart to grate - ful lays; Streams of mer - cy nev - er ceasing, Call for ceaseless songs of praise.
2. Teach me some me - lo-dious measure, Sung by rap - tured saints a - bove; Fill my soul with sa - cred pleasure, While I sing re - deem-ing love.
3. Thou didst seek me when a stranger, Wandering from the fold of God - Thou, to save my soul from danger, Didst re - deem me with thy blood.
1. I would love thee, God and Fa - ther! My Re - deem - er, and my King! I would love thee; for, with - out thee, Life is but a bitter thing.
2. I would love thee; ev - ery bless - ing Flows to me from out thy throne. I would love thee—he who loves thee Nev - er feels himself a - lone.
3. I would love thee; look up - on me, Ev - er guide me with thine eye: I would love thee; if not nourished By thy love, my soul would die.

LANCASTER. 8s & 7s.
1. In the cross of Christ I glo - ry, Tow'ring o'er.... the wrecks of time; All the light of sa - cred sto - ry Gath - ers round its head sub-lime.
2. When the woes of life o'er-take me, Hopes de - ceive, and fears an- noy, Nev - er shall the cross for-sake me; Lo! it glows with peace and joy.
3. When the sun of bliss is beam-ing Light and love.... up - on my way, From the cross the radiance streaming, Adds new lus - ter to the day.
RUHE. 8s & 7s.
D.
1. Lo! the day of rest de - clin - eth, Gath-er fast the shades of night; May the sun that ev - er shin - eth Fill our souls with heavenly light.
2. While thine ear of love ad-dress-ing, Thus our parting hymn we sing: Fa - ther, give thine eve-ning bless - ing, Fold us safe be-neath thy wing.

FOUNT. 8s & 7s.
O. R. BARROWS.
1. Come, thou Fount of ev - ery bless - ing, Tune my heart to sing thy grace; Streams of mer - cy, nev - er ceas - ing, Call for songs of loud - est praise.
2. Teach me some me - lo - dious meas-ure, Sung by flam - ing tongues a - bove; Oh the vast, the boundless treas - ure Of thy free, un-chang-ing love!
3. Je - sus sought me when a stran-ger, Wandering from the fold of God; He, to res - cue me from dan - ger, In - terposed his precious blood.
ALNA. 8s & 7s.
1. Hark! what mean those ho-ly voic - es, Sweet-ly sound-ing thro' the skies! Lo! th'angel - ic host re - joic - es; Heavenly hal - le - lu - jahs rise.
2. Hear them tell the wondrous sto - ry, Hear them chant in hymns of joy: "Glo-ry in the high - est, glo - ry! Glo - ry be to God most high!
3. "Peace on earth, good-will from heaven, Reaching far as man is found; Souls redeem'd, and sins for - giv - en! Loud our gold - en harps shall sound."

ELLA. 8s. & 7s.
1. Take my heart, O Fa-ther, take it! Make and keep it all thine own; Let thy Spir-it melt and break it— This proud heart of sin and stone.
2. Fa-ther, make it pure and low-ly, Fond of peace, and far from strife; Turn-ing from the paths un-ho-ly Of this vain and sin-ful life.
3. Ev-er let thy grace sur-round it; Strengthen it with power di-vine, Till thy cords of love have bound it: Make it to be whol-ly thine.
HUMILITY. 8s & 7s.
1. O'er the gloom-y hills of dark-ness Look, my soul! be still,—and gaze; See the prom-is-es ad-vanc-ing To a glo-rious day of grace.
2. Let the dark, be-nighted pa-gan, Let the rude bar-ba-rian see That di-vine and glo-rious con-quest, Once ob-tained on Cal-va-ry.
3. Kingdoms wide that sit in dark-nes—Grant them, Lord, the glorious light; Now from east-eru coast to west-eru May the morning chase the night

OTELLA. 8s & 7s. Double.

1. Hark! what mean those ho-ly voic-es, Sweetly sounding through the skies! Lo! th' an-gel-ic host re-joic-es; Heavenly hal-le-lu-jahs rise.
2. "Christ is born, the great A-noint-ed; Heaven and earth his prais-es sing! Oh, re-ceive whom God ap-point-ed For your Prophet, Priest, and King!
Hear them tell.... the wondrous sto-ry, Hear them chant in hymns of joy: "Glo-ry in the highest, glo-ry! Glo-ry be to God most high!
Haste, ye mor-tals, to a-dore him; Learn his name, and taste his joy: Till in heaven ye sing be-fore him, 'Glo-ry be to God most high!'"

KENT. 8s & 7s.

1. { With my substance I will hon - or My Re - deem - er and my Lord;
Were ten thousand worlds my man - or, All were noth - ing to his [OMIT.] word.
While the her - alds of sal - va - tion
1. { Be his king - dom now pro - mot - ed, Let the earth her Mon - arch know;
Be my all to him de - vot - ed; To my Lord my all I [OMIT.] owe.
Praise the Sav - iour, all ye na - tions!
His a - bound - ing grace pro - claim, Let his friends, of ev - ery sta - tion, Glad-ly join to spread his fame.
Praise him, all ye hosts a - bove! Shout, with joy - ful ac - cla - ma - tions, His di - vine, vic - to - rious love!

FAITH. 8s & 7s.

1. { Peace be to this sa-cred dwell-ing, Peace to ev-ery soul there-in; }
{ Peace, of heav'nly joy fore-tell-ing, Peace, the fruit of conquer'd sin; }
Peace, that speaks its heavenly Giv-er; Peace to worldly minds unknown;
2. { Prince of peace! for-ev-er near us, Fix in all our hearts thy home; }
{ With thy bright ap-pear-ing cheer us, Let thy bless-ed king-dom come! }
Come with sweet-er con-so-la-tion, Come, and give our souls to prove
Peace di-vine, that flows for-ev-er From its source, the Lord a-lone!
All the joys of thy sal-va-tion, All the joys that spring from love!
RESURRECTION. 8s & 7s. (Peculiar.)
1. Lo! the seal of death is breaking; Those who slept its sleep are wak-ing;
2. There, no more at eve de-clin-ing, Suns without a cloud are shin-ing
Heaven opes its port-als fair! Hark! the harps of God are ring-ing, Hark! the seraph's hymn is fling-ing Mu-sic on im-mor-tal air.
O'er the land of life and love; There the founts of life are flow-ing, Flow'rs unknown to time are blow-ing In that ra-diant scene a-bove.

VESPER. 8s, 7s & 7s.

W.

1. Thro' the day thy love has spared us, Now we lay us down to rest; Thro' the si - lent watch-es guard us, Let no foe our peace mo - lest:
2. Pil-grims here on earth, and strangers, Dwell-ing in the midst of foes, Us and ours pre - serve from dan-gers; In thine arms may we re - pose;
Je - sus, thou our guardian be; Sweet it is to trust in thee.
And, when life's short day is past, Rest with thee in heaven at last.
PINE HILL. 8s, 7s & 7s.
W. WOODWORTH.
1. Hark! ten thousand harps and voices Sound the note of praise a - bove:
2. King of glo-ry, reign for-ev - er! Thine an ev - er - last - ing crown:
Je - sus reigns and heav'n re-joic - es; Je - sus reigns, the God of love: See, he sits on yon - der throne; Je - sus rules the world a - lone.
Noth - ing from thy love shall sev - er Those whom thou hast made thine own: Hap - py ob - ject of thy grace, Destined to be - hold thy face.

GREENVILLE. 8s & 7s. Double.
J. J. Rousseau.
227
Far from mor - tal cares re - treat - ing, Sor - did hopes and vain de - sires,
Here our will - ing foot - steps meet - ing, Ev - ery heart to heaven as - pires.
From the fount of glo - ry beam - ing, Light ce - les - tial cheers our eyes.
Mer - cy from a - bove pro - claim - ing, Peace and par - don from the skies.
SICILY. 8s & 7s.
From "Car. Sac."
Lord, dis - miss us with thy bless - ing, Fill our hearts with joy and peace;
Let us each, thy love pos - sess - ing, Tri - umph in re - deeming grace.
Oh re - fresh us, Oh re - fresh us, Traveling thro' this wil - der - ness.
[This tune may be sung as a Duet by Treble voices.]
MOUNT VERNON. 8s & 7s.
Dr. L. Mason.
Sis - ter, thou wast mild and love - ly, Gen - tle as the sum - mer breeze, Pleas - ant as the air of eve - ning, When it floats a - mong the trees.
WILMOT. 8s & 7s.
Arr. from Weber, by Dr. L. Mason.
Let the Lord Je - ho - vah liv - eth! He's my rock, I bless his name; He, my God, sal - va - tion giv - eth; All ye lands, ex - alt his fame.

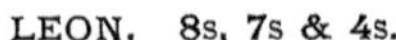
LEON. 8s, 7s & 4s.

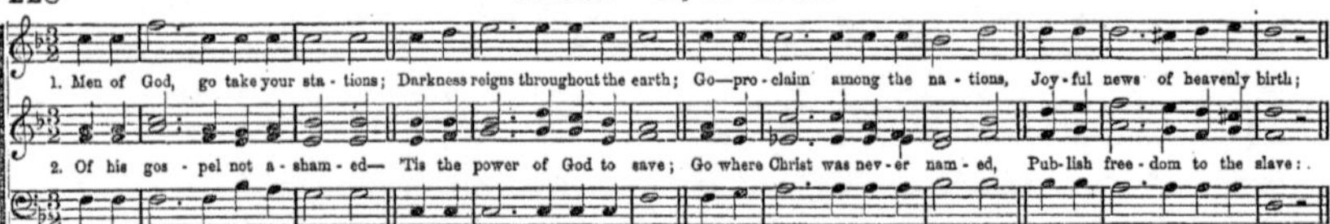
1. Men of God, go take your sta - tions; Darkness reigns throughout the earth; Go—pro - claim among the na - tions, Joy - ful news of heavenly birth;
2. Of his gos - pel not a - sham - ed— 'Tis the power of God to save; Go where Christ was nev - er nam - ed, Pub - lish free - dom to the slave:.

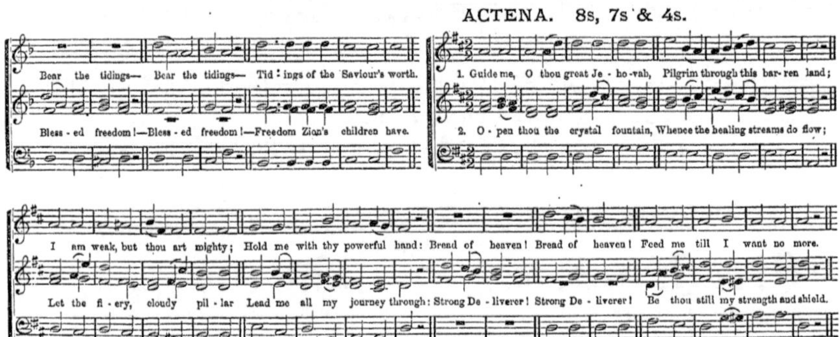
Bear the tidings— Bear the tidings— Tid : ings of the Saviour's worth.
Bless - ed freedom!—Bless - ed freedom!—Freedom Zion's children have.
ACTENA. 8s, 7s & 4s.
1. Guide me, O thou great Je - ho - vah, Pilgrim through this bar - ren land;
2. O - pen thou the crystal fountain, Whence the healing streams do flow;
I am weak, but thou art mighty; Hold me with thy powerful hand: Bread of heaven! Bread of heaven! Feed me till I want no more.
Let the fi - ery, cloudy pil - lar Lead me all my journey through: Strong De - liverer! Strong De - liverer! Be thou still my strength and shield.

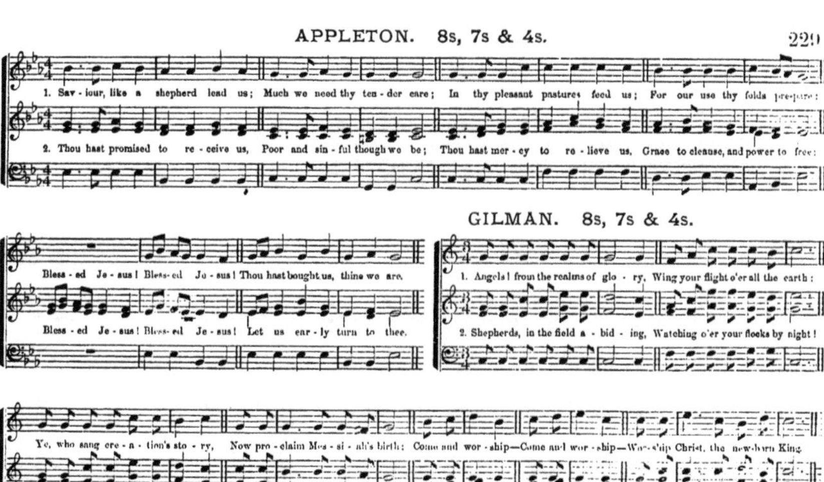
APPLETON. 8s, 7s & 4s.
229
1. Sav - iour, like a shepherd lead us; Much we need thy ten - der care; In thy pleasant pastures feed us; For our use thy folds pre-pare:
2. Thou hast promised to re - ceive us, Poor and sin - ful though we be; Thou hast mer - cy to re - lieve us, Grace to cleanse, and power to free:
Bless - ed Je - sus! Bless-ed Je - sus! Thou hast bought us, thine we are.
Bless - ed Je - sus! Bless-ed Je - sus! Let us ear - ly turn to thee.
GILMAN. 8s, 7s & 4s.
1. Angels! from the realms of glo - ry, Wing your flight o'er all the earth:
2. Shepherds, in the field a - bid - ing, Watching o'er your flocks by night!
Ye, who sang cre - a - tion's sto - ry, Now pro - claim Mes - si - ah's birth: Come and wor - ship—Come and wor - ship—Wor-ship Christ, the new-born King.
God with man is now re - sid - ing, Yon - der shines the heavenly light: Come and wor - ship—Come and wor - ship—Wor-ship Christ, the new-born King.

CLIFTON. 8s, 7s & 4s.

1. Look, ye saints! the sight is glo - rious; See the man of sor-rows now, From the fight re-turned vic - to - rious ;— Ev - ery knee to him shall bow.
2. Crown the Saviour, an-gels crown him; Rich the trophies Je - sus brings: In the seat of power en - throne him, While the vault of heav-en rings:
Crown him—crown him!—Crowns be - come the vic - tor's brow.
Crown him—crown him!—Crown the Sav - iour, King of kings!
JUBILEE. 8s, 7s & 4s.
O. R. BARROWS.
1. O'er the gloom-y hills of dark-ness Look, my soul! be still,—and gaze;
2. Let the dark be - night-ed pa - gan, Let the rude bar - ba - rian see
See the prom - is - es ad - vanc - ing To a glo - rious day of grace: Blessed Ju - bi-lee! Blessed Ju - bi-lee! Let thy glo-rious morn - ing dawn.
That di - vine and glo - rious con-quest, Once ob-tained on Cal - va - ry: Let the gos - pel, Let the gos - pel Loud resound, from pole to pole.

GOULD. 8s, 7s & 4s.

CH. ZEUNER.

Fly abroad, thou might-y gos - pel, Win and conquer—nev - er cease! May thy last - ing, wide do - min - ions Mul - ti - ply and still in - crease;
Sway thy scep - ter, Sway thy scep - ter, Sav - iour, all the world a - round.
CALVARY. 8s, 7s & 4s.
1. Hark! the voice of love and mer - cy Sounds a - loud from Cal-va - - ry; See! it rends the rocks a - sun - der, Shakes the earth, and vails the sky: "It is fin - ished!" Hear the dy - ing Sav - iour cry.
2. "It is finished!"—Oh, what pleasure Do these charming words af - - ford! Heavenly blessings, with-out meas - ure, Flow to us from Christ, the Lord: "It is fin - ished!" Saints, the dy - ing words re - cord.

SPRING. 8s.
W.
1. To Je - sus, the crown of my hope, My soul is in haste to be gone; Oh, bear me, ye che-ru-bim, up, And waft me a - way to his throne.
2. My Sav - iour, whom absent I love; Whom, not having seen, I a - dore; Whose name is ex - alt-ed a - bove All glo - ry, do - minion and power.
3. Dis - solve thou these bands that detain My soul from her portion in thee, Ah! strike off this a - damant chain, And make me e - ter-nal-ly free.
HALE. 8s.
1. My gracious Re-deem-er I love, His prais-es a - loud I'll pro-claim: And join with the armies a - bove, To shout his a - dor - a - ble name.
2. To gaze on his glo-ries di - vine Shall be my e - ter - nal em- ploy; To see them in - ces-sant - ly shine, My boundless, in - ef - fa - ble joy.
3. He free - ly redeemed, with his blood, My soul from the con-fines of hell, To live on the smiles of my God, And in his sweet presence to dwell.

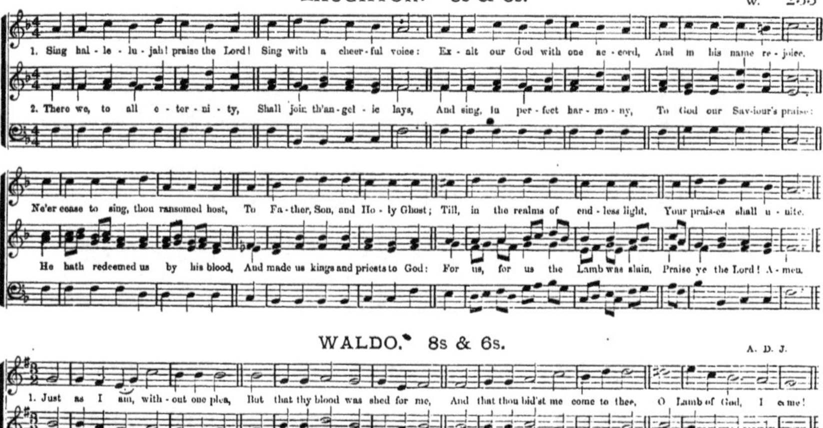
LAUGHTON. 8s & 6s.
W.
1. Sing hal - le - lu - jah! praise the Lord! Sing with a cheer - ful voice: Ex - alt our God with one ac - cord, And in his name re - joice.
2. There we, to all e - ter - ni - ty, Shall join th'an - gel - ic lays, And sing, in per - fect har - mo - ny, To God our Sav-iour's praise:
Ne'er cease to sing, thou ransomed host, To Fa - ther, Son, and Ho - ly Ghost; Till, in the realms of end - less light, Your prais-es shall u - nite.
He hath redeemed us by his blood, And made us kings and priests to God: For us, for us the Lamb was slain, Praise ye the Lord! A - men.
WALDO. 8s & 6s.
A. D. J.
1. Just as I am, with - out one plea, But that thy blood was shed for me, And that thou bid'st me come to thee, O Lamb of God, I come!
2. Just as I am— thy love un-known Hath brok - en ev - ery bar-rier down; Now, to be thine, yea, thine a - lone, O Lamb of God, I come!

STAMFORD. 8s & 4s. Peculiar.

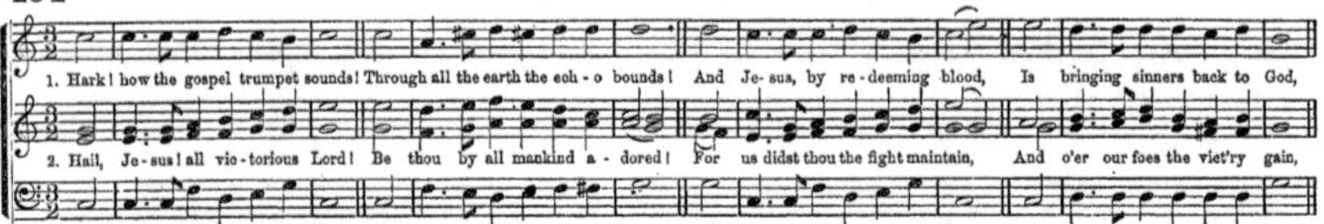
1. Hark! how the gospel trumpet sounds! Through all the earth the ech - o bounds! And Je- sus, by re - deeming blood, Is bringing sinners back to God,
2. Hail, Je - sus! all vic - torious Lord! Be thou by all mankind a - dored! For us didst thou the fight maintain, And o'er our foes the vict'ry gain,

QUIETUDE. 8s & 4. Peculiar.

And guides them safely by his word To end - less day.
That we with thee might ev - er reign In end - less day.
1. Through the love of God our Saviour, All will be well: Free and changeless in his fav-or;
2. Though we pass through tribu-lation, All will be well: Ours is such a full sal - vation;

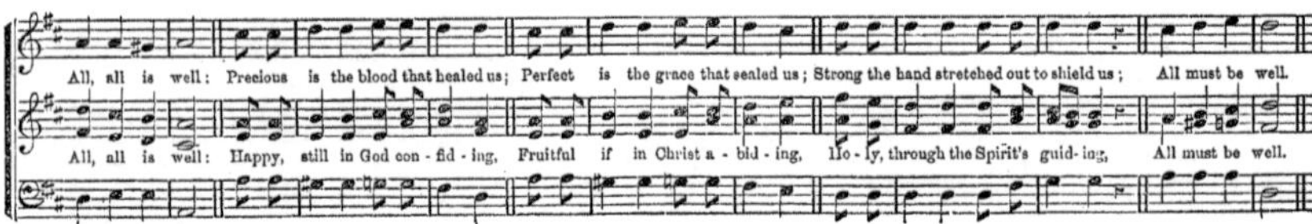
All, all is well: Precious is the blood that healed us; Perfect is the grace that sealed us; Strong the hand stretched out to shield us; All must be well.
All, all is well: Happy, still in God con - fid - ing, Fruitful if in Christ a - bid - ing, Ho - ly, through the Spirit's guid- ing, All must be well.

CALDWELL. 8s, 3s & 6s.

1. Ere I sleep, for ev - ery fav - or This day showed By my God, I do bless my Sav - iour.
2. Leave me not, but ev - er love me; Let thy peace Be my bliss Till thou hence re - move me.
3. And whene'er in death I slum - ber, Let me rise With the wise, Count-ed in their num - ber.

1.
SHEPHERD, while the flock is feeding,
Take these lambs
In thine arms,
Now for shelter pleading.

2.
While the storm of life is lowering,
Night and day,
Beasts of prey,
Lurking, are devouring.

3.
Shepherd, every grace combining,
Keep these lambs
In thine arms,
On thy breast reclining.

DR. T. HASTINGS.

LITTLE. 4s & 6s.

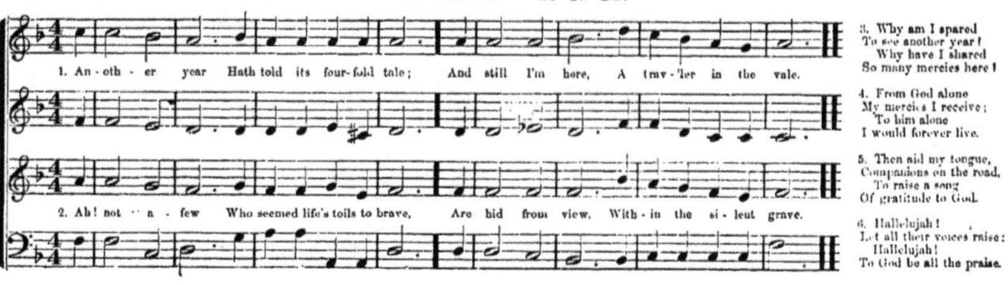
1. An - oth - er year Hath told its four-fold tale; And still I'm here, A trav - 'ler in the vale.
2. Ah! not a - few Who seemed life's toils to brave, Are hid from view, With - in the si - lent grave.

3. Why am I spared
To see another year!
Why have I shared
So many mercies here!

4. From God alone
My mercies I receive;
To him alone
I would forever live.

5. Then aid my tongue,
Companions on the road,
To raise a song
Of gratitude to God.

6. Hallelujah!
Let all their voices raise:
Hallelujah!
To God be all the praise.

SELDEN. 8s & 4.
*
1. My God, my Father, while I stray Far from my home, on life's rough way, Oh, teach me from my heart to say, "Thy will be done!"
2. If but my fainting heart be blest With thy sweet Spirit for its guest, My God, to thee I leave the rest: "Thy will be done!"
3. Then when on earth I breathe no more, The prayer oft mixed with tears before, I'll sing up - on a hap - pier shore: "Thy will be done!"
CRANDON. 6,8,6,4.
*
1. Lo! on th' in-glo - rious tree The might-y Lord of glo - ry hangs; For - sak - en now is he, And pierced with pangs.
2. A shame-ful death he dies, Up - lift - ed with transgres-sor's twain. A lamb for sac - ri - fice, By sin - ners slain.
3. Full is his cup of woe; In death his droop-ing head de - clines; "'Tis done!" he cries, and now His soul re - signs.
4. Oh come, my soul, and gaze On that great grief, that crown of thorn; In deep and dread a - maze, There look and mourn.
5. For thee he shed his blood; Weep till with woe thine eye grow dim; To that ac - curs - ed wood Hast thou nailed him!
6. To thee the mighty Lord, Who washed in blood our sins a - way, Our bound-less grat - i - tude Its thanks would pay.

HAWTHORNE. 6s, 8s & 4s.
1. The goodly land I see, With peace and plenty blest; A land of sa - cred lib - er - ty, And end - less rest: There milk and hon - ey flow,
2. There dwells the Lord, our King, The Lord our righteous-ness: Tri-umphant o'er the world and sin, The Prince of Peace, On Zi - on's sa - cred height,
And oil and wine a - bound; And trees of life for - ev - er grow With mer - cy crowned.
His kingdom still main - tains, And glorious, with his saints in light, For - ev - er reigns.
ROULSTONE. 6s & 10s.
1. Thou who didst stoop below To drain the cup of woe,
2. It was no path of flowers, Through this dark world of ours,
And wear the form of frail mor - tal - i - ty, Thy blessed labors done, Thy crown of vict'ry won, Hast passed from earth—passed to thy home on high.
Be - lov - ed of the Father! thou didst tread; And shall we in dis - may Shrink from the narrow way, When clouds and darkness are a - round it spread!

BLOOMFIELD. 6s & 5s. Iambic and Trochaic.

D.

PAYSON. 6s & 7s.

1. I close my heav-y eye, Sav-iour, ev - er near! I lift my soul on high, Thro' the dark-ness drear: Be thou my light I cry, Be
2. I feel thine arms a - round, Sav-iour, ev - er near! With thee if I am found, Nev-er can I fear, What-ev - er ills a - bound, What-
thou my light, I cry, Saviour, ev - er dear!
- ev-er ills a - bound;—Saviour, ev - er dear!
1. Will that not joy - ful be, When we walk by faith no more, When the Lord we loved be-fore,
2. Will that not joy - ful be, When to meet us rise and come All our bur-ied treasures home,
As Brother-man we see; When he welcomes us a - bove, When we share his smile of love, Will that not joy-ful be? Will that not joy - ful be?
A glad-some compa - ny! When our arms embrace a - gain Those we mourned so long in vain, Will that not joy-ful be? Will that not joy - fu be?

WREATH. 6s & 5s. Peculiar.
D.
1. When shall we meet a - gain? Meet ne'er to sev - er? When will peace wreathe her chain Round us for ev - er? Our hearts will ne'er repose, Safe from each blast that blows, In this dark vale of woes, Never— no, never!
2. When shall love free-ly flow Pure as life's riv - er? When shall sweet friendship glow Changeless for ev - er? Where joys ce - les-tial thrill, Where bliss each heart shall fill, And fears of part-ing chill Never— no, never!
WARREN. 6s & 5s. Trochaic.
W.
1. Hark! the sounds of glad-ness From a dis - tant shore; Like re - lief from sad - ness, Sor-row now no more; 'Tis the Lord hath done it, In his day of power; His own arm hath won it, Praise him ev - er - more.
2. Welcome, sounds of glad - ness From a dis - tant shore; Now a - way with sad - ness, And despond no more. Ye who mourn with Zi - on, And her wel - fare seek, Think of Ju - dah's Li - on, Nev - er faint nor weak

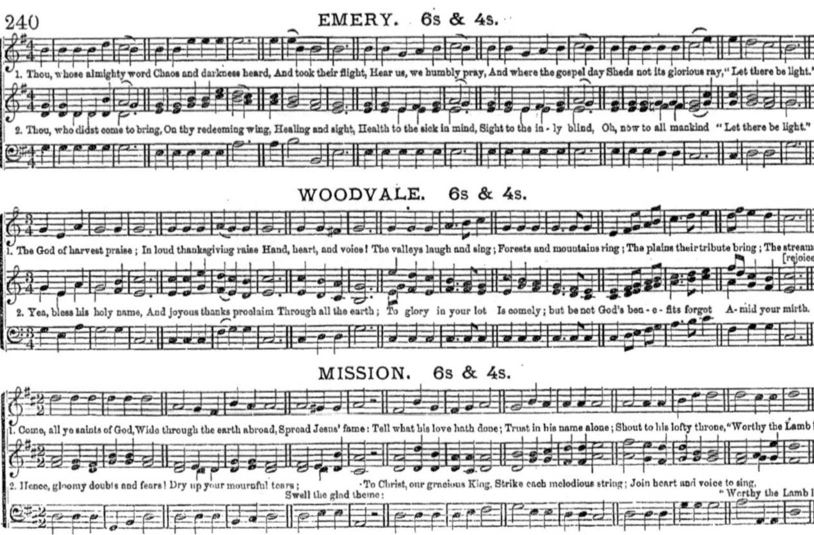
EMERY. 6s & 4s.
1. Thou, whose almighty word Chaos and darkness heard, And took their flight, Hear us, we humbly pray, And where the gospel day Sheds not its glorious ray, "Let there be light."
2. Thou, who didst come to bring, On thy redeeming wing, Healing and sight, Health to the sick in mind, Sight to the in - ly blind, Oh, now to all mankind "Let there be light."
WOODVALE. 6s & 4s.
1. The God of harvest praise; In loud thanksgiving raise Hand, heart, and voice! The valleys laugh and sing; Forests and mountains ring; The plains their tribute bring; The streams [rejoice.
2. Yea, bless his holy name, And joyous thanks proclaim Through all the earth; To glory in your lot Is comely; but be not God's ben - e - fits forgot A- mid your mirth.
MISSION. 6s & 4s.
1. Come, all ye saints of God, Wide through the earth abroad, Spread Jesus' fame: Tell what his love hath done; Trust in his name alone; Shout to his lofty throne, "Worthy the Lamb!"
2. Hence, gloomy doubts and fears! Dry up your mournful tears; Swell the glad theme: To Christ, our gracious King, Strike each melodious string; Join heart and voice to sing, "Worthy the Lamb!"

AMERICA. 6s & 4s.
English
241
1. My country, 'tis of thee, Sweet land of lib-er-ty, Of thee I sing; Land, where my fathers died; Land of the pilgrim's pride; From ev'-ry mountain side Let free-dom ring.
2. My na-tive country! thee, Land of the no-ble free, Thy name I love: I love thy rocks and rills, Thy woods and templed hills; My heart with rapture thrills, Like that a-bove.
3. Let mu-sic swell the breeze, And ring from all the trees Sweet freedom's song: Let mortal tongues a-wake; Let all that breathe partake; Let rocks their si-lence break, The sound pro-long.
ITALIAN HYMN. 6s & 4s.
Giardini.
1. Come, thou almight-y King, Help us thy name to sing, Help us to praise! Father all glo-ri-ous, O'er all vic-to-ri-ous, Come and reign over us, Ancient of Days.
2. Je-sus, our Lord, descend; From all our foes de-fend, Nor let us fall; Let thine almighty aid Our sure defense be made, Our souls on thee be stay'd: Lord, hear our call.
OLIVET. 6s & 4s.
Dr. L. Mason.
1. My faith looks up to thee, Thou Lamb of Calvary, Sa-viour di-vine: Now hear me while I pray; Take all my guilt away; O let me from this day Be whol-ly thine.
2. May thy rich grace impart, Strength to my fainting heart. My zeal inspire; As thou hast died for me, O may my love to thee Pure, warm, and changeless be, A liv-ing fire.

GLENWOOD. 6s & 4s.
*
1. Praise ye Jehovah's name, Praise thro' his courts proclaim; Rise and adore: High o'er the heavens above Sound his great acts of love, While his rich grace we prove, Vast as his [power.
2. Now let the trumpet raise Sounds of triumphant praise, Wide as his fame: There let the harp be found; Organs, with solemn sound, Roll your deep notes around, Filled with his [name.
JARVIS. 6s & 4s.
W.
1. My faith looks up to thee, Thou Lamb of Calvary, Saviour Divine! Now hear me while I pray; Take all my guilt away; Oh, let me, from this day, Be wholly thine!
2. May thy rich grace impart Strength to my fainting heart,—My zeal inspire! As thou hast died for me, Oh, may my love to thee Pure, warm, and changeless be—A living fire!
GORDON. 6s & 4s. Peculiar.
1. Child of sin and sorrow, Filled with dismay, Wait not for to-morrow, Yield thee to-day: Heaven bids thee come, While yet there's room; Child of sin and sorrow, Hear and obey.
2. Child of sin and sorrow, Why wilt thou die! Come, while thou canst borrow Help from on high: Grieve not that love, Which from above, Child of sin and sorrow, Would bring thee nigh.

ADAMS. 6s & 4s. Peculiar.

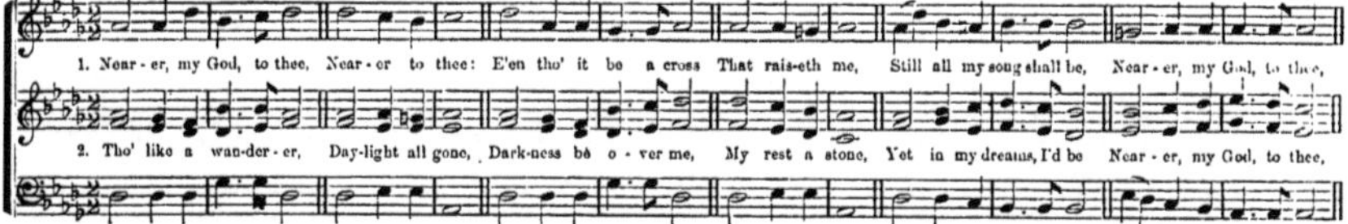
1. Near - er, my God, to thee, Near - er to thee: E'en tho' it be a cross That rais-eth me, Still all my song shall be, Near - er, my God, to thee,
2. Tho' like a wan-der - er, Day-light all gone, Dark-ness be o - ver me, My rest a stone, Yet in my dreams, I'd be Near - er, my God, to thee,

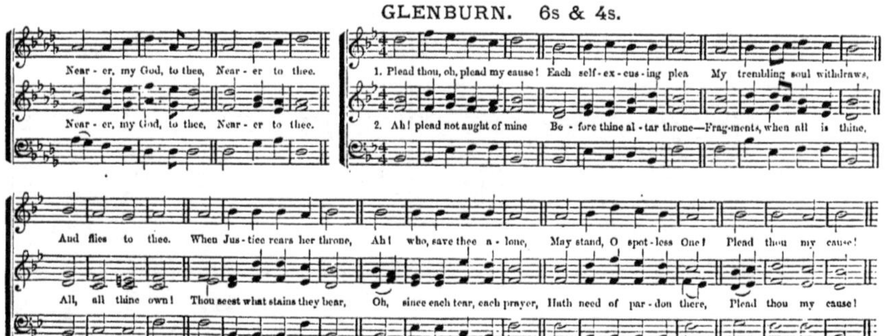
Near - er, my God, to thee, Near - er to thee.
Near - er, my God, to thee, Near - er to thee.
GLENBURN. 6s & 4s.
1. Plead thou, oh, plead my cause! Each self - ex - cus - ing plea My trembling soul withdraws,
2. Ah! plead not aught of mine Be - fore thine al - tar throne—Frag-ments, when all is thine,
And flies to thee. When Jus - tice rears her throne, Ah! who, save thee a - lone, May stand, O spot - less One! Plead thou my cause!
All, all thine own! Thou seest what stains they bear, Oh, since each tear, each prayer, Hath need of par - don there, Plead thou my cause!

244
BETHANY. 6s & 4s. Peculiar. Dr. L. Mason. From "Sab. Hymn & Tune Book."
1. Near - er, my God, to thee. Near - er to thee: Ev'n though it be a cross That rais - eth me, Still all my song shall be, Near - er, my
2. Though like a wan-der - er, Day - light all gone, Dark - ness be o - ver me, My rest a stone, Yet in my dreams, I'd be Near - er, my
3. There let the way ap - pear Steps up to heaven; All that thou send-est me In mer - cy given, An - gels to beck-on me Near - er, my
God, to thee, Near - er, my God, to thee, Near - er to thee.
God, to thee, Near - er, my God, to thee, Near - er to thee.
God, to thee, Near - er, my God, to thee, Near - er to thee.
OAK. 6s & 4s. Peculiar. Dr. L. Mason.
1. I'm but a stran-ger here, Heaven is my home; Earth is a
2. What tho' the tem - pest rage, Heaven is my home; Short is my
3. There, at my Saviour's side, Heaven is my home; I shall be
des - ert drear, Heaven is my home. Dan - ger and sor - row stand Round me on ev - ery hand; Heaven is my fa - ther-land, Heaven is my home.
pil - grim-age, Heaven is my home. Time's cold and win - try blast Soon will be o - ver - past; I shall reach home at last, Heaven is my home.
glo - ri - fied, Heaven is my home. There are the good and blest, Those I loved most and best, There too I soon shall rest; Heaven is my home.

SANFORD. 6s & 4s. Peculiar.
1. Fa - ther, oh, hear me now! Fa - ther di - vine! Thou, on - ly thou canst see The heart's deep ag - o - ny: Help me to say to thee, "Thy will, not mine!"
2. O God! be thou my stay In this dark hour; Kind - ly each sor - row hear, Hush ev-ery trou-bled fear, Thee let me still re - vere, Still own thy power.
HOLMAN. 6s.
1. My soul doth long for thee To dwell with - in my breast; Un - worth - y though I be Of so di - vine a Guest!
2. Of so di - vine a Guest Un-worth - y though I be, Yet hath my heart no rest Un - til it come to thee!
BATES. 6s.
B. C. CHASE.
When will the morning come, The blessed day a - rise, When God shall call me home! To meet him in the skies: When will the moment come, When will the moment come!
When will the morning come, The blessed day a - rise, When God shall call me home! To meet him in the skies: When will the moment come, When will the moment come!

SUBMISSION. 6s.

W.

1. Thy way, not mine, O Lord, How - ev - er dark it be! Lead me by thine own hand; Choose out the path for me.
2. I dare not choose my lot: I would not, if I might; Choose thou for - me, my God, So shall I walk a - right.
LINDELL. 6s.
Go up, go up, my heart! Dwell with thy God a - bove; For here thou canst not rest, Nor here give out thy love.
Go up, go up, my heart! Dwell with thy God a - bove; For here thou canst not rest, Nor here give out thy love.
FIDES. 6s.
1. Once more be - fore we part Bless the Re - deem - er's name; Let ev - ery tongue and heart Praise and a - dore the same.
2. Lord, in thy name we came, Thy bless - ing still im - part, We met in Je - sus' name, In Je - sus' name we part.

MALTBY. 7s & 6s.
1. Broth - er, thou art gone to rest, We will not weep for thee; For thou art now where oft on earth Thy spir - it longed to be.
2. Broth - er, thou art gone to rest, Thine is an earth-ly tomb; But Je - sus summoned thee a - way; Thy Sav - iour bid thee come.
LYNDE. 6s & 10s.
1. Wilt thou not vis - it me! The plant be - side me feels thy gen - tle dew; Each blade of grass I see, From thy deep earth its quick'ning mois-ture drew.
2. Wilt thou not vis - it me! Thy morn-ing calls on me with cheering tone; And ev - ery hill and tree Lend but one voice, the voice of thee a - lone.
CONQUEST. 5s & 8s.
1. Be-hold how the Lord Has girt on his sword; From conquest to conquest proceeds! How hap-py are they Who live in this day, And wit-ness his wonder-ful deeds.
2. His word he sends forth, From south to the north; From east and from west it is heard: The reb - el is charm'd; The foe is dis - armed; No day like this day has appeared.

MONADNOCK. 7s & 6s.
W.
1. Go, when the morning shin - eth, Go, when the noon is bright, Go, when the eve de - clin - eth, Go, in the hush of night;
2. Re - mem - ber all who love thee, All who are loved by thee; Pray, too, for those who hate thee, If a - ny such there be:
Go, with pure mind and feel - ing, Put earthly thoughts a - way, And, in God's presence kneel - ing, Do thou in se - cret pray.
Then for thy - self, in meek - ness, A bless - ing humbly claim, And blend with each pe - ti - tion Thy great Re - deemer's name.
ELLIOT. 8s & 4s.
1. My God! is a - ny hour so sweet, From blush of morn to eve - ning star, As that which calls me to thy feet— The hour of prayer?
2. Blest is the tran - quil hour of morn, And blest that hour of sol - emn eve, When, on the wings of prayer up-borne, The world I leave.

HOSANNA. 7s & 6s. Iambic.
1. Now be the gos - pel ban - ner In ev - ery land un - furled, And be the shout, Ho - san - na, Re - ech - oed through the world;
2. Yes, thou shalt reign for - ev - er, O Je - sus, King of kings! Thy light, thy love, thy fav - or, Each ransomed cap - tive sings.
Till ev - ery isle and na - tion, Till ev - ery tribe and tongue, Re - ceive the great sal - va - tion, And join the hap - py throng.
The isles for thee are wait - ing, The des - erts learn thy praise, The hills and val - leys greet - ing, The song re - spon - sive raise.
DION. 8,3,3,6.
1. Rise, my soul! a - dore thy Mak - er, Angels praise, Join the lays, With them be par - tak - er.
2. Sov'reign Lord of ev - ery spir - it, In the light Lead us right, Through our Saviour's mer - it.
3.
Thou, O Lord, art our Protector,
With us stay
Day by day,
Ever our Director.
4.
Glory, honor, thanks and blessing;
Songs of praise
We will raise,
Never, never ceasing.

ARMAGH. 7s & 6s. Iambic.
1. When shall the voice of sing - ing Flow joy - ful - ly a - long! When hill and val - ley, ring - ing With one tri - umph - ant song,
2. Then from the crag - gy mount - ains The sa - cred shout shall fly; And sha - dy vales and fount - ains Shall ech - o the re - ply:
Pro - claim the con - test end - ed, And him who once was slain, A - gain to earth de - scend - ed, In right - eous - ness to reign!
High tower and low - ly dwell - ing Shall send the hymn a - round, All hal - le - lu - jah swell - ing In one e - ter - nal sound!
COBDEN. 8s, 7s & 4.
1. { Keep us, Lord, oh, keep us ev - er! Vain our hope, if left by thee; }
{ We are thine; oh, leave us nev - er, Till thy glo - rious face we see! }
Then to praise thee Through a bright e - ter - ni - ty.
2. { Pre - cious is thy word of prom - ise, Pre - cious to thy peo - ple here; }
{ Nev - er take thy pres - ence from us, Je - sus, Sav - iour, still be near: }
Liv - ing, dy - ing, May thy name our spir - its cheer.

ARNOLD. 7s & 6s. Trochaic.
D.
1. Time is wing - ing us a - way To our e - ter - nal home; Life is but a win - ter's day— A jour - ney to the tomb:
2. Time is wing - ing us a - way To our e - ter - nal home; Life is but a win - ter's day— A jour - ney to the tomb:
Youth and vig - or soon will flee, Bloom-ing beau - ty lose its charms; All that's mor - tal soon shall be En - closed in death's cold arms.
But the Christ-ian shall en - joy Health and beau - ty, soon, a - bove, Far be-yond the world's al - loy,— Se - cure in Je - sus' love.
CONRAD. 7s & 5s.
D.
1. When our heads are bow'd with woe, When our bit - ter tears o'er - flow, When we mourn the lost, the dear, Gra - cious Sav - iour, hear!
2. Thou our fee - ble flesh hast worn; Thou our mor - tal griefs hast borne; Thou hast shed the hu - man tear: Gra - cious Sav - iour, hear!

252
PARDON. 7s & 6s. Peculiar.
1. Drooping souls, no long - er mourn, Je - sus still is pre - cious; If to him you now re - turn, Heaven will be pro - pi - tious.
2. He has par - dons, full and free, Drooping souls to glad - den; Still he cries—"Come un - to me, Wea - ry, hea - vy -. la - den."
Je - sus now is pass - ing by, Call - ing wanderers near him; Drooping souls, you need not die, Go to him and hear him.
Though your sins like mountains high, Rise, and reach to heav - en. Soon as you on him re - ly, All shall be for - giv - en.
PERKINS. 7s & 4s.
W.
1. { When the vale of death ap - pears, Faint and cold this mor-tal clay— Kind Fore-run - ner, soothe my fears, Light me through the darksome way; } Break the shadows, Ush - er in e - ter - nal day.
2. { Upward from this dy - ing state, Bid my wait - ing soul as - pire; O - pen thou the crys - tal gate, To thy praise at-tune my lyre; } Then, tri - umphant, I will join the im - mor - tal choir.

MONROE. 8s & 4s.

1. Haste, trav'ler, haste! the night comes on, And many a shin - ing hour is gone; The storm is gathering in the west, And thou art far from home and rest:
2. The ris - ing tempest sweeps the sky; The rains descend, the winds are high; The waters swell, and death and fear Be - set thy path; no ref - uge near:
Haste, trav'ler, haste! Haste, trav'ler, haste!
Haste, trav'ler, haste! Haste, trav'ler, haste!
VIOLET. 8s & 4s.
1. Our blest Redeemer, ere he breathed His last farewell, A Guide, a Comforter bequeathed With us to dwell.
2. He came in tongues of living flame, To teach, subdue; All-powerful as the wind he came, As view - less too.
REPOSE. 8s & 4s.
W.
There is a calm for those who weep, A rest for wea - ry pilgrims found; They softly lie, and sweetly sleep, Low in the ground. Low in the ground.
2. The storm that racks the wint - 'ry sky No more dis-turbs their deep re - pose Than summer evening's la - test sigh, That shuts the rose. That shuts the rose.

JUNIPER. 8s & 6s. Peculiar.
A. D. J.
1. Lo! the storms of life are break-ing; Faith-less fears our hearts are shak-ing: For our suc - cor un - der - tak - ing, Lord and Sav - iour, help us!
2. Lo! the world, from thee re - bell - ing, Round thy church in pride is swell-ing! With thy word their madness quell-ing, Lord and Sav - iour, help us!
KENDERWOOD. 8s, 7s & 6s.
A. D. J.
Watchman! onward to your sta - tion; Blow the trumpet long and loud:
Preach the gos-pel to the na - tions; Speak to every gath'ring crowd:
See the day is break-ing, See the saints a-wak - ing, No more in sad - ness bowed.
Watchman! onward to your sta - tion; Blow the trumpet long and loud:
Preach the gos-pel to the na - tions; Speak to every gath'ring crowd:
See the day is break-ing, See the saints a-wak - ing, No more in sad - ness bowed.
FATHERLAND. 5s & 8s.
W.
1. Jesus, still lead on, Till our rest be won; And although the way be cheerless, We will follow, calm and fearless: Guide us by thy hand To our Fa - ther - land!
2. If the way be drear, If the foe be near, Let not faithless fears o'ertake us, Let not faith and hope forsake us; For, thro' many a foe, To our home we go!

HELEN. 9s & 7s.

w. 255

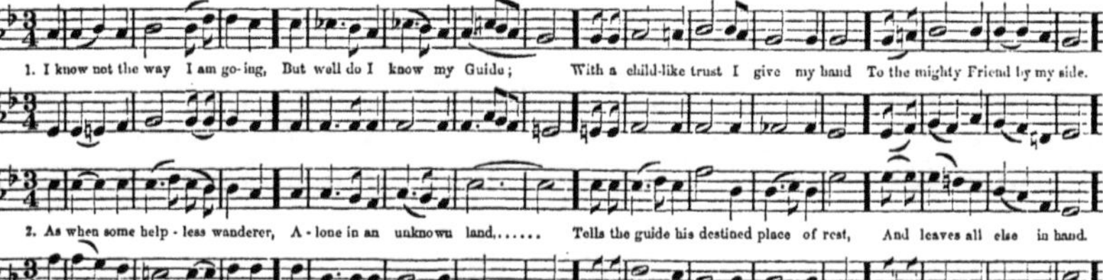

1. I know not the way I am go- ing, But well do I know my Guide; With a child-like trust I give my hand To the mighty Friend by my side.
2. As when some help - less wanderer, A - lone in an unknown land,...... Tells the guide his destined place of rest, And leaves all else in hand.

The on - ly thing I say to him As he takes it is, "Hold it fast!" Suffer me not to lose my way, And bring me home at last.
'Tis home, 'tis home we wish to reach,— He who guides us may choose the way; Little we heed what path we take, If near - er home each day

256
VERONA. 10s.
Hail! happy day! Thou day of holy rest! What heav'nly peace and transport fills my breast, When Christ, the God of Grace, in love descends, And kindly holds communion with his friends.
Hail! happy day! Thou day of holy rest! What heav'nly peace and transport fills my breast, When Christ, the God of Grace, in love descends, And kindly holds communion with his friends.
NEWELL. 10s & 9s.
D.
1. Not in vain I pour'd my supplica-tion, Voiced in anguish that was nigh despair: God—henceforth the Rock of my sal-va-tion—Hears in pit-y, and re-ceives my prayer.
2. On his name from 'midst the darkness calling, He my soul hath ransom'd from its fears; By his strength my feet are sav'd from falling, And his love hath dried my flowing tears.
RADWAY. 11s & 10s.
1. Come, ye disconsolate! where'er you languish, Come to the mercy-seat, fervently kneel: Here bring your wounded hearts, here tell your anguish; Earth has no sor-row that heaven can-not heal.
2. Joy of the des-o-late, Light of the straying, Hope of the pen-itent; fadeless and pure;—Here speaks the Comforter, tender-ly say-ing, Earth has no sor-row that heaven can-not cure.

PLUMMER. 8s & 7s. Peculiar.

1. Head of the church tri - umphant, We joy - ful - ly a - dore thee; Till thou appear, thy members here, Shall sing like those in glory. We lift our hearts and voi - ces In
2. While in af - flic - tions furnace, And passing thro' the fire, Thy love we praise, that knows our days, And ever brings us nigher. We lift our hands, ex - ult - ing In
blest an - ti - ci - pation; And cry aloud, and give to God The praise of our salvation.
thine almighty favor; The love divine that made us thine, Shall keep us thine forever.
OSSAGON. 10s, 5s, 6s & 12s.
J. FENNELL.
1. Come, let us a - new our journey pursue—Roll round with the year, And
2. Our life is a dream; our time, as a stream, Glides swiftly away, And the
nev - er stand still till the Master ap - pear; His a - dor - a - ble will let us gladly ful - fill, And our talents improve By the patience of hope, and the labor of love.
fu - gi - tive moment re - fuses to stay: The ar - row is flown; the moment is gone; The mil - len - i - al year Rushes on to our view, and e - ter - nity's near.

CEREAL. 10s.

1. A - gain the day returns of ho - ly rest, Which, when he made the world, Jehovah blest; When, like his own, he bade our labors cease, And all be pi - e - ty, and all be peace.
2. Let us devote this con-se - crated day To learn his will, and all we learn o - bey; So shall he hear, when fervently we raise Our choral harmony in hymns of praise.
PRINCEBURG. 11s & 8s.
J. S. BROOKS.
1. Be joy - ful in God, all ye lands of the earth; Oh, serve him with gladness and fear: Ex - ult in his presence with music and mirth, With love and devotion draw near.
2. The Lord he is God, and Je - ho - vah a - lone, Cre - a - tor and Ruler o'er all; And we are his people, his scepter we own,—His sheep, and we follow his call.
VERNON. 11s & 8s. Peculiar.
1. The Lord is great! ye hosts of heav'n, adore him; And ye, who tread this earthly ball, In ho - ly songs rejoice aloud before him, And shout his praise who made you all.
2. The Lord is great! his majesty, how glorious! Resound his praise from shore to shore; O'er sin, and death, and hell, now made victorious, He rules and reigns for ev - er-more.

259
(To sing the second hymn, use the small notes.)
ISRAEL. 11s & 10s.
1st Hymn. Hail to the bright-ness of Zi - on's glad morn - ing, Joy to the lands that in dark - ness have lain; Hushed be the ac - cents of sor - row and mourn-ing, Zi - on in tri - umph be - gins her mild reign.
2d Hymn. Daugh - ter of Zi - on, a - wake from thy sad - ness, A - wake! for thy foes shall op - press thee no more; Bright o'er thy hills dawns the day - star of glad - ness; A - rise! for the night of thy sor - row is o'er.
BENTON. 11s & 10s.
1. Bright-est and best of the sons of the morn - ing! Dawn on our dark-ness, and lend us thine aid; Star of the East, the ho - ri - zon a - dorn - ing, Guide where our in - fant Re-deem - er is laid.
2. Cold on his cra - dle the dew-drops are shin - ing; Low lies his head with the beasts of the stall: An - gels
in slum-ber re - clin - ing, Mak - er, and Monarch, and Sav iour of all!

CHARTON. 11s.
D.
1. O eyes that are wear - y, and hearts that are sore! Look off un - to Je - sus, now sor - row no more! The light of his coun - te - nance
2. While look - ing to Je - sus, my heart can - not fear; I trem - ble no more when I see Je - sus near; I know that his pres - ence my
shin - eth so bright, That here, as in heav - en, there need be no night.
safeguard will be, For, "Why are ye troubled?" he said un - to me.
MASONDA. 11s.
1. Tho' faint, yet pur - su - ing, we go on our way; The Lord is our
2. He rais - eth the fall - en, he cheer - eth the faint; The weak, and op -
Lead - er, his word is our stay; Though suffering, and sor - row, and tri - al be near, The Lord is our re - fuge, and whom can we fear!
- press'd—he will hear their complaint, The way may be wea - ry, and thorn - y the road, But how can we fal - ter! our help is in God!

CONWAY. 12s.

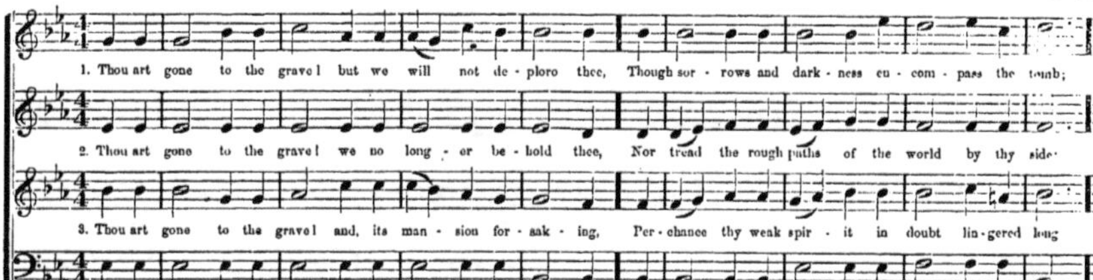
1. Thou art gone to the grave! but we will not de - plore thee, Though sor - rows and dark - ness en - com - pass the tomb;
2. Thou art gone to the grave! we no long - er be - hold thee, Nor tread the rough paths of the world by thy side.
3. Thou art gone to the grave! and, its man - sion for - sak - ing, Per - chance thy weak spir - it in doubt lin - gered long

The Sav - iour hath passed through its por - tals be - fore thee, And the lamp of his love is thy guide through the gloom.
But the wide arms of mer - cy are spread to en - fold thee, And sin - ners may hope, for the Sin - less hath died.
But the sun - shine of glo - ry beamed bright on thy wak - ing, And full on thine ear burst the ser - a - phim's song.

UNITY. 12s.

1. The voice of free grace cries, "Escape to the mountain," For Adam's lost race Christ hath opened a fountain; For sin and un-cleanness, and ev - ery transgression,

2. Ye souls that are wounded, oh, flee to the Saviour; He calls you in mer - cy—'tis in - fin - ite fav-or; Your sins are in - creasing; es- cape to the mountain;

3. When Zi - on we see, having gained the blest shore, With harps in our hands, we will praise him the more; We'll range the sweet plains on the banks of the river,

His blood flows most freely in streams of salvation. Hal-le - lu- jah to the Lamb who has bought us a pardon! We'll praise him again, when we pass over Jordan.

His blood can remove them, it flows from the fountain. Hal-le - lu- jah to the Lamb who has bought us a pardon! We'll praise him again, when we pass over Jordan.

And sing of sal - vation for ev- er and ev- er! Hal-le - lu- jah to the Lamb who has bought us a pardon! We'll praise him again, when we pass over Jordan.

HYMN. "Dear comrade pilgrims of the cross.'
1 Dear com - rade pil-grims of the cross, Although the way be drea-ry, Yet faint not, fail not, onward press, Tho' wounded, worn and wea - ry.
2 Tho' sore be - set, not o - ver - come, Cast down, but not des - pair-ing. We're traveling toward a heavenly home, Our mas-ter's stan-dard bear-ing.
3 We'll one an - oth - er's bur-dens bear, The toil - some jour-ney cheering; Our joys and all our sorrows share, Each day our home we're nearing.
4 Our Lord is God; his prom-ise sure, His help shall fail us nev - er; And they who to the end en-dure Shall reign with him for - ev - er!
Toil on - ward still Thro' eve - ry ill, Con - fi - ding in the Sav-iour; The jour - ney done, And glo - ry won, We'll sing his praise for - ev - er!
Toil on - ward still Thro' eve - ry ill, Con - fi - ding in the Sav-iour; The jour - ney done, And glo - ry won, We'll sing his praise for - ev - er!
Toil on - ward still Thro' eve - ry ill, Con - fi - ding in the Sav-iour; The jour - ney done, And glo - ry won, We'll sing his praise for - ev - er!
HYMN. "Sion, wake, all praise accord."
1 Si - on, wake, all praise accord, To thy Saviour, and thy Lord, Fountain he, for sin outpoured; The Mes - si - ah, the Mes - si-ah, The Prince of Peace is here.
2 He who reigns on heav'nly steep, Comes to seek his wandering sheep, Willing eve - ry soul to keep; The Mes - si - ah, the Mes - si-ah, The Prince of Peace is here
3 Si - on lift thy songs of praise: With the faithful, now upraise Carols sweet, and hymned lays: The Mes - si - ah, the Mes - si-ah, The Prince of Peace is here.

264 Words by Dr. BONAR. HYMN. "A little while." W.

1. Be - yond the smil - ing and the weep - ing, I shall be soon; Be - yond the wak - ing and the sleep - ing, Be - yond the
2. Be - yond the blooming and the fad - ing, I shall be soon; Be - yond the shin - ing and the shad - ing, Be - yond the
3. Be - yond the ris - ing and the set - ting, I shall be soon; Be - yond the calm - ing and the fret - ting, Be - yond re -
4. Be - yond the part - ing and the meet - ing, I shall be soon; Be - yond the fare - well and the greet - ing, Be - yond the
sow - ing and the reap - ing, I shall be soon. Love, rest, and home, Sweet home, Sweet home, Lord, tar - ry not, but come.
hop - ing and the dread - ing, I shall be soon. Love, rest, and home, Sweet home, Sweet home, Lord, tar - ry not, but come.
- membering and for - get - ting, I shall be soon. Love, rest, and home, Sweet home, Sweet home, Lord, tar - ry not, but come.
puls - es' fev - er beat - ing, I shall be soon. Love, rest, and home, Sweet home, Sweet home, Lord, tar - ry not, but come.

HYMN. "Saviour, breathe an evening blessing." 8s & 7s. Double.

D.
1. Saviour, breathe an evening blessing, Ere re-pose our spir-its seal: Sin and want we come con-fess-ing; Thou canst save, and thou canst heal.
2. Though the night be dark and dreary, Darkness can-not hide from thee: Thou art he, who, nev-er wea-ry, Watcheth where thy peo-ple be.
Though de-struc-tion walk a-round us, Though the ar-row near us fly, An-gel-guards from thee surround us; We are safe, if thou art nigh.
Should swift death this night o'er-take us, And our couch be-come our tomb, May the morn in heaven a-wake us, Clad in light and deathless bloom!

HYMN. "Fading, still fading." D.

1. Fading, still fad-ing, the last beam is shin-ing, Fa-ther in heav-en! the day is de-clin-ing; Safe-ty and in-nocence flee not with light: We
p
pp
2. Fa-ther in heaven! on thee do we call, Thou, the Pro-tect-or and Sav-iour of all; Fee-ble and fainting, we trust in thy might; In
Organ.
trust thee by day, and we trust thee by night. From the fall of the shade till the morning bells chime, Shield us from dan-ger, and save us from crime.
mf
pp
mf
doubting and darkness, thy love be our light. Let us sleep on thy breast while the night taper burns, Wake in thine arms when the morning re-turns.

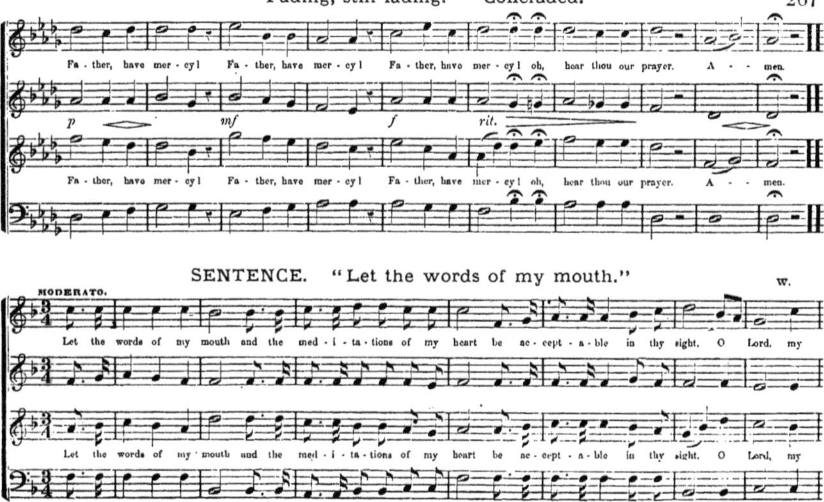
Fa - ther, have mer - cy! Fa - ther, have mer - cy! Fa - ther, have mer - cy! oh, hear thou our prayer. A - - men.
p mf f rit.
Fa - ther, have mer - cy! Fa - ther, have mer - cy! Fa - ther, have mer - cy! oh, hear thou our prayer. A - - men.
SENTENCE. "Let the words of my mouth."
W.
MODERATO.
Let the words of my mouth and the med - i - ta - tions of my heart be ac - cept - a - ble in thy sight, O Lord, my
Let the words of my mouth and the med - i - ta - tions of my heart be ac - cept - a - ble in thy sight, O Lord, my

Strength and my Re - deem - er. Let the words,............ Let the words,............ Let the words of my mouth and the
of my mouth, of my mouth,
Strength and my Re - deem - er. of my mouth, of my mouth, Let the words of my mouth and the
med - i - ta - tions of my heart be ac - cept - a - ble in thy sight, O Lord, my Strength and my Re - deem - er. A - men.
med - i - ta - tions of my heart be ac - cept - a - ble in thy sight, O Lord, my Strength and my Re - deem - er. A - men.

SENTENCE. "The Lord is in his holy Temple."

ADAGIO.
The Lord is in his ho - ly tem - ple, The Lord is in his ho - ly tem - ple. Let all the
The Lord is in his ho - ly tem - ple, The Lord is in his ho - ly tem - ple. Let all the
earth keep si - lence be - fore him, Let all the earth keep si - lence be - fore him, keep si - lence be - fore him.
earth keep si - lence be - fore him, Let all the earth keep si - lence be - fore him, keep si - lence be - fore him.

SENTENCE. "The Lord is in his holy Temple."

ADAGIO.
The Lord is in his ho - - ly tem ple, The Lord is in his ho - ly tem - ple, Let all the earth keep
The Lord is in his ho - - ly tem - ple, The Lord is in his ho - ly tem - ple, Let all the earth keep
si - lence, Let all the earth keep si - lence be - fore him; keep si - lence, keep si - lence be - fore...... him.
si - lence, Let all the earth keep si - lence be - fore him; keep si - lence, keep si - lence be - fore...... him.

Seek ye the Lord, while he may be found, and call up - on him, while he is near; Let the wick-ed for - sake his way, and the
Seek ye the Lord, while he may be found, and call up - on him, while he is near; Let the wick-ed for - sake his way, and the
un-righteous man his thoughts, and re - turn, and re - turn un - to the Lord, and he will have mer-cy up - on him; he will a -
un-righteous man his thoughts, and re - turn, and re - turn un - to the Lord, and he will have mer-cy up - on him; he will a

"Seek ye the Lord." (Concluded.)

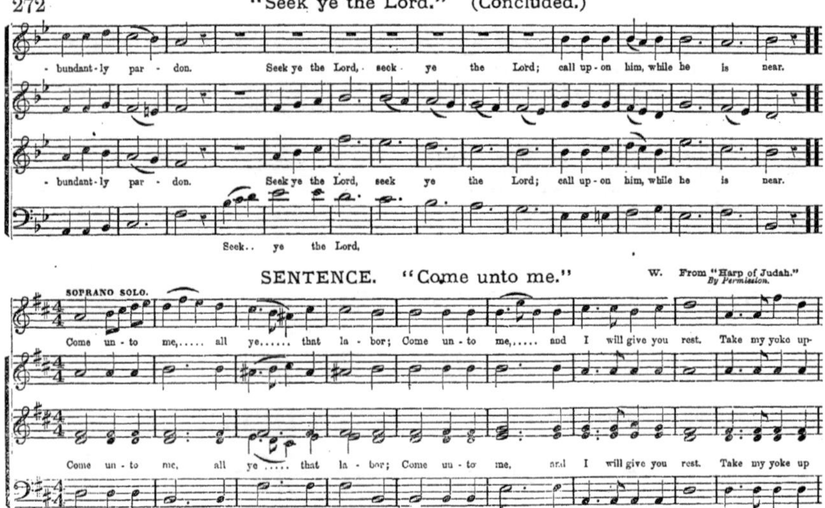

- bundant-ly par - don. Seek ye the Lord, - seek - ye the Lord; call up-on him, while he is near.
- bundant-ly par - don. Seek ye the Lord, seek ye the Lord; call up-on him, while he is near.
Seek.. ye the Lord,
SENTENCE. "Come unto me."
W. From "Harp of Judah." By Permission.
SOPRANO SOLO.
Come un - to me,..... all ye...... that la - bor; Come un - to me,..... and I will give you rest. Take my yoke up-
Come un - to me, all ye..... that la - bor; Come un - to me, and I will give you rest. Take my yoke up

- on you and learn of me,........ for I am meek and low - ly of heart;.... and ye shall find rest un-
ritard.
cres.
rit.
- on you and learn of me, for I am meek and low - ly of heart;.... and ye shall find rest un-
- to your souls: For my yoke is ea - sy, and my bur - den is light, my yoke is ea - sy, and my bur - den is light.
- to your souls: For my yoke is ea - sy, and my bur - den is light, my yoke is ea - sy, and my bur - den is light.

SENTENCE. "Heavenly Father."

D.

MODERATO.
Heaven - ly Fa - ther, heaven- ly Fa - ther, gra - cious-ly hear us, hear us; hear the pe - ti - tions we of - fer be -
p
Heaven - ly Fa - ther, heaven- ly Fa - ther, gra - cious- ly hear us; hear the pe - ti - tions we of - fer be -
gra - cious - ly hear us, hear - us,
fore thee; hear us, oh, gra - cious-ly hear us. May thy blessing rest up - on us, may thy blessing rest up - on.... us. Heaven-ly
p
mf
pp
- fore thee; hear us, oh, gra - cious-ly hear us. May thy blessing rest up on us, may thy blessing rest up - on.... us. Heaven-ly

Fa - ther, hear us; heavenly Fa - ther, hear us, hear our prayer. Heavenly Fa - ther, heaven- ly Fa - ther, gra - cious - ly
Fa - ther, hear us; heavenly Fa - ther, hear us, hear our prayer. Heavenly Fa - ther, heaven- ly Fa - ther, gra - cious - ly
gra -
gra- cious- ly hear us. May thy blessing rest up - on us, May thy blessing rest up - on us; Hear our prayer, hear our prayer.
hear us, hear us.
hear us, hear us. May thy blessing rest up - on us, May thy blessing rest up - on us; Hear our prayer, hear our prayer.
cious - ly hear us.

mind is stayed on thee. whose mind is stayed on thee, whose mind is stayed on
Thou wilt keep him in per - fect peace, whose mind is stayed on
mind is stayed on thee. Thou wilt keep him in per - fect peace, whose mind is stayed on thee, whose mind is stayed on
whose mind is stayed on thee,

A LITTLE FASTER.
thee. Thou wilt keep him in perfect peace, whose mind is stayed on thee. Trust ye in the Lord, Trust ye in the
Thou wilt keep him in per - fect peace, whose mind is stayed on thee. Trust ye in the Lord,
thee. Thou wilt keep him in per - fect peace, whose mind is stayed on thee. Trust ye in the Lord, Trust ye in the
Thou wilt keep him in perfect peace, whose mind is stayed on thee. Trust ye in the Lord,
Lord, Trust ye in the Lord. Oh, trust in the Lord, Oh, trust in the Lord; for in the Lord Je - ho - vah is
Trust ye in the Lord, Trust ye in the Lord.
Lord, Trust ye in the Lord, Oh, trust in the Lord, Oh, trust in the Lord; for in the Lord Je - ho - vah is
Trust ye in the Lord, Trust ye in the Lord.

ev- er- last-ing strength; for in the Lord Je - ho - vah is ev- er- last-ing strength, is ev- er- last-ing strength, is ev- er- last-ing strength, is ev- er- last-ing strength.
ritard.
ev- er- last-ing strength; for in the Lord Je - ho - vah is ev- er- last-ing strength, is ev- er- last-ing strength, is ev- er- last-ing strength, is ev- er- last-ing strength.
ANTHEM. "Calm on the list'ning ear of night."
J. E. GOULD.
By permission.
MODERATO.
Tenor.
p
Calm on the list - 'ning ear of night, Come heaven's me - lo - dious strains, Where wild Ju - de - - a stretch-es far, Her
Soprano.
p

sil - ver - man - tled plains.
Tenor.
O'er the blue depths of Gal - i - lee, There
Alto.
SYM.
Soprano.
O'er the blue depths of Gal - i - lee, There
Base.
comes a ho - lier calm;
SOLO.
And Sha-ron waves, in sol - emn praise,
CHORUS.
Her si - - lent groves of palm.
SOLI.
pp
CHORUS.
SOLI.
CHORUS.
comes a ho - lier calm;
And Sha-ron waves, in sol - emn praise,
Her si - - lent groves of palm.
SOLI.
CHORUS.

MODERATO.
Un - to thee, O Lord, do I lift up my soul; O my God, I trust in thee, let me not be a - shamed,
p
Un - to thee, O Lord, do I lift up my soul; O my God, I trust in thee, let me not be a - shamed,
let me not be a - shamed, let me not, let me not be a - shamed. Lead me in thy truth, and teach me,
let me not be a - shamed, let me not, let me not be a - shamed. Lead me in thy truth, and teach me,

for thou art the God of my sal - va - tion; on thee do I wait all the day. Lead me in thy truth, and
f
pp
for thou art the God of my sal - va - tion; on thee do I wait all the day. Lead me in thy
teach me; lead me in thy truth, and teach me, for thou art the God of my sal - va - tion, on
pp
cres - cen-dc.
truth; lead me in thy truth, for thou art the God of my sal - va - tion, on
for thou art the God &c.

thee do I wait all the day. Re - mem-ber, O Lord, thy lov - ing kind - ness, which has ev - er been of old; re-
p
thee do I wait all the day. Re - mem-ber, O Lord, thy lov - ing kind - ness, which has ev - er been of old; re-
- mem-ber, O Lord, thy lov - ing kind - ness, which has ev - er been of old, which has ev - er been of old.
f
pp
rit.
mem-ber, O Lord, thy lov - ing kind - ness, which has ev - er been of old, which has ev - er been of old.

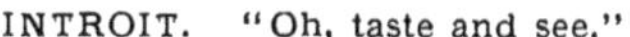

INTROIT. "Oh, taste and see."

Oh taste and see that the Lord is good; Oh, taste and see that the Lord is good. Bless-ed is the man that trust-eth in
Oh, taste and see that the Lord is good; Oh, taste and see that the Lord is good, Bless-ed is the man that trust-eth in
him; bless-ed is the man that trust-eth in him, blessed is the man, is the man that trust-eth in
blessed is the man, is the man............
him; bless-ed is the man that trust-eth in him, blessed is the man, is the man................ that trust-eth in
blessed is the man

him. Oh, taste and see, taste and see that the Lord, that the Lord is good. A - men, A - men.
him. Oh, taste and see, taste and see that the Lord, that the Lord is good. A - men, A - men.
SENTENCE. "The Spirit and the Bride say, Come."
W.
ADAGIO.
The Spir - it and the Bride say, Come; and let him that hear - eth say, Come; and let him that is a - thirst
The Spir - it and the Bride say, Come; and let him that hear - eth say, Come; and let him that is a - thirst

come; And who - so - ev - er will let him take of the wa - ter of Life free - ly, free - ly; and
come; And who - so - ev - er will let him take of the wa - ter of Life free - ly, free - ly; and

who - so - ev - er will, and who - so - ev - er will, who - so - ev - er will let him take of the wa - ter of Life.
f
rit. e dim.
who - so - ev - er will, and who - so - ev - er will, who - so - ev - er will let him take of the wa - ter of Life.

ANTHEM. "Oh, how great is thy goodness."

MODERATO.
Oh, how great, how great is thy good - ness, which thou hast laid up for them.. that fear thee: Oh, how great, how great is thy
Oh, how great, how great is thy good - ness, which thou hast laid up for them.. that fear thee: Oh, how great, how great is thy
good - ness, which thou hast laid up for them.. that fear thee, which thou hast wrought for them that fear thee, which thou hast
good - ness, which thou hast laid up for them.. that fear thee, which thou hast wrought for them that fear thee, which thou hast

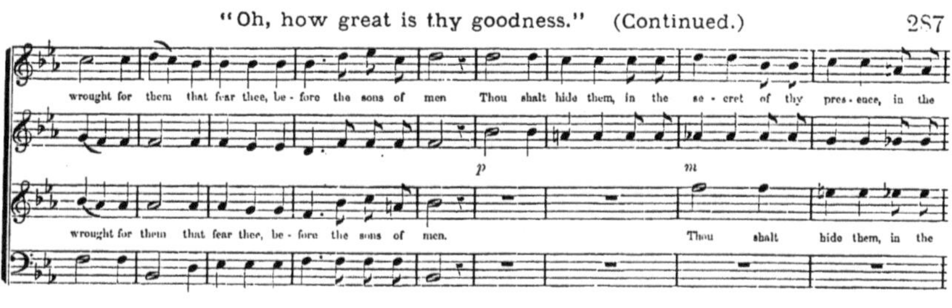
wrought for them that fear thee, be - fore the sons of men Thou shalt hide them, in the se - cret of thy pres - ence, in the
p
m
wrought for them that fear thee, be - fore the sons of men.
Thou shalt hide them, in the

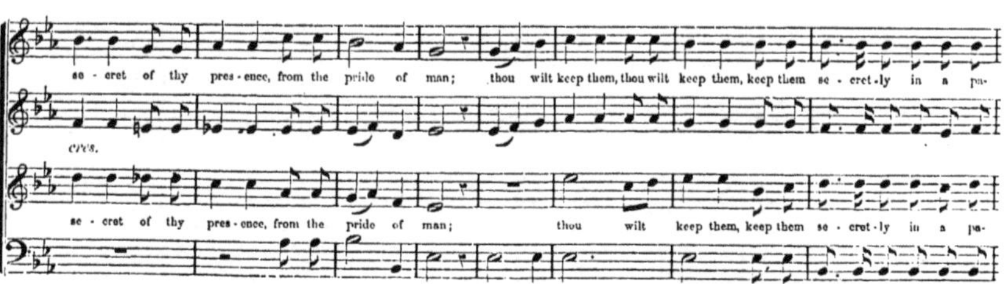
se - cret of thy pres - ence, from the pride of man; thou wilt keep them, thou wilt keep them, keep them se - cret - ly in a pa-
se - cret of thy pres - ence, from the pride of man; thou wilt keep them, keep them se - cret - ly in a pa-
thou wilt keep them,

- vil - ion from the strife of tongues, from the strife of tongues; thou wilt hide them, thou wilt hide.. them, in the se - cret of thy
- vil - ion from the strife of tongues, from the strife of tongues; hide them, hide them in the se - cret of thy
thou wilt hide them, thou wilt hide them,
pres-ence, of thy pres-ence, from the pride of men. Thou wilt keep him, thou wilt keep him, keep him se - cret - ly in a pa-
pres-ence, of thy pres-ence, from the pride of men. Thou wilt keep him, thou wilt keep him, keep him se - cret - ly in a pa-

- vil - ion from the strife, the strife of tongues. Oh, how great, how great is thy good - ness, which thou hast laid up for
p cres. f
- vil - ion from the strife, the strife of tongues. Oh, how great, how great is thy good - ness, which thou hast laid up for
them that fear thee; Oh, how great, great is thy good-ness, how great thy good-ness; how great!..........
great is thy good-ness; oh, how great!
ritard.
them that fear thee; Oh, how great,......... how great is thy good-ness, great is thy good-ness; oh, how great!
Oh, how great, great is thy good-ness,

QUARTETTE. "Oh, that I had wings."*

D.

ADAGIO
pp Oh! that I had wings, had wings like a dove, that I might fly a - way, and be at rest, that I might fly a -
- way, and be at rest. Oh! that I had wings, had wings like a dove, that I might fly a - way, and be at
Soprano ad lib.
- way, and be at rest, fly a - - way and be at rest, that I might fly a - way, and be at

* *By permission of* O. Ditson & Co., *by whom this Quartette is published in sheet form.*

rest. Oh! that I had wings, had wings like a dove, that I might fly a - way and be at rest, and be at rest,
mf
p
rest. Oh! that I had wings, had wings like a dove, that I might fly a - - way,.... and be at rest, and
that I might fly a - way, and be at rest, and be at rest.
and be at rest, and be at rest, and be at rest, and be at rest, and be at rest.
pp
pp
rit. poco a poco.
ppp
be at rest, and be at rest, and be at rest, and be.... at rest, and be at rest.
and be at rest. and be at rest.

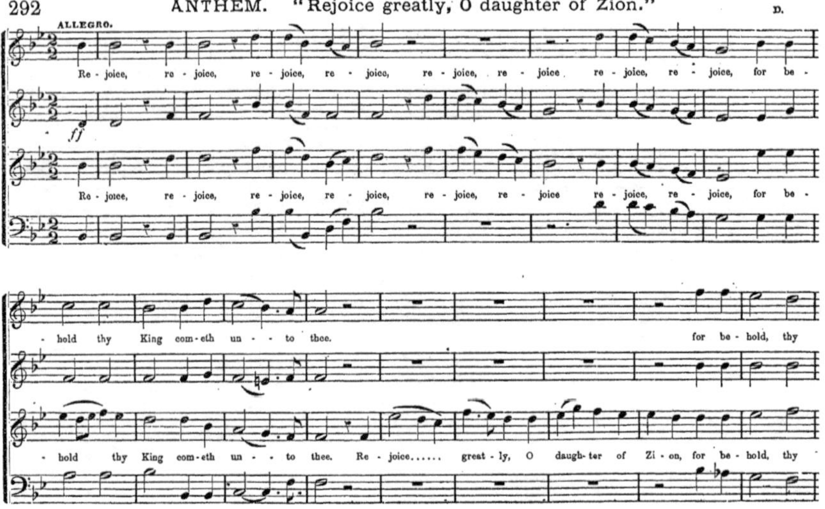
ALLEGRO.
Re - joice, re - joice, re - joice, re - joice, re - joice, re - joice re - joice, re - joice, for be -
ff
Re - joice, re - joice, re - joice, re - joice, re - joice, re - joice re - joice, re - joice, for be -
- hold thy King com - eth un - - to thee. for be - hold, thy
- hold thy King com - eth un - - to thee. Re - joice...... great - ly, O daugh - ter of Zi - on, for be - hold, thy

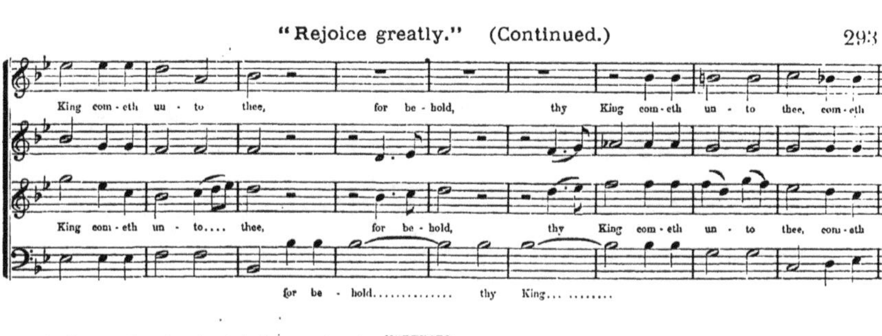
King com - eth un - to thee, for be - hold, thy King com - eth un - to thee, com - eth
King com - eth un - to.... thee, for be - hold, thy King com - eth un - to thee, com - eth
for be - hold.............. thy King... ....

MODERATO.
un - - to thee, com - eth un - - to thee. He is the righteous Sav - iour, He is the righteous Sav - iour, and
rit.
p
un - - to thee, com - eth un - - to thee. He is the righteous Sav - iour, He is the righteous Sav - iour, and

he shall speak peace un - to the hea - - then, He is the right-eous Sav - iour, He is the right-eous Sav - iour; and
he shall speak peace un - to the hea - - then, He is the right-eous Sav - iour, He is the right-eous Sav - iour; and
he shall speak peace un - to the hea - - then, he shall speak peace un - to the hea - - then. Re - joice, re - joice, re-
pp ritard.
A tempo primo. ff
he shall speak peace un - to the hea - - then, he shall speak peace un - to the hea - - then. Re - joice, re - joice, re-

- joice, re - joice, re - joice great - ly, O Daugh - ter of Zi - on; for be - hold, thy King, for be - hold,.... thy
- joice, re - joice, re - joice..... great - ly, O Daugh - ter of Zi - on; for be - hold, thy King, for be - hold, thy
King, for be - hold, thy King com - eth un - to thee, com - eth un - to thee, com - eth un - - to thee.
ritard. Maestoso.
King, for be - hold,.... thy King com - eth un - - to thee, com - eth un - to thee, com - eth un - - to thee.

SENTENCE. "Hear our prayer."

D. From "Harp of Judah." *By Permission.*

Hear our prayer, Hear our prayer, O God, in - cline thine ear; Hear our prayer, Hear - our
p
cres.
Hear our prayer, Hear our prayer, O God, in - cline thine ear; Hear...... our prayer, Hear...... our
Hear our prayer, Hear our
prayer, O God, in - cline thine ear; hide not thy - self from our pe - ti - tion, Hide not thy - self from
mf
prayer, O God, in - cline thine ear; hide not thy - self from our pe - ti - tion, Hide not thy self from

my pe - ti - tion. Un-to us, Un-to us, Un-to us, O God, in - cline thine ear.
Un - to us Un - to us, Un - to us,
f mf p
my pe - ti - tion. Un - to us, Un - to us, Un - to us, O God, in - cline thine ear.
Un-to us, Un-to us, Un-to us,
ADAGIO.
Hear our prayer, Hear our prayer, O God, in - cline thine ear, O God, in - cline thine ear. A - men.
p p
ppp
Hear our prayer, Hear our prayer, O God, in - cline thine ear, in - cline thine ear. A - men.

ANTHEM. "Make a joyful noise unto the Lord."

ALLEGRO.
Make a joy-ful noise un-to the Lord, Make a joy-ful noise un-to the
Make a joy-ful noise un-to the Lord,........
Make a joy-ful noise un-to the Lord,........ Make a joy-ful noise un-to the
Make a joy-ful noise un-to the Lord,
Lord, un-to the Lord, all the earth, all the earth; make a loud noise, and re-joice, and sing praise.
all.... the earth, all.... the earth;
Lord, un-to the Lord, all.... the earth, all.... the earth; make a loud noise, and re-joice, and sing praise.

SOPRANO SOLO.
MODERATO.
Sing un - to the Lord, Sing un-to the Lord with the harp, with the harp, with the harp, and the
TENOR.
Oh, sing un-to the Lord, Sing un-to the Lord, with the harp, with the harp, with the harp,
SOPRANO.
ALTO.
Oh, sing un-to the Lord, Sing un-to the Lord, with the harp, with the harp, with the harp
BASS.
voice of a psalm. Let the sea roar, and the full-ness there-of; the world, and they that dwell there-in, The
TENOR.
and the voice of a psalm.
ALTO.
SOPRANO.
and the voice of a psalm. Let the sea roar, and the full-ness there-of; the world, and they that dwell there-in, The

ALLEGRO.
world and they that dwell therein.
Let the floods clap their hands,..................
Let the floods clap their
Let the floods clap their hands,
Let the floods clap their hands,......................
world and they that dwell therein.
Let the floods clap their hands, clap their hands,
Let the floods clap their hands,......................
Let the floods clap their hands, Let the floods........ clap their hands, Let the floods clap their
hands, Let the floods clap their hands,.......... Let the floods clap their hands,
clap their hands, Let the floods clap their hands,
.... Let the floods clap their hands,
clap their hands.
.... Let the floods clap their hands,.......... Let the floods clap their hands, Let the floods clap their hands, Let the floods clap their hands.
hands......... Let the floods clap their hands,
clap their hands,
clap their hands,

Let the hills be joy - ful be - fore the Lord, Let the hills be
Let the hills be joy - ful be - fore the Lord, Let the hills be joy - ful be - fore the Lord,
Let the hills be joy - ful be - fore the Lord, Let the hills be joy - ful be - fore the Lord, Let the hills be
ANDANTE.
joy - ful be - fore the Lord, Let the hills be joy - ful be - fore the Lord. For he com-eth, for he com-eth to
joy - ful be - fore the Lord, Let the hills be joy - ful be - fore the Lord. For he com-eth, for he com-eth to

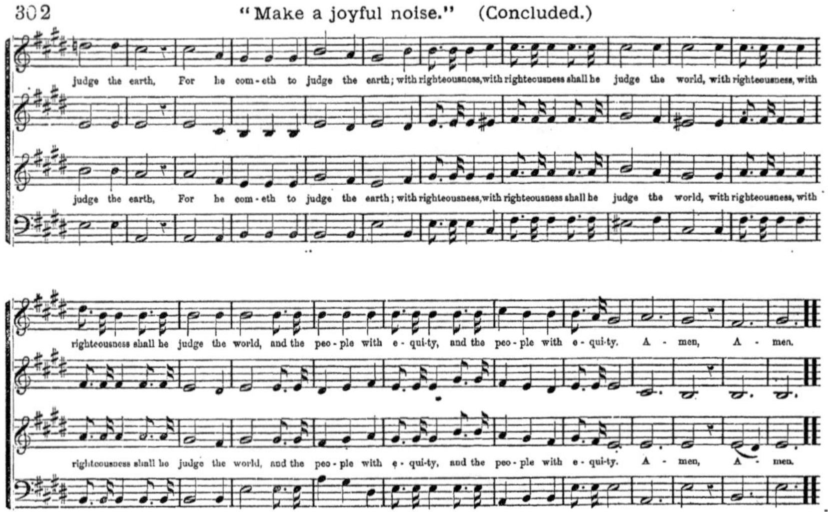
judge the earth, For he com-eth to judge the earth; with righteousness, with righteousness shall he judge the world, with righteousness, with
righteousness shall he judge the world, and the peo-ple with e-qui-ty, and the peo-ple with e-qui-ty. A-men, A-men.

ANDANTE.
Bow down thine ear, O Lord, and hear me, Bow down thine ear, O Lord, and hear me,
me, Bow down thine ear, O
Bow down thine ear, O Lord, and hear me, Bow down thine ear, O
Bow down thine ear, O Lord, and hear me, Bow down thine ear, O Lord, and hear me,
Bow down thine ear, O Lord, and hear me, for I am poor and need-y, I am poor and need-y. Pre-serve my
Lord, and hear me,
pp
Lord, and hear me, O Lord, and hear me, for I am poor and need-y, I am poor and need-y. Pre-serve my
hear me,

soul, Pre-serve my soul, Pre-serve my soul, for I am ho-ly; O thou, my God, save thy ser-vant, who trust-eth in thee.
cres - cen - do.
f
Repeat ad libitum.
soul, Pre-serve my soul, Pre-serve my soul, for I am ho-ly; O thou, my God, save thy ser-vant, who trust-eth in thee.
So will I praise thee, O God, and glo-ri-fy thy name, So will I praise thee, O God, and glo-ri-fy thy name.
f piu mosso.
So will I praise thee, O God, and glo-ri-fy thy name, So will I praise thee, O God, and glo-ri-fy thy name.

So will I praise thee, O..... Lord, So will I praise thee, O Lord, and glo - ri - fy thy name, and
So will I praise thee, O Lord, will I praise thee, O.... Lord,
So will I praise thee, O Lord, and glo - ri - fy thy name, and
So will I praise thee, O Lord,

1st time. 2d time. MAESTOSO.
glo - ri - fy thy name, So will I praise thee and glo - ri - fy thy name, name, and glo - ri - fy thy name. A - men.
pp ppp
glo - ri - fy thy name, So will I praise thee, and glo - ri - fy thy name, name, and glo - ri - fy thy name. A - men.

"How beautiful upon the mountains."

D.

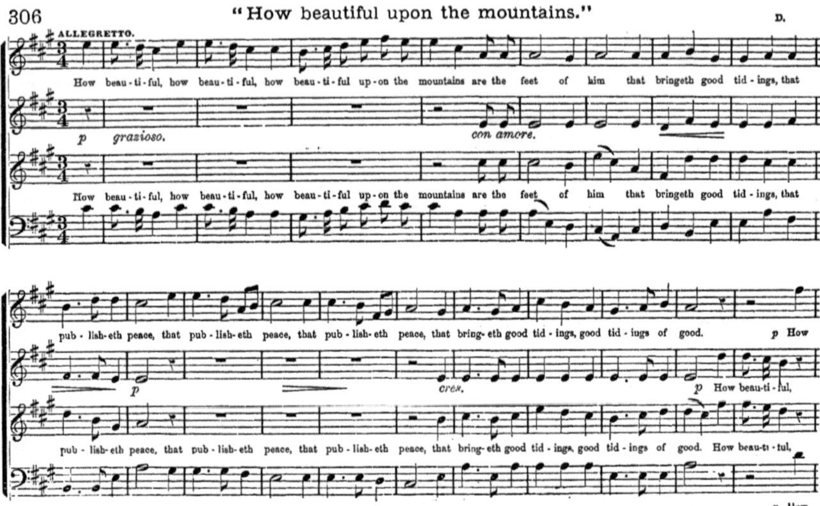
ALLEGRETTO.
How beau-ti-ful, how beau-ti-ful, how beau-ti-ful up-on the mountains are the feet of him that bringeth good tid-ings, that
p grazioso.
con amore.
How beau-ti-ful, how beau-ti-ful, how beau-ti-ful up-on the mountains are the feet of him that bringeth good tid-ings, that
pub-lish-eth peace, that pub-lish-eth peace, that pub-lish-eth peace, that bring-eth good tid-ings, good tid-ings of good. p How
p
cres.
p How beau-ti-ful,
pub-lish-eth peace, that pub-lish-eth peace, that pub-lish-eth peace, that bring-eth good tid-ings, good tid-ings of good. How beau-ti-tul,
p How

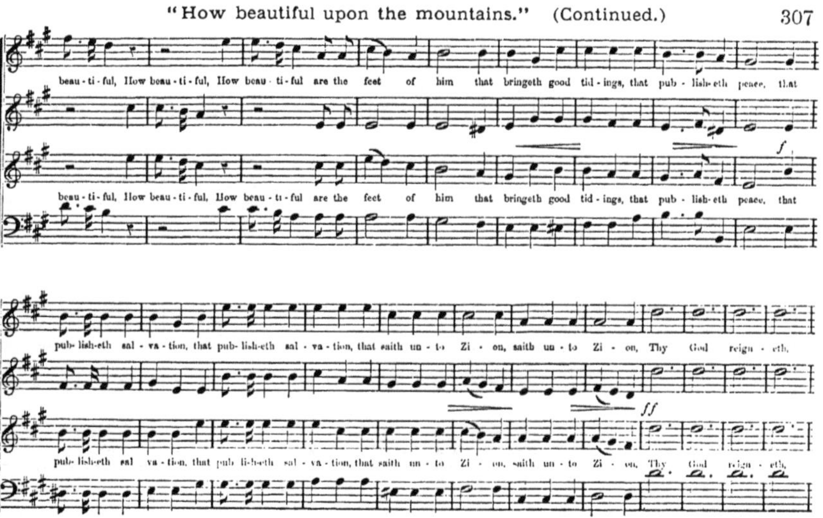
beau - ti - ful, How beau - ti - ful, How beau - ti - ful are the feet of him that bringeth good tid - ings, that pub - lish-eth peace, that
f
beau - ti - ful, How beau - ti - ful, How beau - ti - ful are the feet of him that bringeth good tid - ings, that pub - lish-eth peace, that
pub- lish-eth sal - va - tion, that pub- lish-eth sal - va - tion, that saith un - to Zi - on, saith un - to Zi - on, Thy God reign - eth,
ff
pub- lish-eth sal - va - tion, that pub- lish-eth sal - va - tion, that saith un - to Zi - on, saith un - to Zi - on, Thy God reign - eth,

fff
p
Thy God reign - eth, Thy God reign - eth. How beau - ti - ful, How beau - ti - ful, How beau - ti - ful up - on the mountains, How
beau - ti - ful up - on the mountains, How beau - ti - ful up - on the mountains, are the feet of him that bring - eth good tid - ings, that

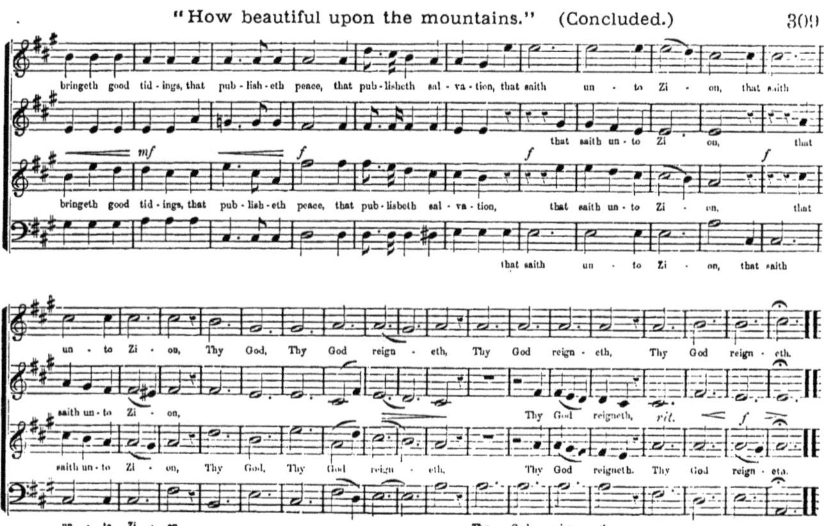
bringeth good tid - ings, that pub - lish - eth peace, that pub - lisheth sal - va - tion, that saith un - to Zi - on, that saith
that saith un - to Zi on, that
mf
f
f
f
bringeth good tid - ings, that pub - lish - eth peace, that pub - lisheth sal - va - tion, that saith un - to Zi - on, that
that saith un - to Zi - on, that saith
un - to Zi - on, Thy God, Thy God reign - eth, Thy God reign - eth, Thy God reign - eth.
saith un - to Zi - on, Thy God reigneth,
rit.
f
saith un - to Zi - on, Thy God, Thy God reign - eth, Thy God reigneth. Thy God reign - eth.
un - to Zi - on, Thy God reign - eth.

ANTHEM. "Lord, have mercy."

HAYDN.
Arranged for this work.

ALLEGRETTO. Four measures for prelude.
p SOLI.
Lord, have mer - cy up - on us, Lord, have mer-cy up - on us, up - on us, Lord, have mer - cy up - on us, O
SOLI.
p SOLI.
Lord, have mer - cy up - on us, Lord, have mer-cy up - on us, up - on us, Lord, have mer - cy up - on us, O
SOLI.
Lord, have mer-cy up - on us, O Lord, have mer - cy, have mer - cy,
Lord, have mer-cy up - on us, O Lord, have mer-cy up - on us,......
have mer - cy

TUTTI.
O Lord! have mer - cy upon us, up on us,
TUTTI. f
O Lord! have mer cy upon us, up on us
SOLI.
Lord, have mer - cy up - on us, for our trust is in......
SOLI
Lord, have mer cy up - on us, for our trust is in thee, for our trust is in
SOLI.
Lord, have mer - cy up - on us, for our trust is in thee, for our trust is in
SOLI.
Lord, have mer cy up - on us, for our trust is in......

thee, our trust........ is in thee,........ is in thee, in......... thee. Lord, have mer - cy up - on....
thee, our trust, our trust is in thee. Lord, have mer - cy up - - - on
thee, our trust... is................ in thee,.............. our trust is in thee. Lord, have mer - cy up - on....
thee, our trust is in thee, is in thee, in thee.
TUTTI.
us, our trust is in thee,...... is in thee,...... is in thee, our trust is in thee. Lord, have mer - cy up - - - on... us,
TUTTI.
us, our trust, our trust is in thee.
f TUTTI.
us, our trust.......... is in thee,........ is in thee,........... our trust is in thee. Lord, have mer - cy up - - - on... us,
our trust.... is in..... thee, in..... thee, is in thee

SOLI.
TUTTI.
Have mer - cy, have mer - cy, for our trust is in thee, is in.... thee, is.. in.... thee.
SOLI.
TUTTI.
Lord, have mer - cy up - - - on us, for our trust is in thee, is in...... thee, is.. in...... thee.
SOLI.
have mer - cy,
"If with all your hearts."
ANDANTE CANTABILE.
D.
If with all your hearts ye tru - ly seek me, ye shall ev - er sure - ly find me, saith our God, saith our God.
If with all your hearts ye tru - ly seek me, ye shall ev er sure - ly find me, saith our God, saith our God.

Ye shall find me, sure - ly find... me, saith our God.
p
SOLO.
Ye shall ev - er sure - ly find me, sure - ly find... me, saith our God. Oh, that I knew where I might
find him, that I might come........ be - fore his pres - ence; Oh, that I knew where I might find him, that I might come be-

If with all your hearts ye tru - ly seek me, ye shall ev - er sure - ly find me, saith our God,
pp
- fore his pres-ence. If with all your hearts ye tru - ly seek me, ye shall ev - er sure - ly find me, saith our God,
saith our God; If with all your hearts ye tru - ly seek me, ye shall ev - er sure - ly find me, saith our God.
mf
p
pp
rall.
ppp
saith our God; If with all your hearts ye tru - ly seek me, ye shall ev - er sure - ly find me, saith our God.

HYMN ANTHEM. "When the worn spirit wants repose."

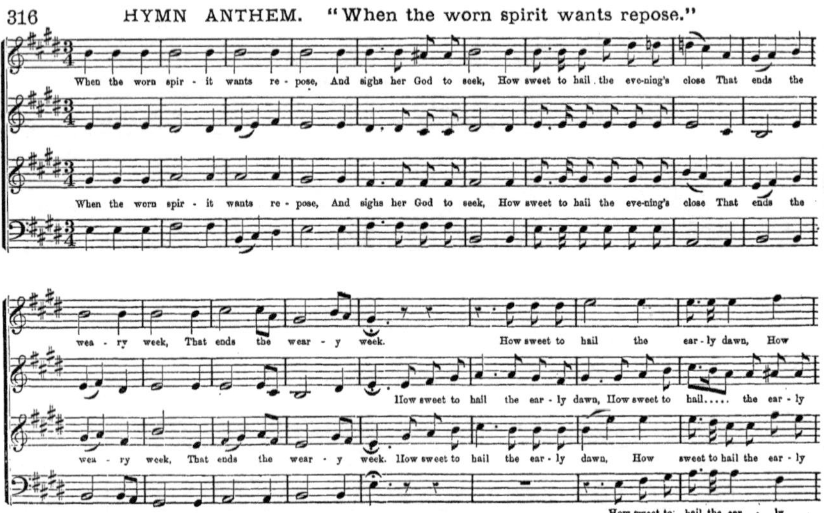
When the worn spir - it wants re - pose, And sighs her God to seek, How sweet to hail the eve-ning's close That ends the
When the worn spir - it wants re - pose, And sighs her God to seek, How sweet to hail the eve-ning's close That ends the
wea - ry week, That ends the wear - y week.
How sweet to hail the ear - ly dawn, How
How sweet to hail the ear - ly dawn, How sweet to hail..... the ear - ly
wea - ry week, That ends the wear - y week. How sweet to hail the ear - ly dawn, How sweet to hail the ear - ly
How sweet to hail the ear - ly

sweet to hail the ear - ly dawn That o - pens to the sight, When first the soul - - re - viv - ing morn Sheds forth its
dawn That o - - - pens to the sight,
dawn That o - - pens to the sight, When first the soul - re - viv - ing morn Sheds
dawn, How sweet to hail the ear - ly dawn That o - pens to the sight, When first the soul - - - - re - viv - ing morn
rays..... of light, Sheds forth its rays of light, Sheds forth its rays of light. Sweet day! thine hours too soon will
forth its rays of light, Sheds forth its rays of light, Sheds forth its rays of light. Sweet day! thine hours too soon will

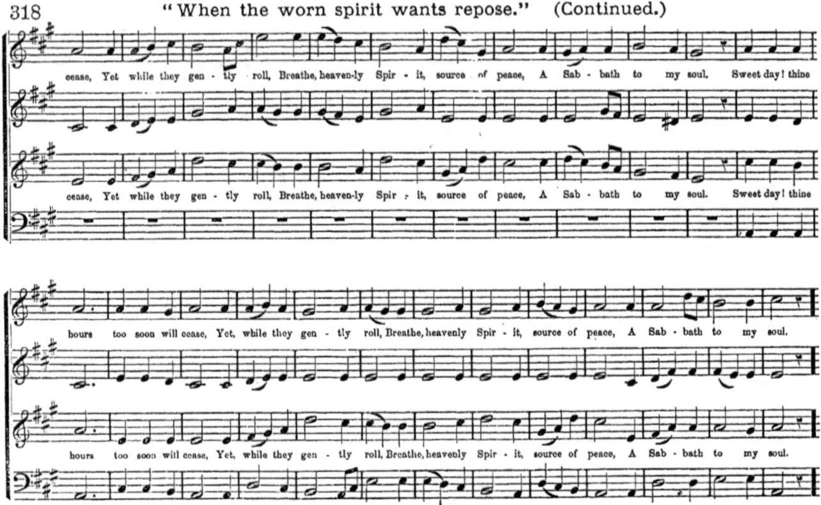
cease, Yet while they gen - tly roll, Breathe, heaven-ly Spir - it, source of peace, A Sab - bath to my soul. Sweet day! thine
cease, Yet while they gen - tly roll, Breathe, heaven-ly Spir - it, source of peace, A Sab - bath to my soul. Sweet day! thine
hours too soon will cease, Yet, while they gen - tly roll, Breathe, heavenly Spir - it, source of peace, A Sab - bath to my soul.
hours too soon will cease, Yet, while they gen - tly roll, Breathe, heavenly Spir - it, source of peace, A Sab - bath to my soul.

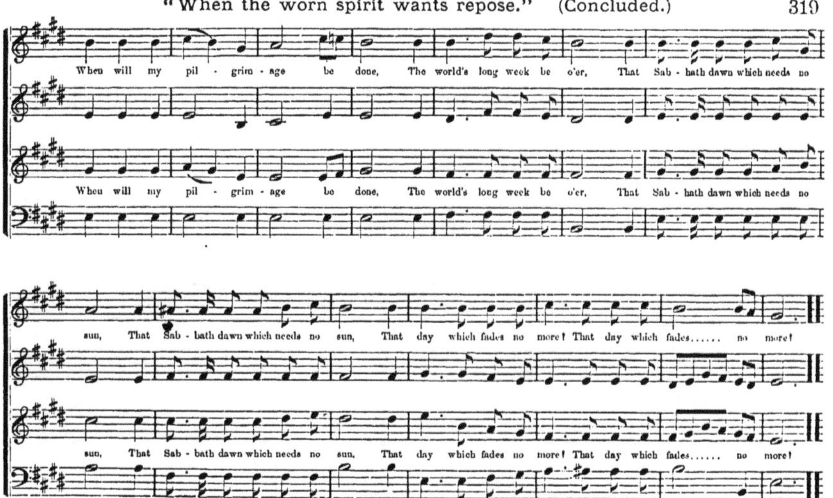
When will my pil - grim - age be done, The world's long week be o'er, That Sab - bath dawn which needs no
When will my pil - grim - age be done, The world's long week be o'er, That Sab - bath dawn which needs no
sun, That Sab - bath dawn which needs no sun, That day which fades no more! That day which fades...... no more!
sun, That Sab - bath dawn which needs no sun, That day which fades no more! That day which fades...... no more!

SOLO for Soprano voice.
Oh, how love-ly, how love-ly is Zi - on, Zi - on, cit - y of our God! Joy and peace shall dwell in thee, thanks-
CHORUS. ANDANTE.
p
cres.
p
Oh, how love-ly, how love-ly is Zi - on, Zi - on, cit - y of our God! Joy and peace shall dwell in thee, thanks-
- giv - ing, thanksgiv - ing and the voice of mel - o - dy.
SOLO. p
Oh, how love - ly how love - ly is Zi - on, Zi - on,
p
- giv - ing, thanksgiv - ing and the voice of mel - o - dy. Oh, how love - ly, how love - ly is Zi - on, Zi - on,

cit - y of our God! Joy and peace shall dwell in thee, thanks - giv - ing, thanks - giv - ing and the voice of mel - o - dy.
cit - y of our God! Joy and peace shall dwell in thee, thanks - giv - ing, thanks - giv - ing and the voice of mel - o - dy.
Oh, how love - ly, how love - ly is Zi - on, Zi - on, cit - y of our God! Oh, how love - - -
Oh, how love - ly is
Oh, how love - ly, how love - ly is Zi - on, Zi - on, cit - y of our God! Oh, how love - ly is

ly is Zi - - - - on, Oh, how love- - ly is Zi - on, cit - y of our God!
Zi - on, Oh, how love - ly is Zi - on, Oh, how lovely is Zi - on, Zi - on, cit - y of our God!
cres.
cres.
Zi - on, Oh, how love - ly is Zi - on, Oh, how lovely is Zi - on, Zi - on, cit - y of our God!
p Joy and peace shall dwell in thee, Joy and
Joy and peace shall dwell in thee, Joy and peace shall dwell in thee, Joy and
p
Joy and peace shall dwell in thee, Joy and peace shall dwell in thee, Joy and peace shall dwell in
Joy and peace shall dwell in thee, Joy and peace shall dwell in thee, Joy and

rit.
peace shall dwell in thee, Joy and peace.............. shall dwell in thee.
peace shall dwell in thee, Joy and peace shall dwell in thee, Joy and peace shall dwell in thee.
rit.
p
pp
thee, Joy and peace shall dwell in thee, Joy and peace shall dwell in thee.
peace shall dwell in thee, Joy and peace shall dwell in thee.
ANTHEM. "Oh, that men would praise the Lord."
MODERATO.
Oh, that men would praise the Lord for his goodness, and for his won-der-ful works to the chil-dren of men; Oh, that men would
Oh, that men would praise the Lord for his goodness, and for his won-der-ful works to the chil-dren of men; Oh, that men would

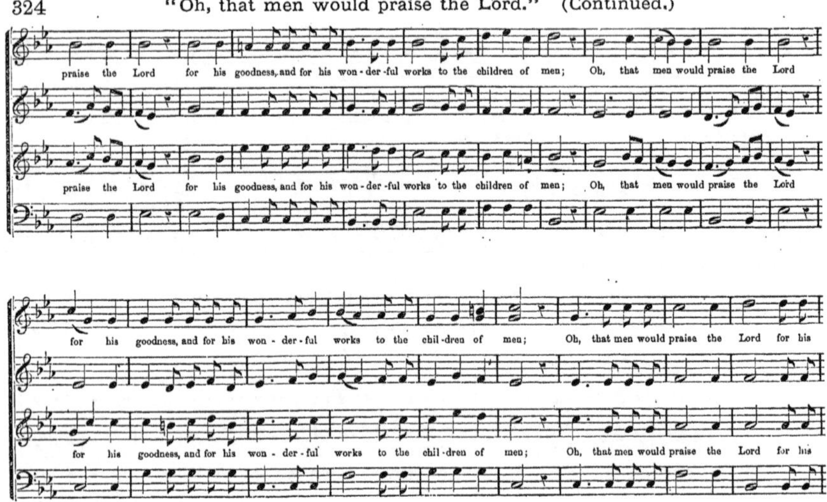
praise the Lord for his goodness, and for his won-der-ful works to the children of men; Oh, that men would praise the Lord
praise the Lord for his goodness, and for his won-der-ful works to the children of men; Oh, that men would praise the Lord
for his goodness, and for his won-der-ful works to the chil-dren of men; Oh, that men would praise the Lord for his
for his goodness, and for his won-der-ful works to the chil-dren of men; Oh, that men would praise the Lord for his

SOPRANO SOLO.
goodness, and for his won - der - ful works to the chil - dren of men. Oh,...... that men would praise the
TENOR.
Oh, that men would praise the Lord, Oh, that men would praise the
SOPRANO.
goodness, and for his won - der - ful works to the chil - dren of men. Oh, that men would praise the Lord, Oh, that men would praise the
ALTO.
BASS.
Lord, praise the Lord...... for his good- ness, and for his won - der - ful works to the chil - dren of men;
Lord, Oh, that men would praise the Lord, Oh, that men would praise the Lord, Oh, that men would praise the Lord,
Lord, Oh, that men would praise the Lord, Oh, that men would praise the Lord, Oh, that men would praise the Lord.

Oh, that men would praise the Lord for his good - ness, and for his won - der - ful works to the chil - dren of men;
Oh, that men would praise the Lord, praise the Lord,
Oh, that men would praise the Lord, praise the Lord for his good - ness, and for his won - der - ful works to the chil - dren of men;
Oh, that men would praise the Lord, would praise the Lord, would praise the Lord, would praise........ the Lord.
Oh, that men would praise the Lord, Oh, that men would praise the Lord, would praise the Lord, would praise the Lord, rit. would praise the Lord.
Oh, that men would praise the Lord, Oh, that men would praise the Lord, would praise the Lord, would praise the Lord, would praise the Lord.

ALLEGRO
Oh, come, let us sing un - to the Lord, let us heart - i - ly re - joice in the strength of our sal - va - tion. Let us come be -
Let us come be - fore his
Oh, come, let us sing un - to the Lord, let us heart - i - ly re - joice in the strength of our sal - va - tion. Let us come be - fore his
Let us come be -
- fore his presence with thanks - giv - ing, and show our-selves glad in him with psalms. Let us come be - fore his presence, Let us come be - fore his
pres - ence with thanks - giv - ing.
pres - ence with thanks - giv - ing, and show our-selves glad in him with psalms. Let us come be - fore his presence, Let us come be - fore his
- fore his presence with thanks - giv - ing.

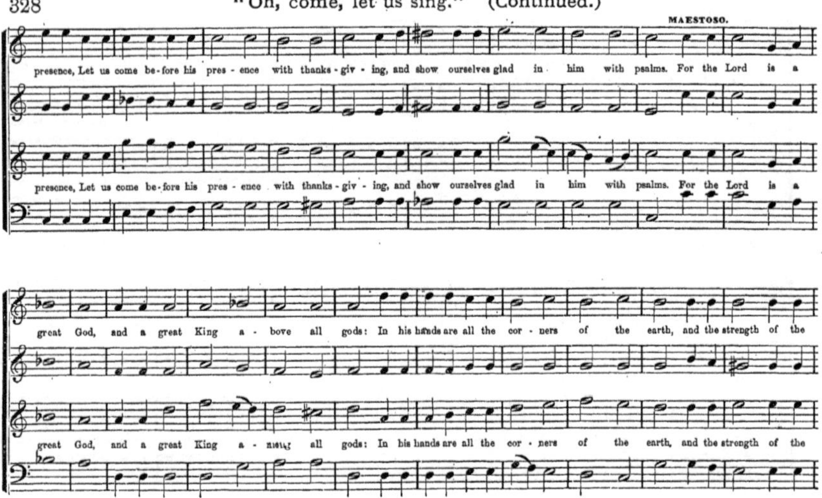
MAESTOSO.
presence, Let us come be-fore his pres - ence with thanks - giv - ing, and show ourselves glad in him with psalms. For the Lord is a
presence, Let us come be-fore his pres - ence with thanks - giv - ing, and show ourselves glad in him with psalms. For the Lord is a
great God, and a great King a - bove all gods: In his hands are all the cor - ners of the earth, and the strength of the
great God, and a great King a - bove all gods: In his hands are all the cor - ners of the earth, and the strength of the

MODERATO.
hills is his al - so. Let us wor - ship the Lord in the beau - ty of ho - liness, Let us wor - ship the Lord in the beau - ty of
p
hills is his al - so. Let us wor - ship the Lord in the beau - ty of ho - liness, Let us wor - ship the Lord in the beau - ty of
ho - li-ness, Let us wor - ship the Lord in the beau - ty of ho li-ness, let the whole earth stand in awe of him; For he
f
mf maestoso.
p
ho - li-ness, Let us wor - ship the Lord in the beau - ty of ho - li-ness, let the whole earth stand in awe of him; For he

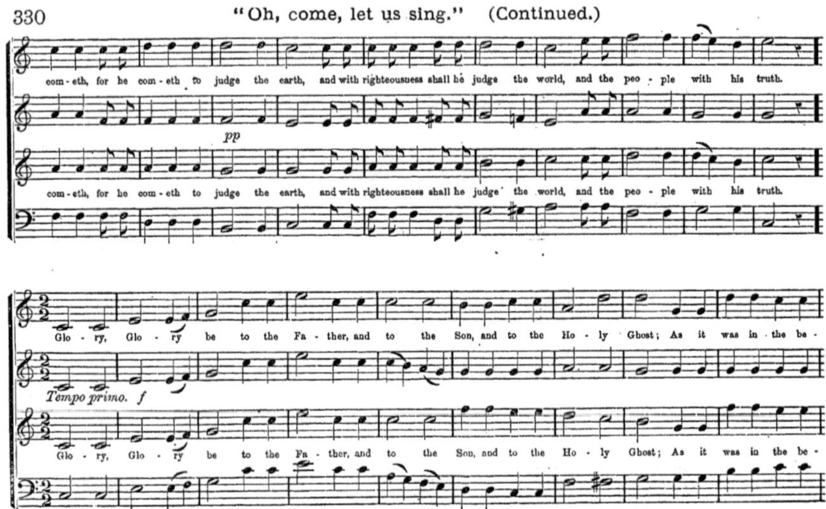
com - eth, for he com - eth to judge the earth, and with righteousness shall he judge the world, and the peo - ple with his truth.
pp
com - eth, for he com - eth to judge the earth, and with righteousness shall he judge the world, and the peo - ple with his truth.
Glo - ry, Glo - ry be to the Fa - ther, and to the Son, and to the Ho - ly Ghost; As it was in the be -
Tempo primo. f
Glo - ry, Glo - ry be to the Fa - ther, and to the Son, and to the Ho - ly Ghost; As it was in the be -

- gin-ning, is now, and ev - er shall be, world with-out end, world with-out end, world with-out end, A - men, A - men; world with-out
- gin-ning, is now, and ev - er shall be, world with-out end, world with-out end, world with-out end, A - men, A - men;
end,........... world with-out end, world with-out end, A - men, A - men; world with-out end, A - men.
world with-out end,
mf
f
ff
ritard. p
world with-out end, world with-out end,........... world with-out end, A - men, A - men; world with-out end. A - men.
world with-out end, world with-out end,..........

SENTENCE. "Whom have I in heaven but thee."

Dr. L. MASON.
From a coll. of church anthems, pub. in London, Eng.

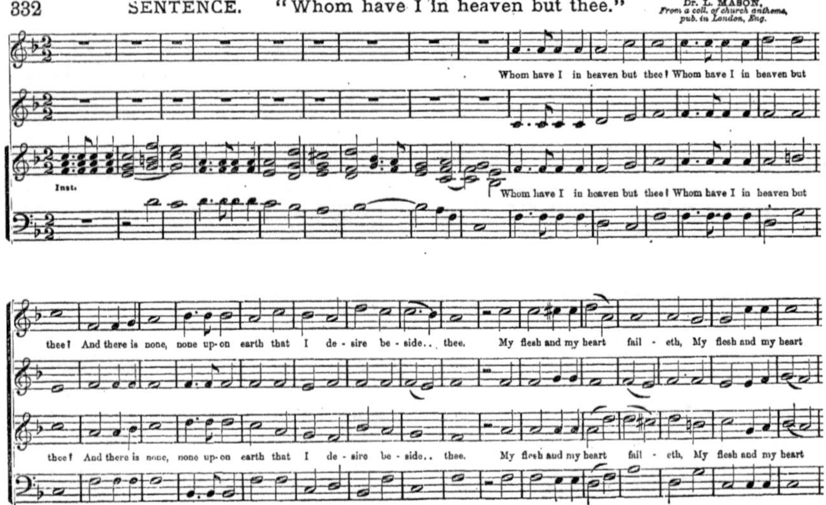
Inst.
Whom have I in heaven but thee! Whom have I in heaven but
thee! And there is none, none up-on earth that I de - sire be - side.. thee. My flesh and my heart fail - eth, My flesh and my heart

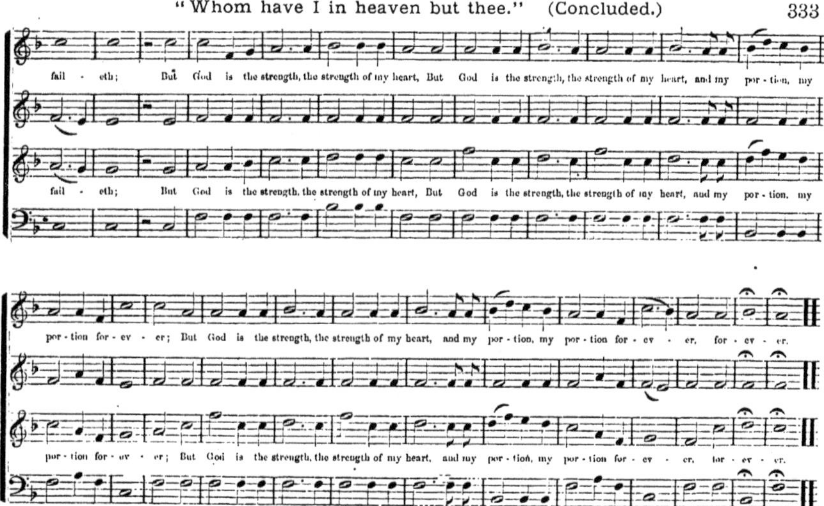
fail - eth; But God is the strength, the strength of my heart, But God is the strength, the strength of my heart, and my por - tion, my
fail - eth; But God is the strength, the strength of my heart, But God is the strength, the strength of my heart, and my por - tion, my
por - tion for - ev - er; But God is the strength, the strength of my heart, and my por - tion, my por - tion for - ev - er, for - ev - er.
por - tion for - ev - er; But God is the strength, the strength of my heart, and my por - tion, my por - tion for - ev - er, for - ev - er.

SENTENCE. "Blessed are the pure in heart."

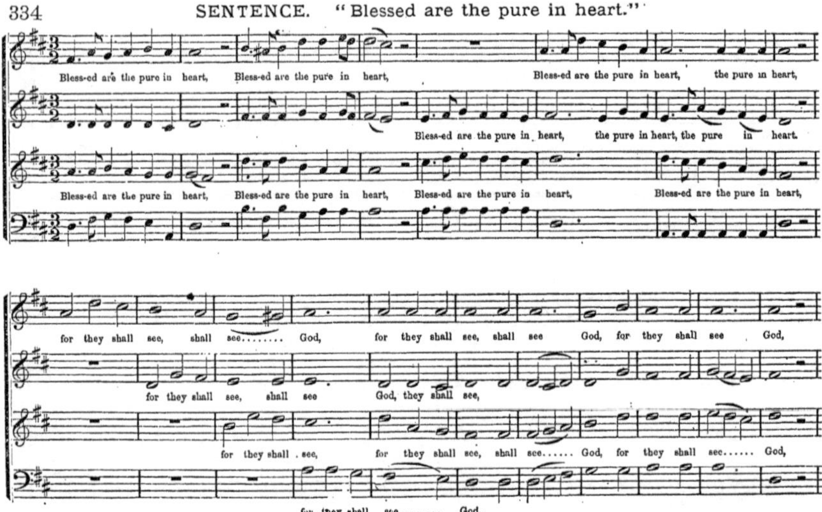
Bless-ed are the pure in heart, Bless-ed are the pure in heart, Bless-ed are the pure in heart, the pure in heart,
Bless-ed are the pure in heart, the pure in heart, the pure in heart.
Bless-ed are the pure in heart, Bless-ed are the pure in heart, Bless-ed are the pure in heart, Bless-ed are the pure in heart,
for they shall see, shall see........ God, for they shall see, shall see God, for they shall see God,
for they shall see, shall see God, they shall see,
for they shall . see, for they shall see, shall see...... God, for they shall see...... God,
for they shall see........ God,

for they shall see, for they shall see, shall see...... God, for they shall see...... God.
for they shall see, shall see God, they shall see,
for they shall see, shall see........ God, for they shall see, shall see...... God, for they shall see...... God.
for they shall see.......... God,
Bless - ed are the pure in heart, Bless - ed are the pure in heart, for they shall see... God.
Bless - ed are the pure in heart, Bless - ed are the pure in heart, the pure in heart,
mf rit. dim. pp
Bless - ed are the pure in heart, Bless - ed are the pure in heart, Bless - ed are the pure in heart, for they shall see... God.
Bless - ed are the pure in heart, the pure in heart.

SENTENCE. "Thou wilt show me."

W.

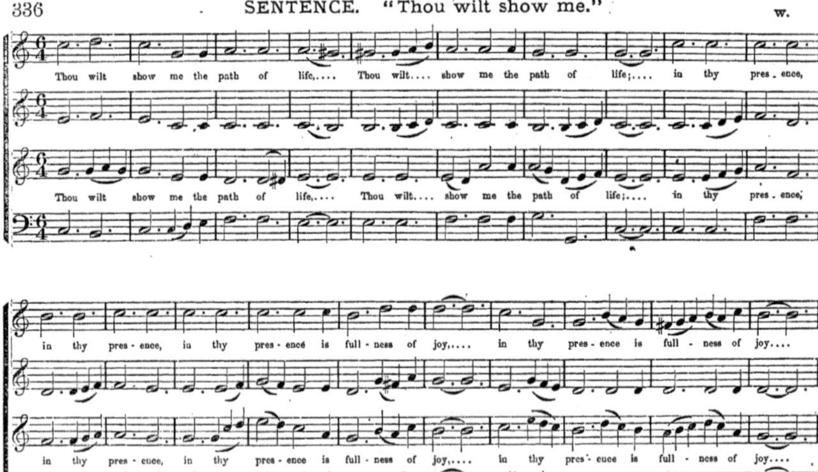
Thou wilt show me the path of life,.... Thou wilt.... show me the path of life;.... in thy pres - ence,
Thou wilt show me the path of life,.... Thou wilt.... show me the path of life;.... in thy pres - ence,
in thy pres - ence, in thy pres - ence is full - ness of joy,.... in thy pres - ence is full - ness of joy....
in thy pres - ence, in thy pres - ence is full - ness of joy,.... in thy pres - ence is full - ness of joy....

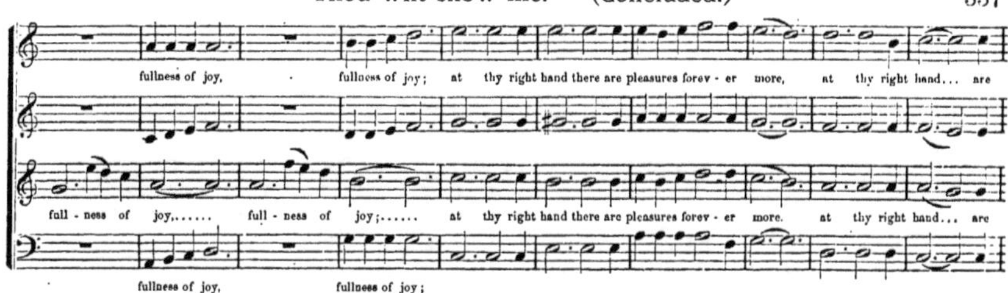

fullness of joy, fullness of joy; at thy right hand there are pleasures forev - er more, at thy right hand... are
full - ness of joy,...... full - ness of joy;...... at thy right hand there are pleasures forev - er more. at thy right hand... are
fullness of joy, fullness of joy;

pleasures forev - er more, at thy right hand there are pleasures forev - er more, at thy right hand there are pleasures forev - er more.
pleasures forev - er more, at thy right hand there are pleasures forev - er more, at thy right hand there are pleasures forev - er more

HYMN. "Hark! what mean those holy voices?"

ALLEGRETTO
Hark! Hark! Hark! what mean those ho - ly voic - es, Sweet - ly sound-ing through the
pp ppp pp Sotto voce.
Hark! Hark! Hark! what mean those ho - ly voic - es, Sweet - ly sound-ing through the
Oboe.
skies! Lo! th' an-gel - ic host re - joic - es, Lo! th' an-gel - ic host re - joic - es, Heaven-ly hal - le - lu - jahs rise:
pp mf cres. ff pp
skies! Lo! th' an-gel - ic host re - joic - es, Lo! th' an-gel - ic host re - joic - es, Heaven-ly hal - le - lu - jahs rise: Hear them

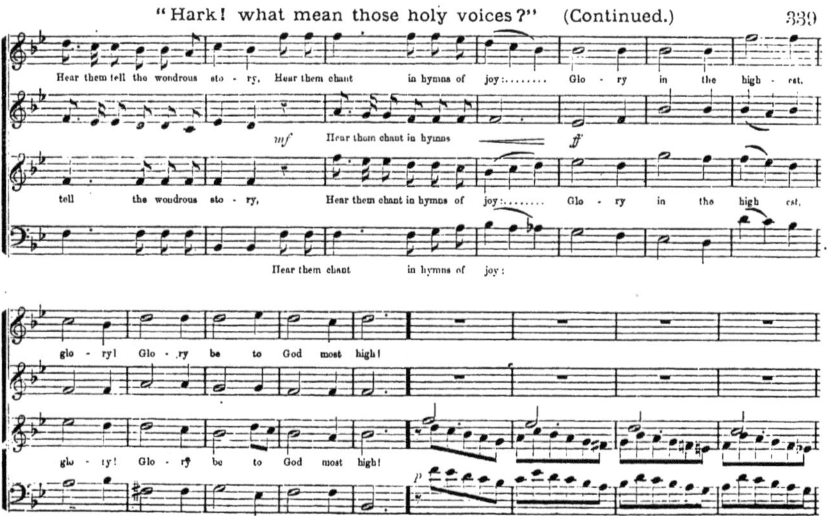
Hear them tell the wondrous sto - ry, Hear them chant in hymns of joy:........ Glo - ry in the high - est,
mf Hear them chant in hymns
ff
tell the wondrous sto - ry, Hear them chant in hymns of joy:........ Glo - ry in the high est,
Hear them chant in hymns of joy:
glo - ry! Glo - ry be to God most high!
glo - ry! Glo - ry be to God most high!
p

ANDANTE.
SOPRANO SOLO.
"Peace on earth, good - will...... from
heav - en, Reach - - ing far...... as man is found;
Souls re - deemed, and
p

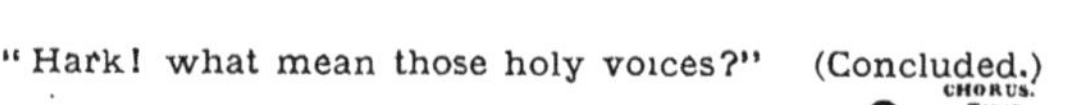

CHORUS.
Tenor.
"Christ is born! the great An -
Alto.
sins...... for - giv - en! Loud.... our gold - en harps shall sound.
"Christ is born! the great An -
Soprano.
f
"Christ is born! the great An -
Base.
- oint - ed; Heav'n and earth his prais - es sing! Oh, re - ceive whom God ap - point - ed, For your Proph - et, Priest, and King!"
- oint - ed; Heaven and earth his prais - es sing!
ff
- oint - ed; Heaven and earth his prais - es sing! Oh, re - ceive whom God ap - point - ed, For your Proph - et, - Priest, and King!"

HYMN. "Our blest Redeemer, ere he breathed."*

GEO. W. FOSTER.

SOLO—Soprano and Tenor.
1. Our blest Re - deem - er, ere he breathed His ten - der, last fare - well, A Guide, a Com - fort - er be-queathed
2. He came, sweet in - fluence to im - part, A gra - cious, will - ing Guest, While he can find one hum - ble heart
SOLO—Alto.
3. And ev - ery vir - tue we pos - sess, And ev - ery vic - tory won, And ev - ery thought of ho - li - ness,
Accompaniment.
With us......... to dwell, With us......... to dwell.
Where - in......... to rest, Where - in......... to rest.
Are his......... a - lone, Are his......... a - lone.
Interlude.

* *Play four measures for a Prelude. First verse, Soprano Solo; second verse, Tenor Solo; third verse, Alto Solo.*

Chorus to first and third Verses.
1. He came in tongues of liv - ing flame, To teach, con - vince, sub - due; All powerful as the wind he came, As view - less, too
FINE.
3. Spir-it of pur - i - ty and grace, Our weakness pit - ying see; O make our hearts thy dwelling-place, And worth - ier thee.
Chorus to second Verse.
2. And his that gen - tle voice we hear, Soft as the breeze of even, That checks each fault, that calms each fear, And speaks of heaven.
p
2. And his that gen - tle voice we hear, Soft as the breeze of even, That checks each fault, that calms each fear, And speaks of heaven.

SANCTUS.

Arranged from L. BORDESE.

ADAGIO.
Ho - ly, ho - ly, ho - ly, Lord, Lord God of Sa - ba - oth; Ho - ly, ho - ly, ho - ly,
p
p
Ho - ly, ho - ly, ho - ly, Lord, Lord God of Sa - ba - oth; Ho - ly, ho - ly, ho - ly,
f
Lord, Lord God of Sa - ba - oth: Heav - en and earth are full of thy glo - ry, Heav - en and
f
Lord, Lord God of Sa - ba - oth:
Heav - en is full of thy glo - ry,
f

earth are full of thy glo - ry; Ho - - san - na in the high - est! Ho - ly,
Ho - san - na, Ho - san - na, Ho - san - na in the high - est!
Ho - san - na, Ho - san - na, Ho - san - na in the high - est! Ho - ly,
Heav - en is full of thy glo - ry; Ho - - - san - na in the high - est!
ho - ly, ho - ly, Lord, Lord God of Sa - ba - oth; Ho - san na! Ho - san - - na!
ho - ly, ho - ly, Lord, Lord God of Sa - ba - oth; Ho - san na! Ho - san - na!

ANTHEM. "I will extol thee."

DUET.
I will ex - tol thee, I will ex - tol. thee, I will ex - tol thee, my God, O King; and I........ will
bless, and I........ will bless thee, and I will praise thy ho - ly name, thy ho - ly name, for ev - er - more.
I will ex - tol thee, I will ex - tol thee, I will ex - tol thee, my God, O King; and I will bless thee, I will
I will ex - tol thee, I will ex - tol thee, I will ex - tol thee, my God, O King; and I will bless thee, I will

bless thee, and I will bless thy ho - ly name for - ev - er more.
Glo - ry be to the Fa - ther, and to the
Glo - ry be to the Fa-ther, and to the Son, and to the Ho-ly
bless thee, and I will bless thy ho - ly name for - ev - er more.
Glo - ry be to the Fa - - - ther, and to the
Son, and to the Ho - ly Ghost, and to the Ho - ly Ghost;
As it
Ghost; Glo - ry be to the Fa-ther, and to the Son, and to the Ho - ly Ghost;
As it was in the be - gin-ning, as it
Son, and to the Ho - ly Ghost, and to the Ho - ly Ghost: As it was in the be - gin - - - ning, as it

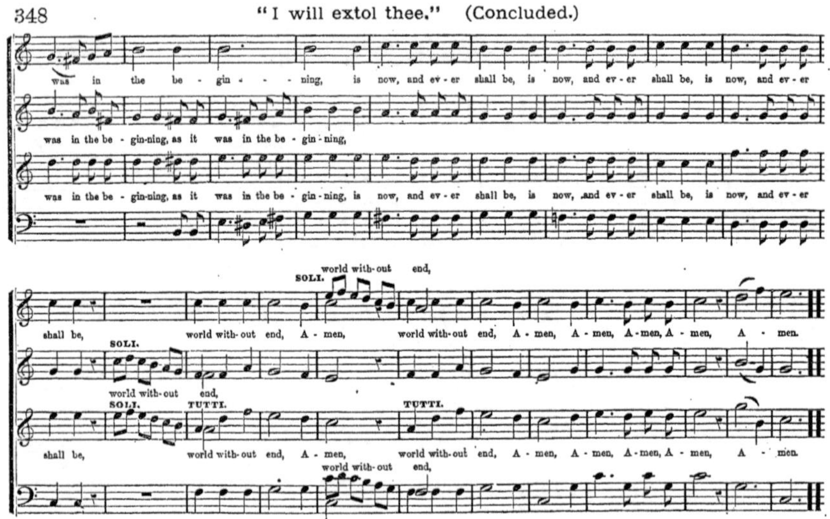
was in the be - gin - - - ning, is now, and ev - er shall be, is now, and ev - er shall be, is now, and ev - er
was in the be - gin-ning, as it was in the be - gin - ning,
was in the be - gin-ning, as it was in the be - gin - ning, is now, and ev - er shall be, is now, and ev - er shall be, is now, and ev - er
world with-out end,
SOLI.
shall be, world with-out end, A - men, world with-out end, A - men, A - men, A-men, A - men, A - men.
SOLI.
world with-out end,
SOLI.
TUTTI.
TUTTI.
shall be, world with-out end, A - men, world with-out end, A - men, A - men, A-men, A - men, A - men.
world with-out end,

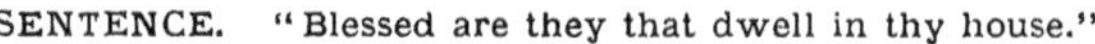

SENTENCE. "Blessed are they that dwell in thy house."

Blessed are they that dwell in thy house, Blessed are they that dwell in thy house; they will be still praising thee, still
they will be still praising thee, they will be still
Blessed are they that dwell in thy house, Blessed are they that dwell in thy house; they will be still praising thee, they will be still praising thee, still
they will be still

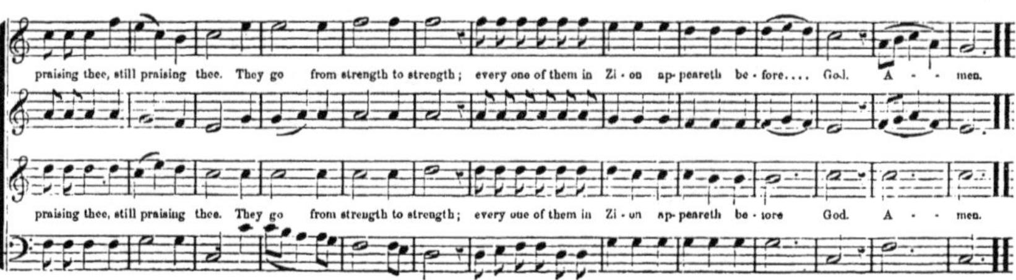
praising thee, still praising thee. They go from strength to strength; every one of them in Zi - on ap- peareth be - fore.... God. A - - men.
praising thee, still praising thee. They go from strength to strength; every one of them in Zi - on ap- peareth be - fore God. A - - men.

"Praise ye the Lord."

Chevalier SIGISMUND NEUKOMM.
From an original MS. furnished for this work by Dr. L. Mason.

Praise ye the Lord, O ye servants of the Lord; praise the name, praise the name, praise the name of the Lord.
p
praise the name, Bless - ed be the
Praise ye the Lord, O ye servants of the Lord; praise the name, praise the name of the Lord. Bless - ed be the
praise the name, praise the name,
Bless - ed be the name of the Lord, from this time forth, and for - ev - - er - more. From the ris - ing of the sun un- to the
name of the Lord, of the Lord,
name of the Lord, of the Lord, from this time forth, and for - ev - - er - more. From the ris - ing of the sun un- to the
Bless - ed be the name of the Lord.

go - ing down of the same, the Lord's name, Lord's name, the Lord's name is to be prais - ed, is to be prais - ed, is to be
same.......... the Lord's name, the Lord's name is to be
go - ing down of the same, the Lord's name, the Lord's name is to be prais - ed, the Lord's name is to be prais - ed, is to be
the Lord's name, the Lord's name, the Lord's name, the Lord's name is to be
prais - ed from this time forth and for ev - er - more, the Lord's name is to be prais - ed, is to be prais - ed, is to be
prais - ed from this time forth and for ev - er - more, the Lord's name is to be prais - ed, is to be prais - ed, is to be

prais-ed. Praise ye the Lord! praise ye the Lord! the Lord is high, is high a - bove all na - tions, and his
p
ff
prais-ed. Praise ye the Lord! praise ye the Lord! the Lord is high, is high a - bove all na - tions, and his
glo - ry, his glo - ry a - bove the heavens. Praise the Lord! praise the Lord! O.... ye serv - ants of the
O ye serv-ants of the Lord, O ye
glo - ry, his glo - ry a - bove the heavens. Praise the Lord! praise the Lord! O ye serv - ants, O ye
f
Praise the Lord! praise the Lord! praise the Lord! O praise the Lord! praise the

Lord, O.... ye serv - ants of the Lord, O ye serv - ants of the Lord, praise the name of the Lord from
servants of the Lord, praise the name of the Lord! praise the name,
servants of the Lord, praise the name... of the Lord! O ye servants of the Lord, praise the name, the name of the Lord from
Lord! praise the Lord! praise the Lord! O ye servants,
this time forth, from this time forth, and for ev - er - more, for ev - er - more, for ev - er - more.
this time forth, from this time forth, and for ev - er - more, for ev - er - more, for ev - er - more.
Ye servants of the Lord, praise the name of the Lord, for ev - er - more,

"Blessed be the Lord God of Israel."

V. NOVELLO, *from an original MS. furnished for this work, by Dr. L. Mason.*

SUBDUED, SLOW, AND SOLEMN.
LOUD.
Bless - ed, bless - ed, bless - ed be the Lord! bless - ed be the Lord God of Is - - ra - el; Bless - ed, bless - ed,
Bless - ed, bless - ed, bless - ed be the Lord! bless - ed be the Lord God of Is - - ra - el; Bless - ed, bless - ed,
bless - ed be the Lord! Bless - ed be the Lord God of Is - ra - el, from ev - er - last - ing and to ev - er - last - ing;
bless - ed be the Lord! Bless - ed be the Lord God of Is - ra - el, from ev - er - last - ing and to ev - er - last - ing;

SOLI.
Bless - ed be the Lord God of Is - ra - el, from ev - er - last - ing to ev - er - last - ing, from ev - er -
Bless - ed be the Lord God of Is - ra - el, from ev - er - last - ing to ev - er - last - ing, from ev - er -
last - ing and to ev - er - last - ing.
CHORUS—With Vigor, but not too fast.
Bless - ed be the
last - ing and to ev - er - last - ing.
Bless - ed be the Lord, God of Is - ra - el from ev - er - last - ing and to

Lord God of Is - ra - el from ev - er - last - ing and to ev - er - last - ing, and to ev - er - last -
Bless - ed be the Lord God of Is - ra - el from ev - er - last - ing and to ev - er -
Bless - ed be the Lord God of
ev - er - last - ing and to ev - er - last - ing.
- ing, and to ev - er - last - ing, ev - er - last - ing to ev - er -
- last - ing, ev - er - last - ing, from ev - er - last - ing to ev - er - last - ing, to ev - er -
Is - ra - el from ev - er - last - ing, from ev - er - last
Bless - ed be the Lord God of Is - ra - el from ev - er -

ev - er - last - - ing, ev - er - last - - - ing, ev - er - last - - - - -
- last - - - - - ing, ev - er, ev - er - last - ing, ev - er - last - - - - - - -
- - - - - - - - ing, ev - er - last - - - - ing.
- last - ing and to ev - er - last - ing, ev - er, ev - er - last - ing, ev - er - last - - - - - -
- - - - ing, from ev - er - last - - ing to ev - - - - - er - last - ing.
- - - - - - ing, from ev - er - last - ing to ev - er - last - - - - ing, ev - er -
- - - - - - - - ing,
ev - er - last -

Bless - ed be the Lord God of Is - ra - el from ev - er, ev - er - last - ing to ev - er, ev - er -
- last - - ing, ev - er - - last - - - ing, from ev - er - last - - - - - ing to ev - er, ev - - er-
Bless - ed be the Lord God of Is - ra - el from ev - er, ev - er - last - ing to ev - er, ev - er - last -
ing to ev - er,....... ev - er-
- last - - - ing, ev - er - last - ing to ev - er - last - ing to ev - er,
- last - - ing, ev - er - last - ing, to ev - - er - last - ing, ev - er -
- ing, ev - er - last - ing, to ev - er - last - ing, to ev - er,
- last - - - ing,

ev - er - last - - ing to ev - er - last - ing, ev - - - - - er - last - - ing, from ev - er -
- last - - - - - - - ing to ev - er - last - - - - - - - - - - - - ing, from ev - er -
ev - er - last - - ing to ev - - er - last - - - - - - - - - - - - - - - - - ing, from ev - er -
Bless - ed be the
- last - - - - ing to ev - er, ev - er - last - ing, and to ev - er - last - ing, ev - er - last - - ing.
last - - - - ing to ev - er - last - - - - ing, and to ev - er - last - ing, ev - er - last - ing.
- last - - - - ing to ev - er - last - - - - ing and to ev - er - last - - - - - - ing.
Lord God of Is - ra - el from ev - er, ev - er - last - - ing, and to ev - er - last - ing, ev - er - last - ing.

VENITE EXULTEMUS DOMINO.

1. Oh, come, let us sing un- | to the | Lord: |
Let us heartily rejoice in the | strength of | our sal- | vation.

2. Let us come before his presence | with thanks- | giving, |
And show ourselves | glad in | him with | psalms.

3. For the Lord is a | great — | God, |
And a great | King a- | bove all | gods.

4. In his hands are all the corners | of the | earth; |
And the strength of the | hills is | his — | also.

5. The sea is his, | and he | made it; |
And his hands pre- | pared·the | dry — | land.

6. Oh, come, let us worship | and fall | down, |
And kneel be- | fore the | Lord our | Maker.

7. For he is the | Lord our | God; |
And we are the people of his pasture, and the | sheep — | of his | hand.

8. Oh, worship the Lord in the | beauty·of | holiness; |
Let the whole earth | stand in | awe of | him.

9. For he cometh, for he cometh to | judge the | earth, |
And with righteousness to judge the world, and the | people | with his | truth.

GLORIA PATRI.

10. Glory be to the Father, | and·to the | Son, |
And | to the | Holy | Ghost;

11. As it was in the beginning, is now, and | ever·shall | be, |
World without | end. — | A- — | men.

No. 1. Single. J. BATTISHILL.

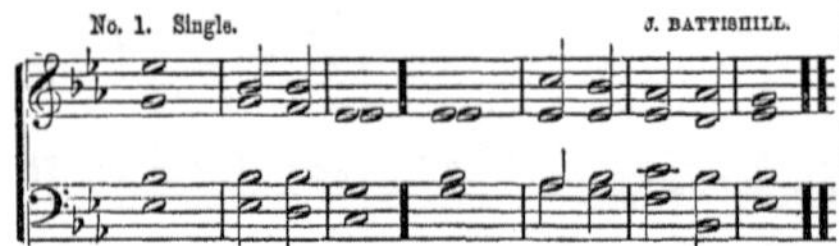

No. 2. Double.
D.
No. 3. Double.
W.
Solo or Unison.
Solo or Unison.

JUBILATE DEO.

1. OH, be joyful in the Lord, | all ye | lands; |
Serve the Lord with gladness, and come before his | presence | with a | song.

2. Be ye sure that the Lord | he is | God; |
It is he that hath made us, and not we ourselves; we are his people, and the | sheep of | his — | pasture.

3. Oh, go your way into his gates with thanksgiving, and into his | courts with | praise; |
Be thankful unto him and | speak good | of his | name.

4. For the Lord is gracious, his mercy is | ever- | lasting; |
And his truth endureth from gener- | ation·to | gener- | ation.

GLORIA PATRI.

5. Glory be to the Father, | and·to the | Son, |
And | to the | Holy | Ghost;

6. As it was in the beginning, is now, and | ever·shall | be; |
World without | end. — | A- — | men.

BENEDICTUS.

1. BLESSED be the Lord | God of | Israel, |
For he hath visited | and re- | deemed·his | people.

2. And hath raised up a mighty sal- | vation | for us, |
In the house | of his | servant | David.

3. As he spake by the mouth of his | holy | prophets, |
Which have been | since the | world be- | gan.

4. That we should be saved | from our | enemies, |
And from the | hand of | all that | hate us.

GLORIA PATRI.

5. Glory be to the Father, | and·to the | Son, |
And | to the | Holy | Ghost;

6. As it was in the beginning, is now, and | ever·shall | be, |
World without | end. — | A- — | men.

No. 4. Double.
No. 5. Single.
No. 6. Single.

CANTATE DOMINO.

1. Oh, sing unto the Lord a | new — | song; |
For he hath | done — | marvel-·lous | things.
2. With his own right hand and with his | holy | arm, |
Hath he | gotten·him- | self the | Victory.
3. The Lord declared | his sal- | vation; |
His righteousness hath he openly showed | in the | sight·of the | heathen.
4. He hath remembered his mercy and truth toward the | house of | Israel; |
And all the ends of the world have seen the sal- | vation | of our | God.
5. Show yourselves joyful unto the Lord, | all ye | lands; |
Sing, re- | joice, and | give — | thanks.
6. Praise the Lord up- | on the | harp; |
Sing to the harp with a | psalm — | of thanks- | giving.
7. With trumpets | also, ·and | shawms; |
Oh, show yourselves joyful be- | fore the | Lord the | King.
8. Let the sea make a noise, and all that | therein | is; |
The round world, and | they that | dwell there- | in.
9. Let the floods clap their hands, and let the hills be joyful together be- | fore the | Lord; |
For he | cometh·to | judge the | earth.
10. With righteousness shall he | judge the | world; |
And the | people | with — | equity.

GLORIA PATRI.

11. Glory be to the Father, | and·to the | Son, |
And | to the | Holy | Ghost.
12. As it was in the beginning, is now, and | ever·shall | be, |
World without | end. — | A- — | men.

BONUM EST CONFITERI.

1. It is a good thing to give thanks un- | to the | Lord; |
And to sing praises unto thy | name, — | O Most | Highest.
2. To tell of thy loving-kindness early | in the | morning; |
And of thy truth | in the | night — | season.
3. Upon an instrument of ten strings, and up- | on the | lute; |
Upon a loud instrument, | and up- | on the | harp.
4. For thou, Lord, hast made me glad | through thy | works; |
And I will rejoice in giving praise for the ope- | rations | of thy | hands.

GLORIA PATRI.

5. Glory be to the Father, | and·to the | Son, |
And | to the | Holy | Ghost.
6. As it was in the beginning, is now, and | ever·shall | be, |
World without | end. — | A- — | men.

No. 7. Double.
D.
No. 8. Single.
D.
No. 9. Single.
DUPUIS.

DEUS MISEREATUR.

1. God be merciful unto | us, and | bless us; |
And show us the light of his countenance, and be | merci-·ful | unto | us.
2. That thy way may be | known up-·on | earth: |
Thy saving | health a- | mong all | nations.
3. Let the people praise | thee, O | God; |
Yea, let | all the | people | praise thee.
4. Oh, let the nations rejoice, | and be | glad; |
For thou shalt judge the folk righteously, and govern the | nations | up-on | earth.
5. Let the people praise | thee, O | God; |
Yea, let | all the | people | praise thee.
6. Then shall the earth bring | forth her | increase; |
And God, even our own | God, shall | give us·his | blessing.
7. God shall | bless — | us, |
And all the ends of the | world shall | fear — | him.

GLORIA PATRI.

8. Glory be to the Father, | and·to the | Son, |
And | to the | Holy | Ghost;
9. As it was in the beginning, is now, and | ever·shall | be, |
World without | end. — | A- — | men.

BENEDIC ANIMA MEA.

1. Praise the Lord, | O my | soul; |
And all that is within me | praise his | holy | name.
2. Praise the Lord, | O my | soul; |
And for- | get not | all his | benefits.
3. Who forgiveth | all thy | sin; |
And healeth | all — | thine in- | firmities.
4. Who saveth thy life | from de- | struction, |
And crowneth thee with | mercy·and | loving- | kindness.
5. Oh, praise the Lord, ye angels of his, ye that ex- | cel in | strength; |
Ye that fulfil his commandment, and hearken unto the | voice — | of his | word.
6. Oh, praise the Lord, all | ye his | hosts; |
Ye servants of | his that | do his | pleasure.
7. Oh, speak good of the Lord, all ye works of his, in all places of | his do- | minion; |
Praise thou the | Lord, — | O my | soul.

GLORIA PATRI.

8. Glory be to the Father | and·to the | Son, |
And | to the | Holy | Ghost;
9. As it was in the beginning, is now, and | ever·shall | be, |
World without | end. — | A- — | men.

No. 10. Double.
D.
No. 11. Single.
All the voices in unison.
Gregorian.
No. 12. Single.
D.

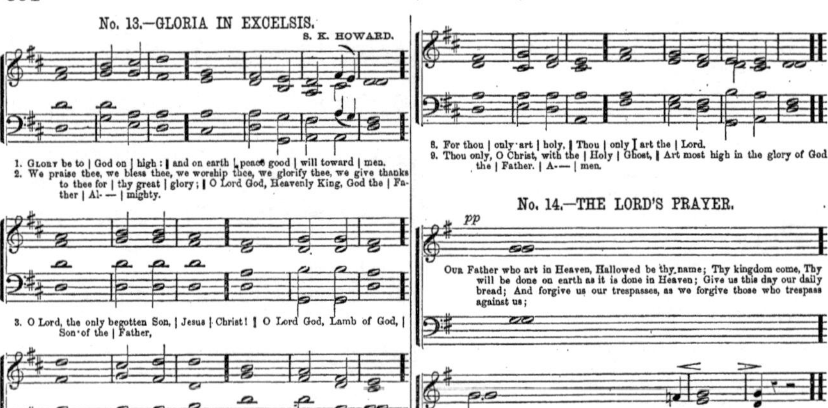
No. 13.—GLORIA IN EXCELSIS.
S. K. HOWARD.
1. Glory be to | God on | high : ‖ and on earth | peace good | will toward | men.
2. We praise thee, we bless thee, we worship thee, we glorify thee, we give thanks to thee for | thy great | glory ; ‖ O Lord God, Heavenly King, God the | Father | Al- — | mighty.
3. O Lord, the only begotten Son, | Jesus | Christ ! ‖ O Lord God, Lamb of God, | Son·of the | Father,
4. That takest away the | sins·of the | world, ‖ Have mercy | upon | us.
5. Thou that takest away the | sins·of the | world, ‖ Have mercy | upon | us.
6. Thou that takest away the | sins·of the | world, ‖ Re- | ceive our | prayer.
7. Thou that sittest at the right hand of | God the | Father, ‖ Have mercy | upon | us.
8. For thou | only·art | holy, ‖ Thou | only | art the | Lord.
9. Thou only, O Christ, with the | Holy | Ghost, ‖ Art most high in the glory of God the | Father. | A- — | men.
No. 14.—THE LORD'S PRAYER.
pp
Our Father who art in Heaven, Hallowed be thy name; Thy kingdom come, Thy will be done on earth as it is done in Heaven; Give us this day our daily bread; And forgive us our trespasses, as we forgive those who trespass against us;
And lead us not into temptation, But deliver us from evil; For thine is the kingdom, and the power, and the glory for..........ev-er. A - men.

No. 15.—TE DEUM LAUDAMUS.

1. *Decani* (or *Minister.*) We praise thee, O God; we acknowledge thee to be the | Lord.
Cantoris (or *Choir.*) All the earth doth worship thee, the Father ever- | lasting.
Dec. To thee all Angels cry a loud; the Heavens, and all the powers there- | in.
Chorus. To thee, Cherubim and Seraphim con- | tinual- | ly do | cry,

2. *Chorus.* Holy, Holy, Ho- | ly,
Lord God of | Sabaoth:
Heaven and Earth are | full
Of the | Majesty | of thy | Glory.

3. *Dec.* The glorious company of the Apostles praise | thee;
Cant. The goodly fellowship of the Prophets praise | thee;
Dec. The noble army of Martyrs praise | thee;
Chor. The holy Church, throughout all the world, | doth ac- | knowledge | thee,

4. *Dec.* The Father of an infinite Majesty; thine adorable, true, and only | Son;
Cant. Also, the Holy Ghost, the | Comforter.
Dec. Thou art the King of Glory, O | Christ;
Chor. Thou art the everlasting | Son — | of the | Father.

5. *Dec.* When thou tookest upon thee to deliver | man,
Cant. Thou didst humble thyself to be born of a | Virgin.
Dec. When thou hadst overcome the sharpness of | death,
Chor. Thou didst open the kingdom of | Heaven to | all be- | lievers.

6. *Dec.* Thou sittest at the right hand of God, in the glory of the | Father.
Cant. We believe that thou shalt come to be our | Judge.
Dec. We therefore pray thee, help thy servants, whom thou hast redeemed with thy precious | blood.
Chor. Make them to be numbered with thy Saints, in | glory | ever- | lasting.

7. *Dec.* O Lord, save thy people, and bless thine | heritage.
Cant. Govern them, and lift them up for- | ever.
Chor. Day by day we magnify | thee:
Chor. And we worship thy Name ever, | world with- | out — | end.

8. *Dec.* Vouchsafe, O Lord, to keep us this day without | sin.
Cant. O Lord, have mercy upon us, have mercy up- | on us.
Dec. O Lord, let thy mercy be upon us, as our trust is in | thee.
Chor. O Lord, in thee have I trusted; let me | never | be con- | founded.

No. 16.—MY GOD, MY FATHER.

1. My God, my Father, while I stray Far from my home, on | life's rough | way,
Oh, teach me from my heart to say, "Thy | will, my | God, be | done."

2. Though dark my path and sad my lot, Let me be still, and | murmur | not,
And breathe the prayer divinely taught, "Thy | will, my | God, be | done."

3. What though in lonely grief I sigh For friends beloved no | longer | nigh;
Submissive still would I reply, "Thy | will, my | God, be | done."

4. If thou shouldst call me to resign What most I prize,—it | ne'er was | mine,—
I only yield thee what is thine; "Thy | will, my | God, be | done."

5. Renew my will from day to day, Blend it with thine, and | take a- | way
Whate'er now makes it hard to say, "Thy | will, my | God, be | done."

6. Then when on earth I breathe no more, The prayer oft mixed with | tears be- | fore
I'll sing upon a happier shore: "Thy | will, my | God, be | done."

ABBOTSFORD, 168
Abbie, 164
Actena, 228
Adams, 243
Addie, 209
Advent, 131
Agnus, 140
Alard, 143
Alna, 221
Alpha, 166
America, 241
Annie, 94
Appleton, 229
Armagh, 250
Armor, 67
Arnim, 99
Arnold, 251
Arville, 96
Ashland, 118
Ashland, 119
Atrem, 95
Auburn, 135
Aurora, 100
Aybol, 82
BACON, 130
Baden, 186
Baker, 75
Balerma, 160
Barrows, 107
Bath, 83
Bates, 245
Bayonne, 180
Beames, 167
Belleville, 80
Bemis, 177
Benevento, 217
Benham, 214
Benedictus, 152
Benton, 259
Berlin, 102
Berrean, 135
Berne, 78
Bethany, 244
Bloomfield, 238
Bondee, 172
Bowman, 167
Boyd, 64
Boylston, 165
Bradford, 125
Bradbury, 182
Briery, 188
Buckminster, 157
Bufford, 78
CALAMINT, 72
Calais, 218
Caldwell, 285
Calvary, 281
Canby, 176
Cantor, 124
Caroline, 173
Carroll, 96
Carrie, 79
Cavare, 147
Cereal, 258
Claflin, 106
Chauncey Street, 154
Champney, 184
Charton, 200
Chesuncook, 146
Clifton, 230
Cobden, 250
Compassion, 66
Companionship, 214
Contrition, 87
Conquest, 247
Conrad, 251
Conway, 261
Corry, 88
Cowper, 161
Crandon, 236
Credo, 149
Cronstadt, 150
Crosby, 128
Currier, 212
Cutler, 218
DALE, 130
Dante, 118
Dalston, 198
Deane, 81
Dedham, 159
Denfield, 161
Dennett, 174
Dennis, 186
Devotion, 215
Dion, 249
Downs, 160
Drake, 141
Drummond, 187
Duke Street, 109
Dundee, 159
Dunning, 92
Duren, 164
EBENE, 116
Eidda, 182
Elsdale, 118
Elden, 179
Ella, 292
Elliot, 248
Emery, 240
Emerson, 145
Emma, 121
Empire, 75
Energy, 69
Engelhart, 114
Enstein, 60
Evandale, 84
Evan, 161
Everett, 202
FAIRSTAR, 87
Faith, 225
Farmington, 167
Fatherland, 254
Federal Street, 110
Fides, 246
Field, 187
Finland, 129
Fisher, 146
Fletcher, 157
Flint, 169
Flora, 97
Florence, 97
Forest Hill, 70
Forester, 88
Fount, 221
Franklin, 206
Freeman, 190
Fribourg, 148
GASCONY, 169
Germain, 208
Georgia, 101
Gilman, 229
Glade, 201
Gladness, 204
Glenburn, 243
Glenwood, 242
Goodwin, 147
Goodrich, 216
Gordon, 242
Gorton, 186
Gould, 281
Grace, 207
Gratitude, 197
Greenville, 227
Greenwood, 71
Greenbush, 188
Grover, 137
Guest, 95
HALE, 232
Hall, 84
Halle, 158
Halsey, 172
Hamburg, 108
Hanson, 188
Happy Home, 115
Harrington, 100
Hartland, 99
Hartwell, 180
Hartford, 189
Hart, 166
Hawthorne, 237
Heavenly Rest, 209
Hebron, 110
Hedge, 183
Helmweh, 175
Helen, 255
Homewell, 94
Himmel, 184
Holman, 245
Hooper, 181
Hosanna, 249
Howland, 150
Hudson, 156
Hullah, 182
Hume, 162
Humility, 222
IDA, 205
Ilba, 158
Invitation, 210
Irving, 72
Israel, 209
Italian Hymn, 241
Janvrin, 120
Jarvis, 242
Jasper, 158
Jewett, 206
Jones, 117
Josquin, 112
Jubilee, 230
Juniper, 254
Justin, 183
KATAHDIN, 115
Kenderwood, 254
Kent, 224
Kimball, 71
Kindness, 178
Kineo, 186
LABAN, 186
Lancaster, 220
Lacy, 65
Lanzon, 91
Laudamus, 68
Laudate, 122
Laughton, 233
Leira, 191
Leon, 228
Lille, 210
Lily Cove, 184
Lime Street, 188
Lindner, 219
Lindell, 246
Lincoln, 102
Linwood, 143
Little, 285
Lizzie, 202
Leshe, 156
Lowe, 85
Lynde, 247
Lynne, 165
MALTBY, 247
Manton, 76
Margate, 86
Marie, 151
Martyn, 217
Marlow, 159
Marshfield, 194
Masardis, 85
Masonda, 200
Meditation, 128
Menville, 64
Merlin, 196
Mentor, 211
Mercy Seat, 98
Merrill, 212
Mernet, 74
Messer, 195
Millinoket, 131
Milton, 207
Minden, 199
Minnie, 215
Mission, 240
Missionary Chant, 108
Monadnock, 248
Monroe, 258
Monson, 98
Montville, 198
Moore, 177
Mortland, 205
Morton, 65
Mount Vernon, 227
Munich, 165
Myrtle, 112
NAOMI, 161
Nellie, 101
Newell, 256
Newtonville, 171
Noonday, 77
Norway, 68
Nuremberg, 217
Nutbush, 179
OAK, 244
Oakland, 201
Olivet, 241
Olmutz, 185
Onge, 120
Orland, 184
Ortonville, 160
Otella, 223
Ossagon, 257
PARDON, 252
Parker, 128
Parma, 89
Patrius, 67
Patten, 108
Payson, 238
Pearson, 187
Pembroke, 122
Perkins, 252
Perth, 142
Peterson, 208
Petition, 192
Pierpont, 98
Pine Hill, 226
Pleyel, 204
Pleyel's Hymn, 217
Plummer, 257
Pope, 104
Porter, 211
Praise, 198
Princeburg, 258
Princeton, 140
Purity, 188
Putney, 163
QUAIN, 149
Quietude, 284
Quito, 163
RADWAY, 256
Redeemer, 128
Reflection, 170
Reign, 198
Repose, 253
Rest, 89
Restoration, 121
Resignation, 200
Resurrection, 225
Rheims, 91
Roberts, 196
Rockingham, 109
Rockland, 116
Roche, 192
Rolliston, 190
Rosedale, 110
Roseland, 144
Roulstone, 237
Rowland, 175
Ruhe, 220
SABBATH, 77
Sacrifice, 111
Sadie, 219
Sanford, 245
Sanctus, 92
Sargent, 168
Seldon, 236
Serene, 170
Sharon, 154
Shenley, 68
Shepard, 199
Sherman, 82
Shield, 152
Sicily, 227
Silsby, 174
Spartus, 155
Spencer, 148
Spohr, 117
Spring, 232
Stamford, 234
Stanton, 129
Stanwood, 80
Star, 127
State Street, 185
Stephens, 160
Stillwell, 136
Still Waters, 111
Stonefield, 109
Stowell, 105
Strong, 66
St. Anns, 159
St. Thomas, 185
Submission, 246
Sumner, 158
Sunrise, 189
Sunset, 195
Sympathy, 137
TARSUS, 93
Temple Grove, 218
The Old Hundred, 108
Thornburn, 155
Thurston, 216
Todd, 194
Topsfield, 107
Tower, 74
Townsend, 102
Transport, 127
Truman, 144
Twilight, 76
ULM, 90
Unity, 262
Upham, 108
Uxbridge, 100
VALE, 203
Vassalboro, 139
Veranta, 188
Vernon, 258
Verona, 256
Vesper, 226
Vienna, 218
Vincent, 145
Vineland, 81
Vining, 200
Violet, 258
Vintner, 73
WACHUSETT, 114
Waldo, 238
Wardwell, 178
Ward, 108
Warren, 239
Waterville, 197
Watkins, 126
Wellman, 106
Wesley, 181
Whittaker, 195
Wiemar, 151
Wien, 120
Willow, 189
Wilmot, 227
Windham, 110
Winner, 182
Woodland, 176
Woodstock, 69
Woodvale, 240
Wreath, 230

METRICAL INDEX.

L. M.

Annie, 94
Armor, 67
Arnim, 99
Arville, 96
Atrem, 95
Aurora, 100
Aybel, 82
Baker, 75
Barrows, 107
Belleville, 80
Berlin, 102
Berne, 78
Boyd, 64
Bufford, 73
Calamint, 72
Carroll, 96
Claflin, 106
Compassion, 66
Contrition, 87
Corry, 88
Deane, 81
Duke Street, 109
Dunning, 92
Empire, 75
Energy, 69
Enstein, 70
Evandale, 84
Fairstar, 87
Federal Street, 110
Flora, 97
Florence, 97
Forest Hill, 70
Forester, 68
Georgia, 101
Greenwood, 71
Guest, 95
Hall, 84
Hamburg, 108
Harrington, 100
Hartland, 99
Hebron, 110
Homewell, 94
Irving, 72
Kimball, 71
Lacy, 65
Lanzon, 91
Laudamus, 63
Lincoln, 102
Lowe, 85
Manton, 76
Masardis, 85
Menville, 64
Mercy Seat, 98
Mernet, 74
Missionary Chant, 108
Monson, 98
Morton, 65
Nellie, 101
Noonday, 77
Norway, 68
Parma, 89
Patrius, 67
Patten, 103
Pierpont, 98
Pope, 104
Rest, 89
Rheims, 91
Rockingham, 109
Rosedale, 110
Sabbath, 77
Sanctus, 92
Shenley, 68
Sherman, 82
Stanwood, 80
Stonefield, 109
Stowell, 105
Strong, 66
Tarsus, 93
The Old Hundred, 108
Topsfield, 107
Tower, 74
Twilight, 76
Upham, 103
Uxbridge, 109
Vineland, 81
Vintner, 78
Ward, 108
Wellman, 106
Windham, 110
Woodstock, 69

L. M. Double.

Bath, 83
Margate, 86

L. M. 6 lines.

Carrie, 79
Ulm, 90

C. M.

Advent, 131
Agnus, 140
Alard, 148
Ashland, Nos. 1 & 2, 118
" " 3 & 4, 119
Anburn, 135
Bacon, 130
Balerma, 160
Benedictus, 152
Berrian, 185
Bowman, 187
Bradford, 125
Bradbury, 132
Briery, 138
Buckminster, 157
Cavare, 147
Chauncey Street, 154
Champney, 134
Chesuncook, 146
Cowper, 161
Credo, 149
Cronstadt, 150
Crosby, 128
Dale, 130
Dante, 118
Dedham, 159
Denfield, 161
Downs, 160
Dundee, 159
Ebene, 116
Elsdale, 118
Emerson, 145
Emma, 121
Engelhart, 114
Evan, 161
Field, 137
Finland, 129
Fisher, 146
Fletcher, 157
Fribourg, 148
Goodwin, 147
Grover, 137
Halle, 158
Happy Home, 115
Howland, 150
Hudson, 156
Iiba, 158
Janvrin, 120
Jasper, 158
Jones, 117
Josquin, 112
Justin, 133
Katahdin, 115
Kinco, 136
Laudate, 122
Lime Street, 133
Linwood, 148
Locke, 156
Marie, 151
Marlow, 159
Meditation, 128
Millinoket, 131
Myrtle, 112
Naomi, 161
Onge, 120
Orland, 134
Ortonville, 160
Parker, 128
Pearson, 137
Pembroke, 122
Princeton, 140
Quain, 149
Redeemer, 128
Restoration, 121
Rockland, 116
Roseland, 144
Sacrifice, 111
Sharon, 154
Shield, 152
Spartas, 155
Spencer, 145
Spohr, 117
Stanton, 129
Star, 127
Stephens, 160
Stillwell, 136
Still Waters, 111
St. Ann's, 159
Sumner, 158
Sunrise, 139
Sunset, 125
Sympathy, 137
Thornburn, 156
Transport, 127
Truman, 144
Vassalboro, 139
Yeranta, 138
Vincent, 145
Wachusett, 115
Watkins, 126
Wiemar, 151
Wien, 126
Winner, 132

C. M. Double.

Cantor, 124
Drake, 141
Perth, 142

S. M.

Abbie, 164
Abbotsford, 168
Alpha, 166
Badea, 186
Bayonne, 180
Beames, 167
Bemis, 177
Bondee, 172
Boylston, 185
Canby, 176
Carolus, 178
Dennett, 174
Dennis, 186
Drummond, 187
Duren, 164
Eilda, 182
Elden, 179
Farmington, 167
Flint, 169
Gascony, 169
Gorton, 186
Halsey, 172
Hartwell, 180
Hart, 166
Hedge, 188
Heimweh, 175
Himmel, 184
Hooper, 181
Hullah, 182
Hume, 162
Kindness, 178
Laban, 166
Lily Cove, 184
Lynne, 165
Moore, 177
Munich, 165
Newtonville (Double), 171
Nutbush, 179
Olmutz, 185
Purity, 188
Putney, 168
Quito, 163
Reflection, 170
Rowland, 175
Sargent, 168
Serene, 170
Silsby, 174
State Street, 185
St. Thomas, 183
Townsend, 162
Wardwell (Double), 178
Wesley, 181
Woodland, 176

L. P. M.

Greenbush, 188
Hanson, 188
Hartford, 189
Willow, 189

C. P. M.

Freeman, 190
Leira, 191
Petition, 192
Rolliston, 190

S. P. M.

Dalston, 198
Montville, 193
Roche, 192

H. M.

Gratitude, 197
Marshfield, 194
Merlin, 196
Messer, 195
Minden, 199
Praise, 198
Reign, 198
Roberts, 196
Todd, 194
Waterville, 197
Whittaker, 195

C. H. M.

Shepard, 199

S. H. M.

Resignation, 200
Villing, 200

7s.

Addie, 209
Benevento, 217
Benham, 214
Calais, 218
Companionship, 214
Currier, 212
Devotion, 215
Everett, 203
Franklin, 206
Germain, 208
Glade, (6 lines,) 201
Gladness, 204
Goodrich, 216
Grace, 207
Heavenly Rest, 209
Ida, 205
Invitation, 210
Jewett, 206
Lilie, 210
Lizzie, (6 lines), 202
Martyn, 217
Mentor, 211
Merrill, 212
Milton, 207
Minnie, 215
Mortland, 205
Nuremberg, 217
Oakland, (6 lines,) 201
Peterson, 208
Pleyel, 204
Pleyel's Hymn, 217
Porter, 211
Temple Grove, 218
Thurston, 216
Vale, 203

8s & 7s.

Alna, 221
Cutler, 218
Ella, 222
Faith (Double), 225
Fount, 221
Greenville, 227
Humility, 222
Kent (Double), 224
Lancaster, 220
Lindner, 219
Mount Vernon, 227
Otella (Double), 228
Resurrection (Peculiar,) 235
Ruhe, 220
Sallie, 219
Sicily, 227
Vienna, 218
Wilmot, 227

8s 7s & 7s.

Pine Hill, 226
Vesper, 226

8s & 7s. Peculiar.

Plummer, 257

8s, 7s & 4s.

Aetona, 228
Appleton, 229
Calvary, 231
Clifton, 230
Cobden, 230
Gilman, 229
Gould, 231
Jubilee, 230
Leon, 228

4s & 6s.

Little, 235

5s & 8s.

Conquest, 247
Fatherland, 254

6s & 4s.

America, 241
Emory, 240
Glenwood, 242
Italian Hymn, 241
Jarvis, 242
Mission, 240
Olivet, 241
Woodville, 240

6s & 4s. Peculiar.

Adams, 248
Bethany, 244
Glenburn, 248
Gordon, 244
Oak, 244
Sanford, 246

6s. & 5s.
Bloomfield, 238
Warren, 239
Wreath, (Peculiar,) 230

6s.
Bates, 245
Fides, 246
Holman, 245
Lindell, 246
Submission, 246

6s & 7s.
Payson, 288

6,8,6,4.
Crandon, 236

6,8,4.
Hawthorne, 237

6s & 10s.
Roulstone, 237
Lynde, 247

7s. & 4s.
Perkins, 252

7s. & 5s.
Conrad, 251

7s. & 6s.
Armagh, 250
Arnold, 251
Hosanna, 249
Maltby, 247
Monadnock, 248
Pardon (Peculiar), 252

8,3,3,6.
Caldwell, 285
Dion, 249

8s & 4s.
Elliot, 248
Monroe, 258
Repose, 253
Quietude, 234
Seldon, 236
Stamford, 284
Violet, 258

8s & 6s.
Juniper, (Peculiar), 254
Laughton, 238
Waldo, 233

8s, 7s & 6s.
Kenderwood, 254

8s.
Hale, 282
Spring, 232

9s & 7s. Peculiar.
Helen, 255

10s.
Cereal, 258
Verona, 256

10s & 9s.
Newell, 256

10s, 5s, 6s & 12s.
Ossagon, 257

11,8.
Princeburg, 258
Vernon, 258

11,10.
Benton, 259
Israel, 259
Radway, 256

11s.
Charton, 260
Masonda, 260

12s.
Conway, 261
Unity, 262

HYMNS, SENTENCES, ANTHEMS, AND CHORUSES.

A little while, *Hymn,* 364
Blessed are they who dwell in thy house, *Sentence,* 349
Blessed are the pure in heart, " 334
Blessed be the Lord God of Israel, *Chorus,* 354
Bow down thine ear, *Anthem,* 303
Calm on the listening ear of night, *Hymn Anthem,* 278
Come unto me, *Sentence,* 272
Dear comrade pilgrims of the cross, *Hymn,* 263
Fading, still fading, " 266
Hark! what mean those holy voices? *Hymn Anthem,* 338
Hear our prayer, *Sentence,* 296
Heavenly Father, " 274
How beautiful upon the mountains, *Anthem,* 306
If with all your hearts, *Sentence,* 318
I will extol thee, *Anthem,* 346
Let the words of my mouth, *Sentence,* 267
Lord, have mercy, *Anthem,* 310
Make a joyful noise unto the Lord, " 298
Oh, come, let us sing, " 327
Oh, how great is thy goodness, " 286
Oh, how lovely is Zion, " 320
Oh taste and see, *Sentence,* 283
Oh, that I had wings, *Quartette,* 290
Oh, that men would praise the Lord, *Anthem,* 323
Our blest Redeemer, *Hymn Anthem,* 342
Praise ye the Lord, *Chorus,* 350
Rejoice greatly, *Anthem,* 292
Sanctus, " 344
Saviour, breathe an evening blessing, *Hymn,* 265
Seek ye the Lord, *Sentence,* 271
The Lord is in his holy temple, " 269
The Lord is in his holy temple, " 270
The Spirit and the Bride say come, " 284
Thou wilt keep him in perfect peace, *Anthem,* 276
Thou wilt show me the path of peace, *Sentence,* 336
Unto thee, oh, Lord, *Anthem,* 280
When the worn spirit, *Hymn Anthem,* 316
Whom have I in heaven but thee, *Sentence,* 332

CHANTS.

Benedic anima mea, 363
Benedictus, 361
Bonum est confiteri, 362
Cantate Domino, 362
Deus Misereatur 368
Gloria in Excelsis, 364
Jubilate Deo, 361
My God, my Father, 365
Te Deum Laudamus, 365
The Lord's Prayer, 364
Venite, exultemus Domino, 360

Singing School Exercises.

Absent Friends, 45
A Farewell 35
Bounding away, 18
By the Sea, 55
Come to me in Cherry Time, 50
Cradle Song, 52
Down by the Riverside, 54
Dreams of Youth, 32
Early Friends, 23
Every Day hath Toil and Trouble, 59
Faintly flow, 49
Fare thee well, 60
Gone, 82
Hunting Song, 28
In Memoriam, 61
Invitation to Flora, 47
I've been roaming, 25
Let all Men praise the Lord, 62
May Morning, 26
May, 27
Morning, 53
Music, 41
Musical Dialogue, 30
Music of Nature, 46
Old Friends together, 36
One by one, 44
Over the Snow, 26
Remembrance, 43
Shepherds in the Vale, 20
Sleep on, Dearest, 37
Softly now the Light of Day, 48
Stars of the Summer Night, 57
Sunshine everywhere, 34
The Cricket, 24
The falling Snow, 39
The Hunting Morn, 56
The loosing of the Silver Chord, 40
The Merry Heart, 17
The New Year's Pastoral Visit, 51
The River, 27
The Schoolhouse Brook, 42
The Silver Stream, 21
The Wayside Well, 38
This World, 16
To the Hayfield, 33

Lightning Source UK Ltd.
Milton Keynes UK
UKHW022058081218
333475UK00006B/586/P

9 780483 990692